Transformation of Collective Intelligences

**Intellectual Technologies Set**

coordinated by
Jean-Max Noyer and Maryse Carmes

Volume 2

# Transformation of Collective Intelligences

*Perspective of Transhumanism*

Jean-Max Noyer

WILEY

First published 2016 in Great Britain and the United States by ISTE Ltd and John Wiley & Sons, Inc.

ISTE Ltd
27-37 St George's Road
London SW19 4EU
UK

www.iste.co.uk

John Wiley & Sons, Inc.
111 River Street
Hoboken, NJ 07030
USA

www.wiley.com

Library of Congress Control Number: 2016950829

British Library Cataloguing-in-Publication Data
A CIP record for this book is available from the British Library
ISBN 978-1-84821-910-6

# Contents

.

# Introduction

## Collective intelligences in the perspective of trans- and posthumanism

The modes of production of knowledge and intelligibility are undergoing a great transformation. Collective assemblages of thought and research are deeply affected by what we call the "digital folding of the world", in concordance with the converging NBIC[1] technologies. The very aims of these assemblages are controversial issues that question the performative becomings of science and technique in general. In particular, issues emerge that increasingly fuel debates about a subject that has several names: "transhumanism, posthumanism or speculative posthumanism". Transhumanism comes as a Great Narrative, the master story of our future becomings as we enter an era defined by humanity making the world become increasingly artificial: the Anthropocene. Furthermore, transhumanism presents itself as a tangible utopia, the harbinger of a major anthropotechnical bifurcation. In this, the transhumanist subject inscribes itself precisely in the tradition of those who once attempted to imagine the "cerebralization" of the world.

In this book, we will therefore attempt to show how collective intelligences stand "right in the heart" of the coupling of, one the one hand, ontological horizons and, on the other hand, processes of biotechnical maturation.

---

1 NBIC: Acronym for the multidisciplinary scientific field that combines the fields of research of Nanotechnology, Biotechnology, Information technology and Cognitive science.

New types of memory, renewal of analogical thought, powerful associationism, irresistible rise of algorithmics, distributed cognition, novel cartographic practices and relational encyclopedism are phenomena that manifest the transformation under way. What we call "nugget encyclopedism" is the open set made of "the community of works (texts, objects, hybrids, etc.) considered as an incompletion in process of production". This is the great system of internal relations that constitute collective enunciation assemblages, the collective equipment of subjectivation that define the community, the vast texture of digital writings, objects and   generalized algorithmics. Altogether, this is the huge Precambrian cauldron of Data, Metadata and Linked Data... a cauldron that enables its own folding. Producing new collective intelligences to be boiled in this cauldron and finding a new cauldron for the intelligences to come are the two issues we aim to address in this book, which is divided into three chapters. We first of all describe in Chapter 1 the most salient characteristics of the transformations currently taking place. These characteristics are mostly determined by the digital folding of the word, expressing the extension of the assemblages of intelligences and we detail how they differentiate and articulate from and with each other. In Chapter 2, an attempt has been made at summarizing trans- and posthumanist narratives, strictly abiding by their modes of enunciation. It also puts them in the perspective of the history of the cerebralization of the human species and sheds light on the symptoms these enunciations reveal. Lastly, in Chapter 3, we investigate the question of what encyclopedism is today underlining several issues it faces as well as some of its concrete modes of embodiment. The main writing apparatuses that affect the conditions of production and circulation of knowledge are thus analyzed.

# Elements of the General Configuration and Adaptive Landscape of Collective Intelligences

The conditions in which intelligence is applied evolve. All encompassing narratives and anthropological accounts are on the rise, and their discourse envisions a very specific future. Sometimes, they relatively boldly predict that humanity will soon overcome the limits of physiology, medical practice, intelligence or creativity. Sometimes, they find allies in key sectors of scientific or technological research as well as in large sections of the most powerful politico-economical agencies and legitimize the implementation of actual apparatuses that aim to redefine the essence of knowledge and existence to set up new ways of collectively inhabiting the world. This chapter explains why we try to relate these transformations and why we stress the lines of tension they bring about.

## 1.1. The intertwined narratives of tangible utopias and brilliant futures

Relating these transformations is indeed nowadays unavoidably necessary because of the very transformations globally affecting the ecologies that constitute our associated milieus and of which we are both the expression and the expressed. This renewed effort to address the issue of the collective intelligences is produced in specific conditions that are worth reminding, if not exhaustively, at least through some of its moments and main characteristics. We will stick to recent history, because we see the decades between the two world wars and the few years that immediately followed WW2 as specifically rich periods of transformations of modes of production and circulation of knowledge, as well as moments of change in the means of semiotic management of societies, organizations and companies.

This period was followed, at the end of the 1950s, by the first massive effects of the process of digitization of the sign, itself the forerunner of what was about to happen, a phenomenon we could call the great disruption. The disruption was caused by this very potent new system of digital, networked writing, whose virtual productions and constant updates increasingly influence and encompass our lives and experiences.

During the 1920s and 1930s, several innovative research projects were carried out, especially in the documentation domain. They epitomized the growing awareness that fundamental issues were becoming prominent concerning document and information management, in societies whose modes of organizing was becoming increasingly complex. These works remind us of the necessity to reflect on the environments of intelligence and on the environments of memory under the constraining weight of complexity and on the constant challenge of always renewed forms of collectives that become increasingly heterogeneous. Vannevar Bush, on his part, developed an interest for the new apparatuses of intelligent access to documents (Memex[1]), showing in his research that accessing issues were somewhat overridden by cognitive navigation practice. Of course, accessing documents involves collecting and classifying them, but only in order to better sort, navigate and associate them. In a nutshell, in order to better exploit and create in an ever-growing indeterminate mass of knowledge and documents whose differentiation keeps increasing.

Many research works were published across the world anound this time, that all pushed in the same direction. The Second World War and the fast rise of the American War Machine, with in particular the Manhattan Project Vannevar Bush was in charge of, strikingly exposed the collective dimensions of (applied and fundamental) research as well as the coexistence of heterogeneous processes and evermore sophisticated mediations. This increase in complexity in turn proved to be urgently in need of

---

1 See https://en.wikipedia.org/wiki/Memex.

collective organization and new intellectual technologies in order to augment the cognitive abilities of the human mind. Vannevar Bush himself expressed this call [BUS 45] in his famous 1945 paper "As we may think"[2], an essay in which he brings to light a number of transformations that affect the modes of production of knowledge. The effects and the posterity of this essay are well known.

To keep a long story short, during the end of the 1950s and the beginning of the 1960s, Carl Robnett Licklider[3] [LIC 58], initially working as a psychoacoustics specialist, promptly imagined the possibility of connecting several computers together with user-friendly interfaces. Licklider therefore played a significant role in the design, financing and management of the research that led to the elaboration of personal computers and the Internet. In *Man-Computer Symbiosis*, he wrote: "Man-computer symbiosis is an expected development in cooperative interaction between men and electronic computers. It will involve very close coupling between the human and the electronic members of the partnership. The main aims are (1) to let computers facilitate formulative thinking as they now facilitate the solution of formulated problems, and (2) to enable men and computers to cooperate in making decisions and controlling complex situations without inflexible dependence on predetermined programs. In the anticipated symbiotic partnership, men will set the goals, formulate the hypotheses, determine the criteria and perform the evaluations. Computing machines will do the routinizable work that must be done to prepare the way for insights and decisions in technical and scientific thinking. Preliminary analyses indicate that the symbiotic partnership will perform intellectual operations much more effectively than man alone can perform. Prerequisites for the achievement of the effective, cooperative association include developments in computer time sharing, memory components, memory organization, programming languages, and in input and output equipment"[4]. Douglas

---

2 Vannevar Bush, As we may think, 1945. http://www.theatlantic.com/magazine/archive/1945/07/as-we-may-think/303881/

3 https://en.wikipedia.org/wiki/J._C._R._Licklider.

4 Carl Robnett Licklider, Ire Transactions on Human Factor in Electronic Man–Computer Symbiosis.

Engelbart[5] also inscribed his work in the perspective of collective and augmented intelligence. His invention of the mouse and more generally his work on the computer were nested in the reflection on the collective dimensions of intellectual activities, within the framework of the emerging systems of digital hypertext.

Nelson[6] [NEL 65] invented digital hypertext (20th National Conference of the Association of Computer Machinery). He developed, with the Xanadu project, a system that aimed at enabling each individual to store information and make it accessible to all. "The aim of Xanadu was to build a universal system for hypertext publishing: in other words, a virtual library that could host infinite numbers of documents, in which we could wander freely via hypertext links. The authors would be automatically remunerated by a 'royalty micropayment mechanism'"[7].

We thus see that the whole process of work began to transform as soon as the Second World War was over, as well as all the modes of production of knowledge, all the organizing types and methods. Far be it from us to immodestly attempt to draw in this book a general history of the concept and notion of collective intelligence. We furthermore would not attempt such a history because we inscribe our reflection in the line of those who think that intelligence "is always-already collective and machined" and that its history is always fundamentally bound to the history of the environments and to the ecologies of the brain-body-(writing-mediation)-world couplings. To keep a long story short, let us only state that we inscribe our work in the continuation of that of Leroi-Gourhan [LER 64], whose research and reflection have been, in recent years, furthered in the powerful works of Stiegler [STI 94] as well as in the ideas

---

5 Douglas Engelbart created the Augmentation Research Center in the Stanford Research Institute, as well as the famous on-line system. https://en.wikipedia.org/wiki/Douglas Engelbart.

6 "Let me introduce the word 'hypertext' to mean a body of written or pictorial material interconnected in such a complex way that it could not conveniently be presented or represented on paper".

7 https://en.wikipedia.org/wiki/Project_Xanadu, http://www.xanadu.com.au/ted/, http://hypermedia. univ-paris8.fr/jean/fiction/Nelson/Nelson.html.

expressed by Goody [GOO 77], Lévy [LEV 93], Herrendschmidt [HER 07] and Latour [LAT 84].

Further back in time, Condorcet during the 18th Century and Durkheim in the 19th Century had already developed ideas about the concept of collective intelligence. Fleck [FLE 05], on his part, insisted during the first half of the 20th Century on the essentially *collective* characteristic of scientific research and proposed, in order to elaborate on this concept, notions such as thought collectives (or thought styles). More recently, Levy in his 1994 book entitled "L'Intelligence collective" ("The collective Intelligence") remarked that in the new digital conditions of networked hypertext memories, "collective intelligence (appears as) the project of a varied intelligence, distributed all over, always building synergies and being valued in real time".

## 1.2. Intelligence is "always already collective and machined"

There is a long history of collective assemblages of intelligence. In only a few millenniums, humanity fostered the vast Nile water resource management system, the cities of ancient Greece, Rome and its empire, collective intelligences of the Arab world, the large network of copyist monks, the rise of merchant capitalism and the invention of the printing press, etc. This long tradition of collective intelligences is constitutive of our history.

Assemblages were complex from the very first times. In Sumer, for example, they combined the invention of writing systems, currencies and the State, all these intertwined with a growing urbanization that, although initially relatively slow, was irresistible.

Nowadays, the milieus of intelligence are heterogeneous and the types of writings that constitute them are legions. The couplings "cortex-mediation-world" are intricately woven together. The alliances that unite texts, images and sounds were initially only slowly varying, but have very recently begun to change rapidly. Semiotics and the diverse non-exclusively linguistic writings have very early played a major part and, today more than ever, the empire of artifacts relentlessly brings new differentiations and intensifications of analogical interplays.

Later in this book we will detail how, nowadays, the complication of the world alters the conditions of exercise of intelligence, the conditions of creativity and the cognitive becomings that affect the imitative and analogical regimes, the regimes of "meme"[8] propagation and translation and, once more, the regimes of memory.

As Stiegler writes in his comments about the current vertiginous deepening of non-exclusively linguistic writings, "digital printing allows to 3D print objects that renew, in depth, the question of the artifact, a question that has been constitutive of the epiphylogenic tertiary retention since the beginning of hominization. As a printed object, the most mundane epiphylogenic tertiary retention becomes altogether hypermnesic, transitional and industrial, all the more because RFID chips as well as other tags embedded in objects. The so-called "communicating" objects, endowed with Internet modules (whose generalization the IPV6 protocol would enable) are constitutive of the Internet of Things (IoT) in a hyperreticulation stage in which not only its inhabitants but the whole world itself is double. It becomes the subject of an interpretation grammar throughout, as realized by, for example, by smart cities. For one thing, the digital tertiary retention has forever upset the functional and oppositional divide between production and consumption. But more importantly, the offset of the function of materialization of industrial design toward the tridimensional printers as robotic terminals seems to complete the industrial metamorphosis: it irreversibly condemns the centralist reticulation that spread through the United States and then Europe via the networks of roads, motorways and audiovisual Hertzian broadcasting".

In this perspective, we seem to be advancing toward complex "cognitive onto-ethologies", according to the scales considered. This movement involves the possibility of combinatorics and appropriate semiotic grammars that should enable wider navigations than in the past. This point will be developed further in what follows. One finds so many phrases that invoke

---

8 Memetics: introduced by Richard Dawkins in 1976 by his book *The Selfish Gene*.
Also see: Francis Heylighen Proc. 15th Int. Congress on Cybernetics, Namur, 1999, What makes a meme successful? Selection criteria for cultural evolution,
Liane Gabora, A DAY IN THE LIFE OF A MEME 1996,
Susan Blackmore, *The Meme Machine*, Oxford University Press, *2000.*

this trend that their repetition sometimes induces a sense of running gag: Smart Cities, Smart Agriculture, Smart Grids, Smart Factories, Smart Buildings, Smart Interfaces, Smart Algorithms, Smart Medicine, etc. The "associated milieu"[9] to which our cerebralities are bound keeps extending itself. What is called the IoT is central to this extension. From the IoT to the hybrid becomings of the Living, a hypernetwork of $n$ dimensions is being deployed, a kind of network shaped by the multiplicity of connections and interfaces that come with or between artifacts, actants (be they organic, non-organic, algorithmic) and writings. A network that relies on operating concepts (linked data, metadata, ontologies, folksonomies)[10], a network that connects billions of human beings as well as billions of things and documents in "clusters" of infinitely varying sizes that can legitimately and concretely be connected in a plastic and open way. This is an emerging anthropological stratum embroidered of an additional synaptic world that seeps in everywhere, weaving into the texture of the world, weaving against it, tightly adhering to the global fabric. This ever-expanding weaving of links and data are therefore complicated by the interweaving of being and things and beings and objects.

These new textures, as we briefly mentioned, are deeply involved in the continuous urbanization movement. More generally, they are at the heart of the transformations that redefine our associated milieus, the ways we inhabit them, the ways we travel across them, we think them, we live them, all the way to the deepest roots of our ways of life according to new or soon-to-be physiological–biological–cerebral conditions. These textures are therefore deeply affected.

---

9 G. Simondon defines the technical individual endowed with an "*associated milieu*" through the functioning of the machine that contributes to the production of his milieu, thus making his functioning possible.

Ars Industrialis (http://arsindustrialis.org/) borrows from G. Simondon the concept of "associated milieu" to analyze the collective individuation that constitutes any human society, in a way that binds the history of human individuation to the history of technical individuation. A techno-symbolic milieu is associated with you if it is the medium and vector of your individuation, which is itself only possible because this milieu associates individuals. On the contrary, a milieu is dissociated if it does not help your individuation, if you do not contribute to your milieu.

10 http://www.w3.org/Metadata/Activity.html, https://www.w3.org/standards/semanticweb/ data.

The movement of artificialization, a concrete expression of the interweaving of texture, is unprecedented and the convergence of NBIC[11] is very powerful. We must live through this evolution with renewed creativity in order to ensure a new stability of our lives in such uncertain ecologies. At the end of the day, it is the very survival of our species that is at stake.

The works and concerns of current and future religions, although we may have no knowledge of them yet, are also constrained by this transformation and by new types of productivity[12]. Among the narratives to come, and although it might be difficult to precisely perceive its borders, part of what we usually agree to call "speculative fiction" seems relevant in exploring the forces and hybrid forms in which the most archaic is mixed with the most futuristic, and narratives of immanence are intertwined with narratives of the great outside.

The emergence of such global assemblages of collective intelligences and the milieu for new forms of reflexivity to develop is central to these processes and the pluralism of writings, semiotics and hitherto unseen narratives, which are more than ever situated as a hub in the powers of algorithmic becomings.

The scales at which cognitive ecologies and the socius do transform are numerous and intertwined. The "problematic" need for new black boxes is pressing. We need to be able to inhabit this, especially because it does not go

---

11 NBIC: Nanotechnology, Biotechnology, Information technology and Cognitive science (NBIC) refers to a multidisciplinary scientific field that combines the domains of nanotechnologies (N), biotechnologies (B), information technologies and artificial intelligence (I) and cognitive sciences (C).

12 For example, see "LAUDATO SI", the encyclical Pope Francis about the *care for Our Common Home* "We are not God. The earth was here before us and it has been given to us. This allows us to respond to the charge that Judaeo-Christian thinking, on the basis of the Genesis account which grants man "dominion" over the earth (cf. *Gen* 1:28), has encouraged the unbridled exploitation of nature by painting him as domineering and destructive by nature. This is not a correct interpretation of the Bible as understood by the Church." "The biblical texts are to be read in their context, with an appropriate hermeneutic, recognizing that they tell us to "till and keep" the garden of the world (cf. *Gen* 2:15). "Tilling" refers to cultivating, ploughing or working, while "keeping" means caring, protecting, overseeing and preserving. This implies a relationship of mutual responsibility between human beings and nature".

without challenging the conditions of collective living. The big data movement, coupled in an essential manner to the IoT[13], is also linked to the sometimes worrisome will to permanently control strategic and political dimensions. It is tightly related to all that sets new conditions for the governance of populations. It strongly echoes the becoming of performative societies that is characterized, at least partly, by the triumph of means and procedures, a "constructal" perspective that invariably raises major anthropological issues. Its complex marriage with the trans- and posthumanist trends therefore needs to be reflected upon. We will come back to this later on.

The IoT also carries political issues that apply to, for example, the fields of hypercontrol and cyber criminality. It deeply alters how individuals, companies and institutions relate, which in turn influences all the domains of co-construction of knowledge, the fields of companies and administration management, including educating technologies. It also affects the modes of production of culture and health. From a sort of "HyperUrban" perspective, the IoT is altering the vast system of internal relations that constitutes our world. This transformation questions forms, arts and new subjectivities and places these issues in a key position, influencing even the still-in-limbo digital immersive becomings.

The IoT is central to all the modern technological developments whereby any object, any living being, any plant or mineral (with its associated data) can instantly be related with any other, through unprecedented semiotic elaborations and through the proliferation of interfaces and their software applications (smartphones, tablet computers, captures, CCTV cameras, etc.). Meanwhile, the consumerist vertigo finds therein new raw material to explore and exploit.

## 1.3. Collective intelligences in the weaving of data

Collective intelligences carve their essence under the aura of a proliferating new species, the "Data". Simultaneously, they are immersed in the intensification of both inherited political economies and the emergence

---

13 https://en.wikipedia.org/wiki/Internet_of_things.

of modes of contribution of various level of novelty[14]. In allying a-signifying semiotics, digital technologies, data and the market, the axiomatic immanence of capitalism has gained an extremely powerful new source of energy. According to Joxe [JOX 12], the global system is now in crisis and, in Guattari's words, "integrated, computerized global capitalism tries to dominate everything through speculation, violence and willful misrepresentations – knowingly lying about the essence of agreements. Its aim therefore is to damage any other type of sovereignty, autonomy or economy. To keep calling it empire is a way of saying that this kind of global power is like the empires of the past, in the same time financial and war based.

Nevertheless, "capitalism [which represents] a paroxystic form of integration of various types of mechanism (not only technological or economy writing machines, but also conceptual machines, religious machines, esthetical machines, perceptual machines, desiring machines)" aims at a "semiotically deterritorialized power". Its semiotic mode – the mode of capital – would thus simultaneously constitute a kind of collective computer of the socius and production, and the spearhead of appropriate innovations (to respond to its internal pulsions). In that case its raw, primary material, staple food, would no longer simply be human or machine work. It would involve all the means of semiotic control related to instrumentalization, insertion in the socius, reproduction, the circulation of the many aspects of this machine integration process. What capital capitalizes on is semiotic power. Not any kind of power, however, or there would be no point in contrasting it with the anterior forms of exploitation. It is a semiotically deterritorialized power. Capitalism endows some social groups with the capacity to selectively control the socius and production through a collective semiotizing system. It is a very specific form of power in so far as it focuses on controlling only the dimensions that contribute to maintaining its processing essence. Capitalism does not try to exert a despotic power on every single thing happening in society. On the contrary, to manage to leave spaces of relative freedom and creativity is essential to its

---

14 On the economy of contribution, or "commons", see Arsindustrialis and the work of Michel Bauwens as well as Elinor Ostrom works. On Jeremy Rifkins: http://www.grico.fr/ articles/lecture-de-the-zero-marginal-cost-society-the-internet-of-things-the-collaborative-commons- and-the-eclipse-of-capitalism-de-jeremy-rifkin-avril-2014/.

survival[15] [GUA 83]. Hence, the central importance of the a-signifying semiotics brought about by digital technologies. Later on, we will elaborate on this.

The context of value creation is situated in the advent of the Internet of objects of hybrids – we could call it the Internet of "everything"; in other words, in a period when a large relational system is created, an extended system connecting individuals, processes, data and things. In this context, value creation will be based on the powers of semiotic creation. More specifically, it will rely on the exploitation of data.

This system is based on producing interfaces and sensors, on the capacity of networked digital writings to leave increasingly numerous and varied marks that bear semantic, behavioral, geolocalized, energy-related value.

It can also be seen as a heteroorganizing system that has an ever-increasing number of recursive loops distributed over its whole extent, involving increasing quantities of applications, software and algorithms: the structural coupling of a "data-centric" society and algorithmic matter.

All the collectives and their associated institutions are affected. Today, more than half of the population has access to the Internet, but by 2025, two-thirds of humanity will be connected. Connected devices are expected to undergo a similar growth. Today, 14 billion of them are connected, and this number is expected to rise to 50 billion by 2030. As for applications, the embodiment of the vast spectrum of desires, their number is currently exponentially growing.

The unstoppable rise of algorithms and the quantitative–qualitative explosion of data production are both relatively brutal. This upsurge is also materialized in the doxic plane of immanence. Public debates of various complexities routinely discuss the impacts the algorithms of the dominant agents of software industry have on research, science, arts, marketing as well as on political governance in so far as it seeks to manage population, territories, wars, etc.

---

15 F. Guattari and E. Alliez, on the role of a-signifying semiotics in capitalism, in Le Capital en fin de Compte, Change, 1983.

The various ways of automating data production processes and their exploitation infuse into the imagination that governs political action. At the same time, they enable the design of apparatuses that striate the powerful human–non-human collectives. We all know how, nowadays, the forms of power are tied up to "statistical rationality". Our modes of being are mediated by value production, the world economy, the collectives, the subjectivation processes, etc. We are well aware of how much their becoming real is mediated by the mathematization of relations, regimes of interfaces and multiplication of applications that come with them.

In the analysis of Galloway [GAL 10], "As one of the leading industrial giants, Google uses the pure math of graph theory for monetary valorization". But he also writes: "... a grand dividing line between two schools of thought: Those who consider today that symbolic logic, geometry, linear analysis, set theory, algorithms, information processing, etc., are outside of ontic history, that is, outside the history of instances, appearance, and existence, and those who recognize that such mathematization exists today at the very heart of the mode of production, and therefore not only drives history, but in some basic way is history itself. It is not simple that "we must always historicize"; it is that there is a particular thing about *today's* mode of production that obligates us to historicize mathematics [GAL 10]. In this context, data mining is presented as an imperial narrative, the master storytelling of performative societies. A narrative that is bound to the holy and obsessive trinity of "performation–prediction–preemption", which characterizes intelligence societies and the marketing hegemony.

In 1990, Gilles Deleuze already wrote in a famous text: "In the societies of control, on the other, what is important is not a signature or a number, but a code: the code is a *password*, while on the other hand the disciplinary societies are regulated by *watchwords* (as much from the point of view of integration as from that of resistance). The numerical language of control is made of codes that mark access to information, or reject it. We no longer find ourselves dealing with the mass/individual pair. Individuals have become 'dividuals' and masses, samples, data, markets or '*banks*'" [DEL 90a]. This imperial narrative paradigm (as well as the digital data and algorithmic matter it produces while in the same time feeding on it) is being materialized in very various forms. It roams through various (relatively autonomous) milieus, not only challenging but also reviving their ability to vary, to transform. Indeed, the complexity of semiotics, narratives and languages, the wealth of cognitive ecologies and the involved risks of chaos bring to the foreground the issue of reflectivity and simplexity in an unprecedented pressing way.

One could think the issues raised by interfaces (and the proliferation of applications that come with them) as the foundation of a kind of "noo-nomadology" that pushes to the foreground the diversity of perspectives and the way they evolve. It also is a noo-nomadology of interstices and a renewal of the notion of "boundary zones", which is based on dispersion–disseminating as well as on the miniaturization of interfaces of translation, connection, exploitation, etc. Productive boundaries are ones that articulate the passageways and translations enabling the analogical freedom of interstices. Data, as elements of various sizes and complexity, are therefore both the means and the ends of the relentless activity of cerebralities and hybrid collective intelligences, that is, under the current conditions [NOY 15].

## 1.4. Semiotics and statistics

We now understand the strength of the ties that bind the "electronic revolution", the computerized management of "markets" and the algorithmic policies that come with them. We perceive the magnitude of the tensions that develop between robotization[16] processes, monopolistic corporate becomings, and inequalities [KRU 12, LYN 10]. These tensions apply at the heart of the new industrial revolution that Anderson promises, or that Rifkins represents in his very political but aseptic prospective vision [RIF 12]. That industrial revolution would be based on the alliance of "3D printers, laser cutters, open source soft and hardware" [AND 12] and on the advent of globalized flexibility.

---

16 Including the robotization of war: A. Joxe, for example, remarks "how much this evolution is a new form of the bio-technical becoming of the military, a process aiming to abstract itself from the presence of the ground, to reduce the costs and maximize the benefits of confronting anthropological asymmetric patterns and especially the differences in the urge to death, whether it be its conjuration or its celebration. Although this falls beyond the scope of this book, the issue of global polemological becomings, obstinately implicit as the promised pacifying processes (both a sort of shadow theater and a promise of violence conjuration modes) carry worrisome oddities, cannot be overlooked" [JOX 12].

Several financial and economy mechanisms are also perceived to be disrupting innovation processes much more than the current robotization phenomenon does. Simultaneously, we cannot but see that the digitization of money – with its humongous trail of data – unceasingly fills the abyss of immanence, there introducing, in Schmitt's words, "a distortion, a convulsion, an explosion. In short a movement of extreme violence" [DEL 72]. We know the extent and the strength to which the forms power and "statistical rationality" are tied together, as statistics and sociology perform an extraordinary fantasist function.

Mathematics, data mining as well as machine (deep) learning[17] [LEC 15] are immanent in the process of production. They are employed to extract value and make novel hermeneutics about the fields of ontology production and combining. They also aim to perform/predict phenomena that ensure specific strategical positions, and therefore involve the production of subjectivities through regimes of desire. In the near future, these learning algorithms will be coupled with our brains, which will certainly open novel smooth spaces, fertile grounds to invent new issues, architectures and configuration with $n$ dimensions of intelligibility.

The everlasting question of writing is asked anew by its constant reelaboration, digitization of the sign and unstoppable rise of a-signifying semiotics [GUA 89], as we pointed out earlier. More precisely,

---

17 LeCun, Facebook AI Research, Center for Data Science, NYU, Courant Institute of Mathematical Sciences, NYU. L'apprentissage Profond: Une Révolution en Intelligence Artificielle Leçon Inaugurale au Collège de France Chaire Annuelle 2015–2016 Informatique et Sciences Numériques, http://www.college-de-france.fr/site/yann-lecun/Recherches-sur-l-intelligence-artificielle.htm.

David Balduzzi Semantics, Representations and Grammars for Deep Learning, ArXiv, 2015 "Let us recall how representation learning is commonly understood. Bengio *et al.* describe representation learning as "learning transformations of the data that make it easier to extract useful information when building classifiers or other predictors". More specifically, "a deep learning algorithm is a particular kind of representation learning procedure that discovers multiple levels of representation, with higher level features representing more abstract aspects of the data". Finally, LeCun *et al.* state that multiple levels of representations are obtained "by composing simple but nonlinear modules that each transform the representation at one level (starting with the raw input) into a representation at a higher, slightly more abstract level. With the composition of enough such transformations, very complex functions can be learned. For classification tasks, higher layers of representation amplify aspects of the input that are important for discrimination and suppress irrelevant variations".

a-signifying semiotics interact with signifying ones in a way that opens new virtuals (that have undefined actualizations) and overflows toward the supremacy of algorithmics and software.

On the plane of the political economy of knowledge, one could say that, nowadays, economy is defined by the algorithm, the software.

From a social–cognitive perspective, we can see in this profound movement flows and dances of data, which find their rhythms and modes of infiltration or propagation "in" the application-equipped interfaces that feed the many recursive loops that themselves open to action and thinking. Obviously, the political does not come out unchanged.

The deployment of numerous and vast relational systems and of their specific cartographic methods indeed echoes the relatively pronounced evolution of "the political" toward a generalized experiment in which the means and performative procedures problematically prevail over the ends, be they political or ethical. Great ecological (social, mental, environmental) crises stem from the transformation of anthropotechnical, economical, cognitive, organizational, military, etc., mechanisms. They arise mostly under the conditions of the digital perspective and its associated technical and scientific becomings. Such crises in turn intensify these transformative tendencies and processes. There are bio-political and psycho-political becomings, then, that develop into new, previously unseen shapes.

One thus understands why so much effort is made to develop a semiopolitical thought about interfaces [CAR 13, NOY 13, LAZ 06]. This research attempts at signaling the new relations of production as well as the new forms of subservience (in the machinic sense) and subjugation. It also aims at detailing their hybridizing and implementation both by and central to various apparatuses. These subjugating apparatuses are informational and digitally communicational. They are apparatuses to create, store and exploit data, but they also involve existential patterns, temporalities and the breaches pierced through the suffocating texture of intelligence societies.

This engaging dance is endless and feeds on the immense flows and stocks of traces we leave behind on the Internet (Big Data). Online, on the N-dimensional labyrinth of the Internet, every single action and behavior, from the most furtive click to the most elaborate trajectories, betrays our personal cartographies and becomes a readable deposit. These cartographies tell the interwoven fabric of our visions, and rhythms and of what we focus on, our preferences for such expression material, our compulsive or hesitant moves, our tremors and consumerist addictions, and also our silences and our "by default" choices of our disappearances.

The dance induces us to build that architecture of uncertain stability, which we constitute with our associations, and/or with all that connects within us, thus creating graphs that are sometimes crude and sometimes subtle, and that display myriads of different patterns. They embody the scientific dream of Tarde [TAR 95].

This movement complicates our skins and our geologies, involving our ways of being with the interactions of urges and passions of violence producing mechanisms. It complexifies our ways of waging wars (from the most archaic to the most futuristic ones). In other words, it alters the core of our "desiring machines".

The current explosion of the Internet therefore leads to a novel dialogue between population of humans and non-humans. Data are produced and they travel through applications, sensors and databanks. The applications and sensors are in a way the cross stitches of various complexities that proliferate and constitute the texture of the worldwide N-dimensional relational system. This texture is threaded on the basis of an ever-extending, increasingly intrusive ichnology. A specter is haunting the new modalities of work, existence and governing – the specter of traceability and associated data. At all scales, from intranets to globalization processes, there are transformations happening, shifts from the nation-state to the market-states (in the framework of the attempt to establish, forcefully and rapidly, a global market), shifts from traditional forms of sovereignty to new digital traces and avenues, or to decentralized pattern territories (in which the privatization of the most regalian functions, including that of war machines goes unfettered). These shifts result in a software issue that is of major politico-strategic importance.

In our perspective, the "digital" allows for the emergence of a new way of "rematerializing the social matter by making interactions visible" (the translation of traces into data), in Bruno Latour's words. Similarly, and within the same move, social physics develop that, as Pentland [PEN 14] writes, "mathematically describe the impact of connections between, on the one hand, information and the flow of ideas and, on the other hand, people's behavior"[18]. It is well known that Pentland considers that the Big Data, in conjunction with powerful algorithmic methods, should enable the development of "a causal theory of local structure". This view has been criticized and argued against many a time, and one can show it is linked with some trends of transhumanism.

## 1.5. Data cities and human becomings: the new milieus of intelligence

Hand in hand with the urbanization of the planet, the digitization of cities (smart cities), agricultural areas and, more generally, of soils, the atmosphere and marine environments generate massive amounts of digital data (their quantity doubles every year).

A significant critique of this trend can be found in Nicolas Carr's article, in the MIT technology review [CAR 14d] "tapping into big data, researchers and planners are building mathematical models of personal and civic behavior. But the models may hide rather than reveal the deepest sources of social ills"), which points some important issues out. For example, he remarks that Pentland's notion of "data-driven society" raises several issues. This strategic choice, in his opinion, favors the status quo. It reinforces established anthropological and political power relations and shuns any possibility of alternative by forcing changes and becomings to conform to some kinds of evolutionary political and strategic creodes that only let change-desiring agents craft computational optimizations within given, stable systems.

This is, by the way, one of the major dangers of "performative societies", of a "constructal" understanding of societies that, once more, the transhumanist ideology fosters.

---

18 See also [PEN 14]: "I believe that the power of Big data is that it is information about people's behavior instead of information about their beliefs. It's about the behavior of customers, employees, and prospects for your new business. It's not about the things you post on Facebook, and it's not about your searches on Google, which is what most people think about, and it's not data from internal company processes and RFIDs. This sort of Big data comes from things like location data off of your cell phone or credit card, it's the little data breadcrumbs that you leave behind you as you move around in the world".

New urban ecologies, from "smart cities" to security driven urban policies, are rapidly developing. They raise profound issues as they constitute the anthropological and political bedrocks on the basis of our societies, organizations, thought collectives and the subjectivation processes.

The intensification of this movement, the rise of hybrid territories and the extension of "becoming indoors" [SLO 13] at the very core of what is expressed, are particularly visible in cities like Dubai where (in Mike Davis's words) [DAV 07] Albert Speer and Walt Disney are merged into odd lines of flight, which we ride between "the anarchy of choice and Disney-fication" (William Gibson). All this increasingly deepens the "milieus" of our lives, our living environments, and relies on the production and exploitation of data.

Smart cities are growing in other areas of the planet, too, as exemplified by the Scientific American when it lists various aspects of a smart city: reduction of its ecological impact and energy optimization; smart management of flows and transportation in the city; creation of services that renew the relations of inhabitants to their city and also transform the modes of social interaction; deployment of armies of sensors that feed database complexes essential to the optimal management of the public action: "truly smart cities will emerge as inhabitants and their many electronic devices are recruited as real time sensors of daily life. Networking the ubiquitous sensors and linking them to government databases can enhance a city's inventiveness, efficiency and services"[19]. In there, data are the majority population.

Several notions, embody the way this urbanization process is infused and born by the digital fold. The notions presented below are the expression of interwoven and hybrid policies, actions and governances.

First of all, there is the notion of cybercities. It puts the emphasis on governance, on control of territories and milieus, relying especially on data capture and on the implementation of specific infrastructures. It also focuses on cybercriminality and involves traceability and identification, which can develop as far as military control of cities. Amongst others, Stephen Graham, in his paper "When Life Itself is War: On the Urbanization of

---

19 See Scientific American, September 2011, and especially "The Efficient City" by Mark Fischetti.

Military and Security Doctrine" particularly clearly links digital urban life to militarized control strategies.

The notion of "digital cities" rather emphasizes the modes of representation of cities in their relatively immersive nature (in the realm of simulated cities, one finds avatars, the cities of Second Life, Sim City, 3D). It highlights the connecting interfaces of urban environments and hybrid territories that are, if not massively, at least partly, digital. The third notion, that of "intelligent cities", focuses on the principles of intelligibility of cities and on the (relatively) collective conditions of intelligence production under the dominion or networks, infrastructures, protocols and citizen assemblages. In other words, all that nurtures the distributed quality of intelligences and cognition, thus complicating the task of governing cities (whether in a polycentric manner or not). It includes processes such as crowdsourcing, bottom-up apparatuses of deliberation and collaboration, etc.

The last, most fashionable and probably most important notion is that of "smart cities". Its various incarnations aim at "optimally" and ecologically managing cities, energy flows, populations, information, mobility, etc. Even in this seemingly inoffensive and energy transition-supported notion of "smart cities", there is, because of the anthropotechnical and political control of our urban "associated milieus" it relies on, a problematic "constructal" purpose[20]. This is indeed in the field of urban management that the generalized digitization of everything is most advanced and extended, expressed by the digitization of grounds and buildings, energy flows, movements of population, etc. This is therefore the main locus of the political tension between big data, open data (OD) and algorithmics. This tension relentlessly comes out in our research as central and very

---

20 The aim of constructal theory is to find the ideal form of a system, that which provides an optimal yield. One easily understands how, applied to human societies, it naturally becomes an ideology of total control wherein creativity must be eradicated as it is a source of change, of alteration... See, for example, on constructal theory and its application to the engineering world, the works of André Bréjean, an engineering Professor that specializes in thermodynamics. (What does "optimal" mean, in that context or even in any context? What about an "optimal" that would evaluate our very existence, how we experience ourselves through our becomings? "Optimal" in Leibniz's calculating God's perspective? "Optimal" in the opinion of the engineers of the *Conservatoire National des Arts et Métiers*? "Optimal" according to the algotrading algorithms? Optimal according to the rules of the Three Great Books?

problematic, whereas a constant ideological propaganda enforces a positive understanding of it on the population, enhancing its positive aspects with what often are mere slogans like "open cities, intelligent cities" or, in the best cases, express present utopias. In any case, this immense field of transformation is being experimented globally.

However, constructal theory keeps repeating and expecting that cities would not be truly intelligent before its inhabitants, their applications and interfaces are finally coupled and become tireless "real time" sensors of daily life activities. To achieve this goal, omnipresent, everywhere-distributed sensors must be connected into a network that feeds the databases of the governing apparatus, in order to improve the inventive qualities of cities and urban worlds, the efficiency of their services. The growing importance of environmentalist territorial policies bears with it the rise of the "open data power"[21]. The latter presents itself as the new horizon of city policies, playing a significant part in an almost infinite data production context and in the invention of the appropriate processing apparatuses that summon the open source, alternative energies, etc.

"The vast amount of data that is emerging is the starting point for making efficient infrastructure programmable so that people can optimize a city's daily processes. Extracting information about real-time road conditions, for example, can reduce traffic and improve air quality. The potential for developing more of this kind of efficient infrastructure is vast and a good fraction can be unleashed through smart systems. It is thus no surprise that many large corporations, such as IBM, Cisco Systems, Siemens, Accenture, Ferrovial and ABB, are setting their sights on the urban space" [RAT 11].

Now may be the time to think beyond the dream sold by smart cities, beyond the fantasies of optimized our ways of being in the world in terms of energy, climate, mobility, with respect to our expanding cerebralities, under a democratic plain would be "cleared" of any developing differentiation of the uneven potential becomings of relatively closed/open local networks that form more or less tree-like, a centered structures (such networks are based on negotiation protocols and translation modes that are more or less arbitrary); now may be the time to think beyond the inequalities that arise

---

21 http://datascienceseries.com/blog/download-open-data-power-smart-cities.

from this sleepless, self-legitimating algorithmic regime. Now may be the time, lastly, for smart cities designers to leave room for urban and existential chaosmosis, the cracks in the digital walls, the freedom of DIY and the rise of underground worlds.

In a way, we think that smart cities will only be inhabitable when they leave room for what could be called an "anti-smart word". Without such openings, they might spur forms or resistance involving the emergence of new pioneers of chaos.

Because, walking in the footsteps of Jean-François Lyotard, big data are an integral part of the "legitimation by power [...] the latter legitimizing itself like a system tuned to optimize its own performance. Indeed, this sort of control on context is precisely" what the alliance of algorithmic methods and big OD promises. One could say that the performativity of a policy increases proportionally with the quantity of information it has about its associated milieu. "Thus, the growth of power, and its self-legitimation, are now taking the route of data storage and accessibility, accessibility, and the operativity of information" of data [LYO 79]. All this leads to a kind of urban machine endowed with some stupid intelligence.

This evolution embarks with us, so to speak, on a galley journey, leaving captaincy up to a divinely digital hetero-organization. Once again, it may time for us to be more deeply concerned by that alliance. We should be more consistently questioning the roots of the association of the insomniac capture of digital, behavioral, socio-semantic and spatio-temporal traces with the desire of prediction taken as a categorical imperative, as well as with the scientific paradigm of Jim Gray and Chris Anderson who see it as the radiant future of thought... Unless it becomes a future of Yawning Heights [ZIN 76, ZIN 78].

Admittedly, although the coupling of the digitization of cities and the Internet of Things certainly generates a major transformation of the environments of intelligence, this transformation must be understood as the advent of a body of learning techniques and "forums". Colin McFarlane advocates "a conception of learning based on three processes: translation, or the relational distributions through which learning is produced as a social-material epistemology of displacement and change; coordination, or the construction of functional systems that enable learning as a means of linking different forms of knowledge, coping with complexity and facilitating adaptation; and dwelling, or the education of attention through which learning operates as a way of seeing and inhabiting the world". He then considers "this conception of learning in relation to tactical learning, i.e. the resources marginal groups use to cope with, negotiate and resist in the city..." [FAR 11].

One can also understand the current changes by considering the hybrid and rhizomatic processes [DEL 87] that shape urban networks. The city can be seen as the expression of a kind of topological conversion of brain worlds in which the intelligences of the city are situated in an $n$-dimensional territory, dominated by relentless folding of which they are both the expression and the expressed. Brain cities again coupled in the immense interplay of interfaces and their proliferation differentiation.

Far from the Big Data of control and from the pathological "constructal" push, there are forces that play with and evade the new regimes of desire, forces that crisscross the cities in cryptospheres, labyrinths of secrets, "semioglyphes". These forces are the heart of the motions and lines of flight of thought.

The approach that consists of thinking such flows and regimes in terms of states of various stabilities and ephemeral quality is called an "exology" by John Weissman (when applied to the city): "The exological is ecological insofar as the ecosphere is also a cryptosphere, a hall of mirrors and infinite labyrinth of secrets, light and darkness: and this duplicity, this infinite complexity, this fractality and fragmentarity is present in physical-ecological systems as well as economic, sociological, psychic, etc."[WEI 12].

These points are important because they replace a whole body of psychological energies, which are far from any equilibrium, at the heart of the becoming urban intelligence, thus contradicting the "smart" embodiments that trust the center stage.

### 1.5.1. *Open Data (OD): a heterogeneous movement, the contribution to novel forms of knowledge in question*

Let us mention here some factors that led to the elaboration of the OD movement. The fact that concerns pertaining to what is called the "open data movement" rose to the forefront is one of the consequences of the exponential growth of the knowledge, information and data that are produced, exchanged and that circulate on digital networks. OD is one aspect of the struggle between the various productive forces that depend on knowledge and significance of semiotic control. Using Marxist terminology, OD is the manifestation of the emergence of new relations of production.

The history of "data" as the instantiation or embodiment of the fundamental relation between knowledge and power, a relation in which the evolution of the political is at stake, is nevertheless a long history. Let us signal a few of the most recent landmarks to keep in mind, such as the co-emergence, during the 21st Century, of the nation-state and statistical rationality. Desrosières [DES 10] published a major contribution on this subject.

Earlier in this book, we mentioned that the very question of digital data began becoming increasingly significant during the end of the 1950s and the beginning of the 1960s, when large databases began to be developed in order to store data of scientific, business, financial, etc., interest. Very rapidly, strategical data bases of scientific research publications were implemented, with scientific policies and scientific governance aims. The beginning of the 1960s was in fact the years when the United States began to equip itself with the first devices and methods to globally evaluate the production of scientists to monitor its internal dynamics and attempt to discern new routes for research. This policy quickly raised the main issues involved with the exploitation of large documentary collections. Presently, databases of companies and patents underwent the same evolution.

The means of semiotic control, derived from the digital sphere, thus became a pressing issue. Many methodologies of various sophistication were imagined to provide the necessarily means of knowledge extraction, and the reflection gained momentum to eventually produce the new fields of research called Scientometry and Infometry[22]. From this point on, the paradigm clearly shifted from "knowledge access" to "knowledge

---

22 See: Xavier Polanco Aux sources de la scientométrie, Dossier Solaris, No. 2, 1995;

Michel Callon, Jean-Pierre Courtial, Hervé Penan, La scientométrie 1993;

Paul Wouters "Aux origines de la scientométrie. La naissance du Science Citation Index", Actes de la recherche en sciences sociales 4/2006 (no. 164), pp. 11–22.

www.cairn.info/revue-actes-de-la-recherche-en-sciences-sociales-2006-4-page-11.htm.

production". In the beginning of the 1990s, an "open" movement gained momentum in the fields of software creation, dissemination of programs and scientific publication. It constituted the tangible, experimental milieu in which political and organizational questions could be put back on the agenda because they were attached to the relatively agonistic variation of the modes of data and knowledge production, circulation, exploitation and consumption. Powered by the free software and open source movements and by the archive initiative, new models were able to challenge the excesses of a seemingly limitless development of property rights. They attempted and still strive to loosen the authoritative grip capitalist forms of intellectual property rights hold on the dynamics of collective intelligence, innovation and creation. On this account, the works of Lawrence Lessig, Richard Stallman, Steven Harnad and Paul Ginsparg are seminal[23].

Advocating forms of free agreements to collective property, relying on the productivity of parallel work practices and on the adaptivity of bottom-up modes of governance, these movements play a central role in the positive transformation of creation processes. In an anthropological and political perspective, they contribute to transforming the culture of democratic deliberation into a culture of controversy and to inventing novel modes of governance that are polycentric and varied.

The conditions in which knowledge and information are produced, circulate and are exploited are not only affected but also intensely discussed. The economic and juridic models are constantly challenged by new agents, new demands, practices and uses (GNU for free software, creative commons and OD commons are significant actants of this field).

Lastly, there are rapidly growing emergent technologies that enable new "distributed" ways of making, collecting and redistributing data in information flows. These technologies are developed hand in hand with the miniaturization of interfaces and with the multiplication of ever-more elaborated software applications.

---

23 http://fr.wikipedia.org/wiki/Lawrence_Lessig, http://www.stallman.org/, http://www.open archives.org/, http://archivesic.ccsd.cnrs.fr, http://arxiv.org/.

The whole of this movement thus forces the centralized, "top-down" modes of governance to compete or coexist with a-centered, distributed and "bottom-up" models. However, since these models establish relatively co-determinating relations, new political fronts appear.

To understand the "open data" movement, we should focus on these short and long stories in order to ground the phenomenon in a tangible reality. Otherwise, we could let the OD movement remain an ethereal notion, suspended in a void that would make it appear as a radically new thing, disconnected from any associated milieu, from any "memories". What this movement creates is not written on an empty, fresh white page. From its very beginning, it comes entangled in the web of all the social-political dimensions of knowledge – power relations. It is inseparable from the individual and/or collective social-cognitive asymmetries and from the asymmetries of appropriation of writing technologies andintellectual technologies in general. Of course, the irruption of digital memories and of new intellectual technologies enables the emergence of new utopias, whether they be tangible or not. Desires of transformations of the political economies of knowledge, desires and projects of transformations of the art of creating value or "values" arise from this irruption. But these trends are only the latest figures drawn on the historical background of anthropological heterogeneses in which cognitive forces, creative forces and political desires have always confronted themselves.

In many countries, the "open data" movement, together with the so-called "Open Government" movement, has gained momentum to the point of becoming, at the international level, a political gauge and a measure of the efficiency of administrations. "Public" data, that which pertains to States, regional authorities, administrations or other organisms whose data can be considered of "public interest"[24] have seen their first prescriptive policies formulated at the beginning of the 21st Century (although, in France, free access to administrative documentation enshrined us in the law since

---

24 In France, the Macron law demands that companies that provide public services of transportation publicize online, in a free and open format, all the details of their schedules (times and stations served). The Lemaire law, at the beginning of 2016 however nuanced this obligation for the SPICs and EPICs (SNCF (train service) and RATP (parisian subway)) whose activity are subject to commercial competition.

1978[25]). Open Government programs, embodied, for example, by the 2009 Obama administration, consider that OD is one of the three pillars of the approach (the two others being citizen partaking to political life and the implementation of methods to enrich the collaboration of local authorities). In these programs, the "transparency" motto is essentially linked to "open data" [LAS 10]. According to the Open Knowledge Foundation and the World Wide Web Foundation, governmental OD pertains to the following domains: election results, geography maps and Land Registry, postal codes, finances (budgets, spending and public procurements), legal texts, national statistics (demography, employment, economy, offenses), companies, public services of transportation, health, education and environment[26]. A city or a county must also provide information on cultural facilities, heritage, air quality, urban planning, etc., which further expands the domain of possibilities[27]. In other words, all the domains of public activity are subjected to the injunction to "free the data", commanded to hop on the "data driven" train, on a global scale[28].

Investments and returns on investments are expected to be huge. For example, in Europe in 2001, the commission announced that it adopted a strategy for OD. According to the communication, the "overall economic gains from opening up this resource could amount to €40 billion a year in the EU"[29]. Also in 2011, McKinsey, an American consulting firm, expected OD to generate several trillions of dollars worth of value creation, including the private sector. However, despite the plethora of slogans and communication elements, we should not forget the many barriers that hinder

---

25 Law no. 78-753 of the July 17, 1978 about the right to access administrative documents. Even the 15th article of the declaration of human rights (Déclaration des Droits de l'Homme et du Citoyen) states: "Members of society have the right to demand that any public agent accounts for his administration".

26 http://index.okfn.org/, http://www.opendatabarometer.org/report/analysis/implementation.html.

27 Each country has a different legislative framework, therefore particular themes may be subject to legal obligation of openness or not.

28 See the 2013 and 2011 McKinsey reports on Open Data and Big data.

29 Communication from the Commission to the European Parliament the council, the European economic and social committee and the committee of the regions, Open data, An engine for innovation, growth and transparent governance.

See also: https://ec.europa.eu/digital-single-market/en/open-data-portals.

the data opening trend [CAR 14b]. Although several works highlight the potential impacts of OD on the transformation of public action, many others conversely detail the limits of this movement and even document its first disappointing achievements [GUR 11, KIT 14, MOR 14].

The way this movement unfolds is sometimes paradoxical, as it does so with the framework that challenges the role of States as centralized regulating bodies (Welfare State) in ways whose radicalism depends on, in broad terms, whether one considers the case of the United States or that of Europe. Interestingly, we see that in the United States, the OD movement is developing in parallel with a strong push to irrevocably impose the Market State.

The great significance of these issues become undeniable when we consider OD as a major political-economical question, a major strategical subject. Similarly, in France, for example, regions, counties and cities gradually provide increasing amounts of various public data to the general population, with various exploitation methods.

This opening process involves data coming from science, the legal system, socio-economy studies. It also involves addressing systems (such as geographical signaling systems that provide the locations of places and events), as well as data pertaining to climatology, geology, agriculture, arts, etc.

Such governmental initiatives[30] are numerous in the democratic countries and also emerge elsewhere. They strengthen the drive to experimenting and thinking about collective intelligences, how they operate and develop abilities to reflect on themselves. They encourage us to explore the capacity of collective intelligences to unfold models of production and diffusion of knowledge that are less centralized and increasingly a-centered (and even bottom-up). These complex issues are key, as they will end up determining the future becomings of open and fluid societies.

---

30  http://fr.wikipedia.org/wiki/Open_Government_Initiative, http://en.wikipedia.org/wiki/Open_ source_governance, http://www.whitehouse.gov/open, Open Government Partnership: http:// www.opengovpartnership.org/.

OD materializes the demand that territorial authority delegations and governments provide some public data to citizen in order for them to "for example reuse them in specific services or applications". Data pertaining to fields of demography, economy, tourism, transportation, cultures, environment, etc., can therefore be published and made accessible (in various formats). All the domains that contribute to the description and management of territories are potentially involved.

The State and its various ministries, the institutions and public companies, the regions, cities, the public service concession holders, etc., all these agents are required to act in response to this movement and to the local, governmental or European Union demands of OD, while maintaining an appropriate and protective trade-off between what pertains to personal data and private life and what is a "common good". The opening of digital records and public domain databases, the developing of new records about an increasing number of domains of the public sector is a movement that must negotiate with the production of novel types of memories and records in civil society because a line must be drawn between private and public (therefore open) data. The understanding of the issues that the OD movement raises is thus made more complex by this negotiation, while the official discourse celebrates transparency as a core virtue of democracy.

We believe that we urgently need to deconstruct this celebration of transparency. Furthermore, "real-time environmental data bases" are being developed in several places, on the basis of a distributed data collection methods involving disseminated sensors carried by parts of the publics and groups of citizens. For example, the ecological bikes of Copenhagen City perform such a distributed sensor scheme. These bases of a new type are linked to sustainable development, environmentalism and the new scientific methods of digital empiricism (Gerard Berry, Jim Gray), as well as to matters of security.

What is called "crowdsourcing" refers to a whole diversity of processes, which should be analyzed more deeply. Crowdsourcing is a method that aims at tapping into new sources and resources, into resources that are non-institutional, ad hoc, and that partake to the production of knowledge or sometimes to their management. These sources sometimes involve processes of data capture and collection that are relatively simple and passive (when one acts as a "consenting" sensor), and sometimes involve more active processes of project definition, processing and exploitation that can in turn involve relatively creative innovation processes, linked at various levels to the local conditions and collective assemblages. How agents are involved also happens very diversely. From volunteering to remunerated work, the models of collaboration can take forms of various complexities. For example, a participant can consent to not only provide, via his mobile phone and during a given time period, the data about his whereabouts but also to qualify it [CAR 14b].

In the context of a growing trend to the popularization of science and attempts to raise awareness and involve an increasing number of citizens in the complex process of scientific co-construction, making the said citizens be vectors of the collecting of information (and even of more complex information production) is a developing strategy: everyone knows about crowd-sourced projects in astronomy and environmental sciences. It is sometimes difficult to evaluate the impact this trend has on the spreading of scientific culture and on the development (in a scientific perspective) of reflectivity. Moreover, a growing number social–technical controversies nowadays arise as the crisis of rationalisms unfolds, which complicates the measure of the effects of scientific crowdsourcing. In a similar perspective, how experts relate to the "layman" word is also being transformed. For example, groups of patients demand to share knowledge and information with doctors, to voice their opinion and propose their own approach to ailments. Although they challenge the knowledge power of doctors, the latter can take advantage of these demands and tap into this "non-specialist expertise" and into the data produced by monitored collection programs. There are numerous examples of this type of experimentation.

Let us mention another example, as it sheds an interesting light on the scale of issues that OD raise.

OD, open sources and data mining are also involved as essential elements of military strategy and "counterinsurgency intelligence". In the case of operations abroad, for example, the implementation of digital networks, digital communication apparatuses and local data bases is a major pillar of the strategy. Developing tactical-operational strategies in the semiotic sphere is fundamental in order to better control the anthropological, cultural and societal dimensions of the conflict or the operation being carried out. This was for instance the aim of the ICON project in 2000 (Figure 1.1).

**An Access Architecture for ICON**

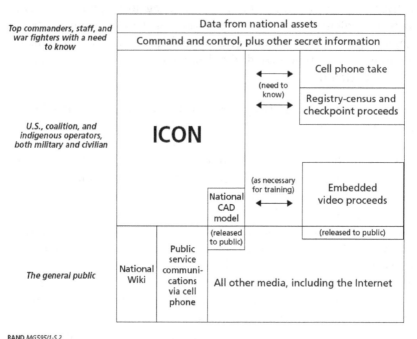

RAND MG595/1-S.2

**Figure 1.1.** *An image of the Icon project of the Rand Corporation*

That is how, since the publication of the report[31], there is a steady effort in furthering research about means of controlling political and anthropological dimensions of conflict and insurgency fields, especially by strategically leveraging the opportunities opened by data proliferation. Such strategies naturally rely on the cultural and political records of the digital space, i.e. the "open data", as well as on the deposits of collaborative

---

31 Martin C. Libicki, David C. Gompert, David R. Frelinger, Raymond Smith, "Byting Back Regaining Information Superiority Against 21st-Century Insurgents", Rand Corporation, 2007.

knowledge constituted by digital social networks of all sorts, which are steadily growing[32] [JUA 07].

Similarly, the multiplication of OD sources and exploitation methods are strongly attached to the increasing security and to the development of military urbanism [GRA 12].

To trace the whereabouts of the citizen–consumer–soldier is indeed the core of control and intelligence society. The infrastructures that support urban life development – although they are often overlooked, considered as normal as long as they keep functioning – are generally central to political violence and the contemporary military doctrine. Data collection involves the military and police force in association with evermore sophisticated algorithmic devices.

The "open data" movement is thus a chance, in its various manifestations, to politically re-negotiate the power – knowledge relationship to transform collective intelligences and liberate the circulating flows of knowledge. Now is also the time to elaborate new criteria to measure the economic and political impact of OD within the context of ecologies of the environment, psychologies and culture, which are themselves subject to the conditions and constraints of capitalistic markets.

The "open data" movement would therefore improve its credibility if it would tackle a specific issue about access to datasets: it consists of open access routes that realistically take into account the actual uses, social-cognitive practice, political economies and constraints that come with the production of novel types of knowledge and know-hows.

Nowadays more than ever, the digital divide echoes cognitive divides. This resonance generates the rise of agonistic narratives and creative forces, even on the basis of the "doxic immanence field", in Philippe Mengue's words [MEN 09]. There are sharp differences in the abilities to use or write on the basis of digital data and in the abilities to produce them. Very

---

32 J.M. Noyer, B. Juanals, "La stratégie américaine du contrôle continu De la "Noopolitik" (1999) à "Byting Back" (2007): une création de concepts et de dispositifs de contrôle des populations" (http://archivesic.ccsd.cnrs.fr/sic_00292207/fr). See also: counterinsurgency FM 3-24, David H. Petraus, James F. Amos, respectivement Lieutenant General, U.S. Army Lieutenant General, paper 9 11 U.S. Marine Corps Commander Deputy Commandant U.S. Army Combined Arms Center Combat Development and Integration.

discriminating mechanisms filter that is able to extract new knowledge from data, which is able to reuse this knowledge and feed it back to the general circulation and production machine. For "open data" to have positive outcomes, we need to think of an education of and by citizens with regard to the pervasive influence that digital and computational practices have on the societal world. This necessity is becoming, day by day, more evident and pressing.

## 1.6. Coupling OD/big data/data mining

The OD movement must also reflect its articulation with the spreading of intellectual technologies and software that aim at the intelligent handling of data in order to foster individual and collective creativity. It must therefore cope with the necessary task of accompanying the development of the social-semantic web, democratic interfaces and the learning processes they imply.

That everything becomes algorithmic can be seen as a social-cognitive and political-anthropological issue. In that perspective and in Deleuzian terms, it opens to novel mechanisms that may striate the metastability of collectives, thus threatening to let elaborate control societies emerge that would make democratic regimes mutate "out of themselves". It also opens itself to mechanisms that may produce new smooth spaces in which to revive the cognitive conditions essential to hybrid intelligences.

Among other things, becoming algorithmic partly renews the process of actualization of new cerebral states and opens novel analogical freedoms in the interstices. However, we must repeat that it does not necessarily mean that, on the basis of the becomings of the technogenesis – sociogenesis coupling, the desire for control and mastery (the most common desire of the world!) would not use the automation of several politico-cognitive tasks, tasks that are attached to modes of governance of populations, to totalitarian ends.

The deployment of digital writings and networks therefore causes, in both the public and personal realm, a transformation of memories, publication mechanisms and ecological niches that are the conditions of our lives and existence. This is planetary and it affects, although with significant differences and inequalities in its actualization, our anthropologies, social and social–cognitive practices, subjectivities and identity processes.

New political economies emerge, attached to new libidinal economies. On the basis of new reticular dimensions, a new onto-ethology of individuals is being deployed. The collectives of thought and work are being recomposed. Contrary to often heard and read nostalgic critiques, we are not facing a loss of connection, nor a thinning out of our associative abilities or of what binds and ties us to each other. No, we are facing a transformation, the advent of something different, which involves the saturation of all this, and in which an essential part of the question of the future of our becomings and of the alteration processes, the becomings of open societies, is at stake.

The world increasingly appears as a vast realm of relational systems, in which new cartographies are necessary for those who want to inhabit it. This indeed echoes the relatively pronounced evolution of "the Political" toward a generalized experiment in which the means and the performative procedures problematically prevail over the ends, be they political or ethical. Great ecological (social, mental, environmental) crises stem from the transformation of the anthropotechnical, economical, cognitive, organizational, military, etc., mechanisms. They arise mostly under the conditions of the digital perspective and its associated technical and scientific becomings. Such crises in turn intensify these transformative tendencies and processes. There are bio-political and psycho-political becomings, then, that develop into new, previously unseen shapes.

One thus understands why so much effort is made to develop a semio-political thought about interfaces [NOY 11, LAZ 06]. Throughout the texture of intelligence societies, threaded on the basis of an ever-extending, increasingly intrusive ichnology[33], a specter is haunting the new modalities of work, existence and governing – the specter of traceability. This generalized interfacing and therefore normalizing strategy is one of the major pillars of the contemporary transformation of the governmental essence, especially when it is understood in the framework of the "becoming Empire" as defined by Negri and Hardt [NEG 00].

A relative weakening of centralized control systems is indeed visible, in parallel with the strengthening of distributed systems of control and

33 Louise Merzeau, http://archivesic.ccsd.cnrs.fr/docs/00/48/32/94/PDF/CITES-MERZEAU.pdf.

intelligence that are immanent to the production system of networked urbanity. These vast and complex systems of a centered networks are managed in a multifractal mode that involves many recursive loops and local rules implemented on increasingly elaborate digital machine interfaces.

At all scales, from intranets to globalization processes, there are transformations happening, shifts from the Nation state to the Market state (in the framework of the attempt to establish, forcefully and rapidly, a global market), shifts from traditional forms of sovereignty to new decentralized and relatively complex forms (in which the privatization of the most regalian functions, including that of war machines goes unfettered). These shifts result in the semiotic and software issue which is of major politico-strategic importance. Those who can extract and exploit the graphs that emerge from the (individual or collective) digital traces gain a superior standpoint within the political, libidinal and strategical economies. He who is able to exploit the variations and differences in speed of the writing systems, he who masters the variations of meme[34] combinations, an essential part of the social-political becomings of the modes of intelligibility and the processes of subjectivation, this one gains a dominant position in the production, circulation and consumption of knowledge.

## 1.7. The semantic web as intellectual technology

In the framework set out above, the notions we call Open, Big and Small Data are entangled in the nexus of major social–cognitive and political tensions. They also involve significant epistemological debates that question, for example, the power of digital empiricism, statistical algorithmics, which challenge the dominant position of theory with regard to the significance of its speculative dimensions and of its conceptual modeling. In 2008, Anderson [AND 08] remarked that: "At the petabyte scale, information is not a matter of simple three- and four-dimensional taxonomy and order but of dimensionally agnostic statistics. It calls for an entirely different approach, one that requires us to lose the tether of data as something that can be visualized in its totality. It forces us to view data mathematically first and establish a context for it later. [...] There is now a better way. Petabytes allow us to say: 'Correlation is enough'. We can stop looking for models.

---

34 See note 19.

We can analyze the data without hypotheses about what it might show. We can throw the numbers into the biggest computing clusters the world has ever seen and let statistical algorithms find patterns where science cannot" [AND 08]. This opinion has since been critiqued with good reason. Later on in this book, we will elaborate on this.

Other questions come up in the fields of Human and Social Sciences. At the core of these paradigmatic issues, we find the measure of the evolutions of digital writings, especially in the form of what is called the semantic web or social-semantic web. We also find questions about the nature of ontologies[35]. Such writing is, once again, at the forefront of change. The control and development of digital memories fully partakes to what Jean-François Lyotard called, in 1979 already, "legitimation by power [...] the latter legitimizing itself like a system tuned to optimize its own performance. Indeed, this sort of control on context is precisely what generalized algorithmic methods promise. The performativity of an enunciation increases proportionally with the quantity of information one has about what it refers to. Thus, the growth of power and its self-legitimation now uses the production, recording, accessibility and operability of information" [LYO 79].

However, as Yannick Maignien writes [MAI 09], the digital revolution is both the subject and the instrument of the contemporary development of social and human sciences. Data exploitation, production of novel types of knowledge, new forms of expression that mostly target the general audience, new ways of accessing data, free (social-political) usage... These new practices force the OD movement to tackle the issues of traces, data and text corpora processing. The issues raised are of cognitive nature and therefore pertain to scientific work, but they are also of political and economical nature, because "value" production also involves costs.

For example, the notion of "Open Content Mining"[36] is currently increasingly attracting attention within the "open" publishing movement as well as in the framework of private publishing.

---

35 In the semantic web sense.

36 http://poynder.blogspot.fr/2012/06/new-declaration-of-rights-opencontent.html; especially the interview of Peter Murray-Rust by Richard Poynder (2012).

In other publications (http://archivesic.ccsd.cnrs.fr/sic_00759618), we have detailed how the movements of "the Open", OD and data mining are connected. Data mining is itself central to the process of commodification of data, knowledge and semiotic domains in the regimes of market economies. For example, the French regional authorities deal with OD on the basis of their institutional heritage, in a "top-down" stance. This framework only allows them to think the political, economic, cognitive and cultural subject of OD from a single point of view: for them, the issue of OD mainly concerns the processing of data access and distribution. They temporarily leave the management of metadata untouched, although this management cannot be separated from the issue of organizational and institutional inter-interoperability[37].

Metadata is thought of in terms of access, in a paradigm of internal performativity of the institution assemblages. So far, no attention is paid to the social–political dimension of innovation or to the question of how to renew democratic practices. Writings, interfaces and document engineering policies are nevertheless influenced by actual conditions, but up until now, the regional and local administration prioritize, as one of their main axis of work, the normalization of the data catalogs of OD portals. They in fact propose a late (and necessary) equivalent to what the Dublin Core was for the web. The project, however, progresses fast and should soon reach issues and questions such as: "what to do?", "what for?", "to which ends create these metadata?".

To interconnect and intelligently process, data are becoming an essential part of OD management. To achieve this, the conditions in which software and applications are created and disseminated must be openly thought about. Here also, strong lines of tensions are drawn between the liberal (and even neo-liberal) paradigm and the various ways of imagining the commons, all the more that the modes of creation and selection of uses as well as the desires of intelligence are not only diverse but also often competing or even conflicting. To conceive commons in the paradigm of multiplicity or in that of unity becomes an opposition between a-centered and centralized modes of governance. The work of Ostrom is still a major reference on this account[38].

---

37 http://fr.wikipedia.org/wiki/Données_ouvertes_en_France.
38 E. Ostrom, Beyond Markets and States: Oolycentric Governance of complex economic systems, Nobel Lecture.

Metadata and the semantic web must therefore be designed without preconceptions with respect to the optimality of organizational forms, especially because the criteria and ends of such an optimization cannot be easily determined. So, the various models of semantic or social-semantic web must be evaluated in the light of the organizational plasticity and combinatorial grammars they enable.

The worst that could happen would indeed be to essentialize the writings and methods, to developed closed ontologies, whereas we live in times when what governance models need is to develop their processuality and the heterogeneity of agents, practices, criteria and ends. They need to open bridges to foster differential relations between microworlds and macro-worlds. What "reusing data" means is a renewal of the definition of the process of work and the struggle for new democratic forms and new forms of creativity. This is a pretty tall order. In a first phase, let us sum up the essential elements: the main standards published by the W3C are called RDF, OWL and SPARQL. Several tools have been developed for these standards. The RDF-based approaches, such as the linked OD or "LOD Cloud" follow its predicative nature and are but one way to apprehend some types of data exploitation to design various processing methods on a data corpus.

There are many different perspectives on the world, and these perspectives are not necessarily unifiable. Being aware of this heterogeneity should be sufficient for ontology and metadata designers to take a reflective step back and avoid falling for the urge (one of the most common temptation of the world) to define writings and standards from a totalitarian and simplistic viewpoint. That is one of the reasons why paying great attention to the works of the "Government Linked Data Working Group", whose mission is to "provide standards and information that will help governments, worldwide, to publish their data in the form of efficient and functional "Linked Data", thanks to semantic web techniques"[39], is important.

Similarly, the Simple Knowledge Organization System defines a data model that allows the sharing and combination of knowledge organizing systems via the web.

---

39 http://www.w3.org/2011/gld/wiki/Main_Page – see also the LOD2 initiative of the European Union: http://lod2.eu/Welcome.html.

As we have mentioned before, the "Open" approach, from its very beginning, involved a shift from the paradigm of access to that of knowledge production-circulation under new conditions. This shift highlighted how essential metadata are to increase the quality and power of inferences that can be made in order to extract knowledge or processing methods such as statistical processing, thus enabling the exploitation of structured, semi-structured or unstructured heterogeneous data, etc. Later on in this book, we will explain how the processes subsumed under the phrase "data mining" are essential to our understanding of the reuse and exploitation of data to our apprehension of the production of novel visibilities and of Value creation. This is why we think that a global reflection on OD cannot separate the following different dimensions and think them apart: the multiple dimension of data mining, the various types of intellectual practice, social-cognitive conditions of usage, citizenship, consumption, the definition of elites... Individuals, organizations and communities, all these bodies experience the opening of data with their own social-cognitive apparatuses, which they support and elaborate according to the political, economic and ethical ends they purport.

This leads us, once more, to the "limits of the current situation: a data-oriented web with a clear line drawn between the fields of social sciences and that of new technologies". Pierre Levy has been considering for a long time the recasting of this divide with the help of a metalanguage (Ieml). This metalanguage would enable the creation of the conditions of an "intelligent" navigation through heterogeneous domains and ontologies. In other words, it would enable its agents to inhabit translation or contact zones in which cognitive practice and the work of thinking can be carried out. His aim is to develop the conditions of reflexivity required for thinking collectives to be used as instances of their own reflective work.

This constitutes a context that can naturally be extended to include the political economy of marketing, the economy of security, urbanization, sustainable development, the extension of the means of semiotic control... In this context, data mining has become a new "great narrative", an underlying but blinding discourse that tends to control the structuring and shaping of the world. Human sciences, marketing and economy, strategic and military aspects... all these data mining actualizations, all these modes of intelligibility spurred alliances that sometimes bear dangerous implications, fostering profiling techniques and inducing strategies of prediction, performation and preemption.

To set up a continuous control of the political, strategic and economic realities and of psycho-politics is a temptation that more than ever feeds on these new trends to develop its insomniac rationalizations. Data mining is the backbone of this shift from societies of control to society of strategic intelligence or "sousveillance".

Some constitutive elements of the limited but seminal open model need to be recalled here. The Open Archive movement brought about the ideas that now force us to think about the so-called OD, Big Data, Linked Data, e-Science, data mining, Algorithmics and relate them (they are constitutive of the various aspects of the transformations of intellectual work processes of the modes of governance and political economies, which are attached to collectives intelligences). These relations are home to a twofold practical research effort. On the one hand, there is the question of how to improve and structure these immense stocks of data (various traces of, for example, behavioral data, all types of documents, scientific and financial data), in order to extract knowledge from them. On the other hand, there is the question of the exploitation of semi- or non-structured data with the same aim.

How, then, to exploit these vast amounts of heterogeneous data to extract knowledge and know-hows, analyses and results that can be reused by other agents? Such approaches are knowingly difficult to design, they involve combinatorial languages that should enable the creation of "ontologies" in a manner that allows them to strike creative relationships. The fact that various ways of modeling social-cognitive behaviors, contents to use and their associated products is undeniably a complex and significant matter. It challenges and undermines the attempts at creating the conditions of a would-be universal combinatorial model (IEML[40] is a very significant example of such attempts). At present, the notion of modularity seems inescapable and singular approaches seem to be the most efficient in a perspective of a multiplicity of models.

The diversity within OD is increasing and differences between various elements are widening, while OD is becoming central to political economies of knowledge and collective intelligences. These tendencies will induce a paradigmatic shift in the domains of ontologies and/or onto-ethologies and especially in the conditions that preside over their production. For reasons

---

40 http://www.ieml.org/french/elements.html.

pertaining to the preservation of the openness of our societies and to the possibility of sustaining healthy controversies at all levels, we believe that it would be beneficial not to remain tied up in limiting traditional perspectives. We should emancipate ourselves from the gray zones of elementary metadata and over-generalizing ontologies, which are designed under the essentialist, predicative logic inherited from the limitations and waking dreams of symbolic artificial intelligence[41].

Ontologies that are developed in a top-down approach under conditions that translate the interests of only a small number of groups and collectives cannot claim to be prescribing the way the world should be, even if their elaboration is a relatively necessary step. As the world is increasingly complex, as the heterogeneses that constitute it throughout diversify, developing, with a "bottom-up" strategy, local, specific ontologies appropriate to the specific applications, software and algorithms that are implemented on the basis on the diverse data sets becomes essential and even vital to the semantic web. The next generations of cognitive architectures, in other words the next intellectual technologies (writings, interfaces, cartographies), must (should) allow some users to become themselves relatively powerful agents, precisely within the cognitive assemblages.

Developing the semantic and socio-semantic web entails designing metadata according to the inferences and exploitation we aim to make with the data at hand, according to the research programs and usage we foresee. What we call "reuse" must therefore be understood in a largely extended sense: usage in different contexts, exploitation, invention of new data and novel knowledge, in order, once more, to create value.

From the design of metadata to the elaboration of ontologies that are at least partially interoperable, even if such elaborations are automatically or semiautomatically performed, profound issues are involved. What is at stake is not only the creation of value, as we said before, but also the various ways

---

41 Douglas Hofstadter, Godel, Escher, Bach, An Eternal Golden Braid, 1979 (French: Les brins d'une guirlande éternelle, Editions Interéditions, 1985). See also Ontologies pour le Web sémantique (Ontologies for the Semantic Web), Jean Charlet, Bruno Bachimont, Rapahël Troncy spécifique 32 CNRS / STIC, Web sémantique, Rapport final, Éditeurs Jean Charlet, Philippe Laublet & Chantal Reynaud V3 – December 2003, Charlet.

we apprehend intellectual work, and how we imagine and practice open and democratic societies.

Can we overcome this normalizing tendency? To which extent? Can we at least leave these normalized systems open to the introduction of metadata that are able to renew the types of knowledge produced? These questions undoubtedly draw out a battlefield on which to fight for democracy and intellectual freedom. In this perspective, the open source and open archive initiative movements sketch the bases of the ideas underlying the political, economic and scientific debates to come. The "commons" paradigm and the private property application programming interface (API) paradigm, their hybridizing, are thus currently the subjects of intense debates[42].

We must keep in mind that the metadata issue, especially within the framework of OD, cannot avoid questioning its relations with the evolution of the modes of social classification, the social and doxic indexing paradigm. How do they, how will they relate? Will users be allowed or able to insert their own metadata, under which protocols and with which freedom? The web indeed evolves toward the possibility for each and everyone to publish, tag, classify, etc. Social "bookmarking" continuously increases and open "tagging" systems, known as folksonomies, bloom.

Folksonomies are a great potential source of semantic richness. This emergent, ascending ("bottom-up") approach to collaborative knowledge

---

42 In terms of free software, the situation is complex. In our opinion, François Bourdoncle accurately summarized it on the basis of his experience as co-founder of Exalead: "In our domain, free software are mainly used on online website by publishers who need to add search functionalities to their software but do not wish to spend any of their added value by using our service. When the search functionality is not too strategical, however, they turn to us. We for example have agreements with societies that develop messaging archives: the vumes to process are so important that the costs of the IT stock they would need to implement a free software solution would be prohibitive.

This is in fact an economic choice between make and buy. Free software is not a miracle, despite what one might dream of. One does not simply download and press the "enter" key. If a company wants to integrate a free software into its programs and ensure ist synchronization with dozens of modules, it needs to hire a dozen of engineers, who come at a cost. Free software solutions therefore have pros and cons like any other proprietary competitor would. For internal applications, customers usually choose to call a software produer who will be in charge of ensuring the seamless integration of the software solution they bought." Lecture in the Ecole de Mines de Paris: EALEAD NEUF ANS APRÈS, (Exalead, 9 years later), by François Bourdoncle, co-founder of Exalead, 23d of September 2009.

resources was soon rightly seen as an approach that could overcome several thorny difficulties that knowledge management practice struggled with.

The exploitation of folksonomies, together with semantic web technologies, although less simple than what one initially imagined, are now seen as an essential step in the evolution from "Web 2.0" to "Web 3.0". Relatively complex research is devoted to create and develop new indexing and description modes. Metadata production, including that of folksonomies, is the core of the concerns of those who wish to develop a socio-semantic vision of the Internet, who wish to influence the relations between a "Web of documents" and a "Web of data". Research is being developed along several axes of which we provide a few examples below.

In the case of OAI-ORE (Open Archives Initiative Object Reuse and Exchange), "the aim is to produce standards for the description and exchange of web resource aggregates".

These aggregates, once named "compound digital objects"[43] can combine parallel resources made of texts, images, videos and data. Such standards aim at making visible the rich content of aggregates and to make it usable by applications that handle their storage, exchange, visualization, reuse and conservation"[44]. So called "Web 2.0" communities and the advocates of the semantic and socio-semantic web are very interested in such user-created metadata.

## 1.8. Towards understanding onto-ethologies

The "tagging" approach, which relies on users autonomously indexing documents because of computerized apparatuses, is interesting because it

---

43 Later on in this book we will detail how, within the great transformation of documentation, these "compound digital objects" are mirrored by "non-unequivocal, N-perspective relational compounds" that constitutes a document of hyper document in the digital realm.

44 OAI-ORE is designed to overcome the barriers found between different storage facilities, to develop a new generation of functionalities and transversal tools. In this perspective OAI-ORE advocates the standardization of the description of the relations between digital documents. By relationships between documents, they for example mean how the various versions of a document relate, or the aggregation of various documents such as the images of a web page or all the chapters of a book. Online: http://www.openarchives.org/ore/1.0/datamodel.

eases the exploitation and organization of one's own resources. It is a (relatively informal) mode of distributed indexing and classification. Let us not forget that Internet indexes and folksonomies are developed by communities of indexers that cooperate throughout the web. Resource lists are in line with the logic of the classification schemes that are characteristic of librarianship, but they do not claim that the patterns they comply with are imbued of any sense of universal disciplinary organization or of any form of theoretical legitimity. "Resource indexes compiled by communities of volunteers unceasingly grow in size and numbers. They contrast with indexes like that of, for example, Yahoo. Where Yahoo uses employees to index documents under the authority of managers and with explicit referencing policies, the process of social indexing deployed by these communities relies on modes of control situated somewhere between that of Wikipedia and the more hierarchical ones of 'Open Source' communities. Virtual community members can control and modify the classification at levels whose importance and criticality grows according to their reputation levels. They can add branches in domains where they have acquired enough 'authority', delete descriptions written in the 'notices' by less well-known contributors, etc." [ZAC 07]. The pros and cons of folksonomies have been extensively debated. The "tagging" activity, as a doxic (and partly intuitive) means of indexing, benefits to cooperative practices of various agents.

The lack of "a minima" tag organization, their heterogeneity weakens the potential benefits of folksonomies, as, for example, they limit their simple reuse and intercommunity exploitation.

These issues are reasons why not only designing standards but also proposing methods that enable the exploitation and sharing of sets of "tags" is a task that should be undertaken. There currently exist several approaches, some of which are already being used while others are being developed. These approaches are either based on semantic methodologies and formal rules paradigms (like the subject verb predicate paradigm of RDF schemes), or on statistical linguistic approaches inspired by mathematical linguistic research or clustering techniques (coming, for example, from the field of infometry)[45].

---

45 For example, there are methods involving associate words et term co-occurrences frequency measures. On this subject, see [COU 90].

The SCOT program (Social Semantic Cloud of Tags) is an example of this first type of approach. It aims to describe the structure and so-called "semantic" relations of a set of "tags" in order to improve their social-cognitive use. Such approaches rely on the fact that "tagging" processes involve people (agents), resources and "tags". From a general point of view, as we mentioned before, the conceptual framework and the tools of the semantic web are already in charge, on the basis of several analyses of social networks, the representation and exchange of items of knowledge in digital social networks. They use formats like RDF, query languages such as SPARQL, RDFS and OWL[46]. Folksonomies can in fact be exploited using graph theory in order to detect user groups and major emergent themes. Another line of research work extended the SPARQL language to expose the semantic connections and pathways between RDF resources. New routes of investigation about "tag ontologies" must also be mentioned.

These new types of ontologies are interesting because, among other characteristics, they integrate aspects of "speech acts", which are attached to tags or rather to "what we do when we tag". They allow any resource to become itself a tag, reusing works that were carried out to solve the "identity crisis" of the semantic web. They underline the semiotic nature of the relation between tags and resources: "beyond what one does with the sign, tag semiotics is a matter of what the sign performs as a sign itself, these two dimensions complementing each other"[47]. Other ideas try to take into account the communicational practices "of organizing short-lived interactions between distant users while proposing representations, which

---

46 The SPARQL language is a set of specifications that define the syntax and semantics required to query and manipulate content from RDF databases on the Web or in an RDF store. It also defines the possible forms of query results. SPARQL is adapted to the specific structure of RDF graphs, leveraging the triplets that constitute it. See online: [https://www.w3.org/2001/sw/]. RDF Schema, or RDFS is a knowledge representation extensible language. It provides the building blocks for the definition of ontologies or dictionaries that structure RDF resources. Web Ontology Language (OWL) is an XML dialect based on an RDF syntax. It enables the definition of structured web ontologies. The OWL language is based on research on descriptive logics.

47 Communication of Alexandre Monin: an ontology proposed by David Laniado from the Polytechnic University of Milan, Freddy Limpens of the INRIA, and Alexandre Monin, helped by Thomas Lörtsch and Ricardo Tasso. See also the account of the VoCamp organized by the Inria, September 2009 [http://vocamp.org/wiki/VoCampNiceSeptember2009].

often are of visual nature, of the so-created social networks". Such approaches advocate a more pragmatic approach to informational and communicational processes, considering linguistics in a more open manner. We believe that they are very interesting because they challenge the hegemony of formalisms inspired by Tim Berneers-Lee's "cake"[48], whose efficacy is dependent on a "semiotic closure" that entails reducing and standardizing the field of behaviors and practices. Again, how do those that act and speak for OD and wish to make new, more appropriate types of intellectual and social practice situate themselves?

Other stances can in fact be held up. They take into account the sociology of practice and usage, as well as the phenomena of co-construction of intelligences. This approach precisely aims at making "syntactically formal languages" efficient. The issue here is to design methods to represent such weakly formal semiotic and socio-cognitive structures in such a way that their weakly formal nature would enable a strongly pragmatic approach. This is why we believe that there is a pressing need to develop critiques and debates over the elaboration of such new alphabets, their grammars and the constraints that affect their combining. There also is a pressing need to imagine new "non-documentary" approaches to the production of open and dynamical onto-ethologies[49] in order to bring back to our awareness the fact that writings are evaluated and emerge on the basis of the creativities and inventions they open up, on the basis of the new combination modes they carry within and of the many new hermeneutics they enable.

Folksonomies that use statistical approaches and methods based on, for example, co-words analysis[50] let particularly appear, in their processing, the

---

48 The Semantic Web infrastucture is often described as a "cake", the cake of Tim Berners-Lee.

49 Conceptual ethology means, in our understanding, the diagram or field from which specific concepts emerge. These are concepts that can be considered as singularities that consist of the weaving of other concepts, percepts, affects, relatively heterogeneous writings and of various combination constraints.

50 Ciro Cattuto, Dominik Benz, Andreas Hotho, Gerd Stumme, Semantic Analysis of Tag Similarity Measures in Collaborative Tagging Systems, arXiv:0805.2045v1, 2008. Research on the semantic-based co-word analysis, Zhong-Yi Wang, Gang Li, Chun-Ya Li, Ang Li, Akade′miai Kiado′, Budapest, Hungary 2011. For a more general perspective, see the body of works on associate wordanalysis and on fractal approaches to the co-elaboration of knowledge. See also [MUT 01].

combinatorial modes mentioned above. Such methods are based on principles of similarity and co-occurrence. They show that "tagging" practices display patterns akin to those found in traditional indexing methods, and that these patterns are quite predictable [KIP 08]. Moreover, the fact that so many folksonomies are developed, that they are heterogeneous and even often not inter-operable, call for the analysis, with a similar rationale, of phenomena that overlap across "tag spaces", especially in collaborative environments [OLD 08].

This is why we should be looking for the definition of "onto-ethologies" rather than for that of ontologies. Onto-ethologies express the social-cognitive structures that corpora carry within, the translations and processuality at work in the very core of communities. We must understand the technical aspects of the "structuring" (formalization) as well as of the filtering of texts and documents in the light of a double constraint. On the one hand, we must be able to process whole populations of digital texts that may always recombine or transform; on the other hand, we must elaborate tools for the intellectual, social-cognitive exploration and exploitation of these populations, tools to represent their constitutive cognitive processuality, which fosters their analogical, associative and combinatorial capacity, on several levels of organization.

For the creative insertion of OD in the digital world to be a success, we need to invest in this increase in reflexivity that, in our opinion, results from the possibilities such tools open and from the associated emerging cartographic practices, be they doxic or scientific. Either OD will enable us to exist within the world as free beings, or it will solidify into something that will partake, as an allegedly unaware accomplice, to the continuation of polemological power relations.

In that perspective, what does the phrase "to open data" mean? Let us consider the example of the Open Archive. The Open Archive provides access to collections of articles or documents produced by people active in the research domain. Its service is based on the digital corpora of a scientific community and on the automatic and semiautomatic data-processing software mentioned above. This apparatus is representative of the associations, associative networks, aggregations and selection modes, constraints and combination modes as well as of the social modes of transmission and selection of such constraints. It applies on the heterogeneous assemblages of researchers, laboratories, texts, journals, themes and concepts. In order to "open data", we need to be able to update one's knowledge of the new research fronts, the influencing networks and the systems that emerge to translate, overlap or percolate notions, concepts or themes. The representations must include networks of agents, networks of citations and references, co-citations[51], the modes in which texts and their associated contexts are repeated, altered as well as the graphs of concepts. The aim is to provide researchers with new means of orienting themselves in the various perspectives, thus enabling a better management and navigation across points of view and the increase in associationist capabilities. In other words, it should enable the ability to relate what at least partly constitutes the structural conditions in which we as researchers become visible, conditions that will always be bounded and particular. This is the profound signification of what we call new cartographic practices, and it should spark off the creation of novel types of interfaces[52].

These approaches raise many issues, as they sometimes seem to rely on an exaggeratively essentialist understanding or interactions and usage, whereas they apply on the lives of populations, on the multiplicities of assemblages as... metastable multiplicities.

These issues also draw attention to the various ways we can attempt to describe and represent hypertextual digital memories and attempt to create meaning from them. They stress the need to show that plurality – according to contexts and corpora, usage and practices – is required in the ways we conceptualize the types of writing we need to inhabit the multiple social-cognitive space times. The various web structuring approaches are not fundamentally incompatible, and an appropriate understanding of plurality is a requirement to develop OD usage as well as their desires.

---

51 Issues pertaining to the field of citations are complex. See, for example, [DER 90, COM 79]. See also [VAN 01, HIG 01, WOU 99, CRO 98, LEY 98].

52 We have already mentioned the "memetic" trend, which, within a similar perspective, generates research based on an evolutionary understanding of the replications and lives of "memes", which are described as semiotic entities or as ant form relational compound. But then, what is it for local authorities and public institutions, as well as for those who will gain access, to "open data for new visibilities"? Which new types of reflectivity will then develop and affect usage and social-cognitive practices?

We thus favor an open approach that would consist of thinking about the differential relationships between different understandings of the semantic web and that would involve precise characterization of their articulations and articulation levels. Such a stance holds dissensual life at the heart of the democratic habitat, as an essential condition of its perpetuation and deepening.

Public sector OD epitomizes the role narratives and slogans have in the construction of an irrepressible desire for data. From a very general perspective, OD advocates free access (and provides the services that enable it) to some public data, for users to develop uses and ways of exploiting them unfettered by patents, copyright or other control mechanisms. This is a very simple definition. Ever since the very beginning of its development, the web fostered a "free" access to documents of heterogeneous nature. This was indeed the original, foundational intent of the creators of the Internet network, who developed it on the basis of a specific model of scientific activity: a mode in which the "free" production and circulation of knowledge optimizes creativity and innovation drives. Although the irenic and simplistic aspects of this model may rightfully be critiqued, the project was developed on the basis of this first, general idea. Moreover, the so-called "Internet of data" (now with its associate the Internet of objects) may be seen – under specific economic and political conditions – as the convergence of several mechanisms that lead to a shared goal: the spreading of data in both the private and public spheres and the "intelligent reuse of data independently from their original digital context" [NOY 12].

Nowadays, tension keeps mounting, to put it sharply, between the advocates of a philosophy of open resources (the web as a smooth space) and those advocating a proprietary approach (the web as a striated space).

This dichotomy however lacks nuance and needs to be refined, as it makes it too easy for us to be "tossed about from the Charybdis of the market and individual property for all and the Scylla of bantustans of primitive communism hailing the new accumulation evangiles" [MOU 10]. New digital records are open every day, as well as public domain databases. New types of records are constantly created and implemented in new sectors that pertain to this very public domain. Parallel to this explosion of available public data, whole sections of civil society are creating new types of open, public but non-institutional records. This sometimes difficult cohabitation can be confusing for those who try to clarify their understanding of the issues raised by the OD movement, which hails transparency as a cardinal virtue of democracy. The evaluations tasks that emerge in France because of a legal background of injunctions and compulsory regulations[53] also become more complex. In fact how can we evaluate the completion of aims such as: "to develop transparency and democracy"; "to make the action of local institutions and elected representatives more readable"; "to provide meaning and to make knowledge emerge"; "to enrich the knowledge of local regions and territory"; "to promote the reuse of data by the research industry, the education system and journalism"; "to promote the development of innovating services"; "to develop citizen empowerment", etc.?

These objectives are far reaching and their evaluation would require far more than counting how many datasets were liberated, how many applications were developed or how many APIs were queried or downloaded. Currently, most of the gauges of public administrations merely provide information about the "activity" of the OD apparatus, but they fail to provide any relevant information about the transformative social processes that might result. The notion of transparency (dominated by a broadcasting engineering perspective) has been extensively used and exploited by now, but one realizes that transparency is not convincing enough for the data owners or managing bodies, which remain skeptical. In order for OD to become desirable, other stances and actions are necessary. Many project leaders acknowledge this lack of enthusiasm: in France, the explicit voicing of a desire (from representatives, CEOs or inhabitants) has not been a salient aspect of OD initiatives. The initiatives were rather carried out as experimentations, and supported by rationalizing narratives of political and managerial flavor.

In our opinion, what is at stake is a true, drastic change in the political economy of territories. In a context where centralized governance systems

---

53 The law of the 17th of July 1978 already required that data be accessible on demand and acknowledged the right to access public information in France. In 2014 the Commission des Finances de l'Assemblée Nationale decided that reforms about open data (access and reuse of public data) would have to be debated in the parliament. See also the PROJET DE LOI *pour une* République numérique, (Project of law for a digital Republic) that was recorded in the Presidency of the National Assembly on the December 9, 2015.

are to various extent losing their grip and in which decentralized or a-centered modes of governance are rising, questions about this transformation could be asked, in crude terms, as follows: "How can open data, or at least some of its forms, transform the modalities of public action and enable the advent of an 'active milieu' different from the current conditions, which are dominated by "constructivist planification"?. This would imply reimagining evaluation protocols, discarding the inherited activity measures, in order to truly make a reflective effort to invent new measures with other methods... How indeed would one understand the impacts of OD on territories, citizens and the relationships the latter establish with the former, as well as, on the way, apprehend these relationships, if one lacks the truly social – technical, anthropological and political surveys or proper knowledge of the lifecycles of data? What could we possibly understand without means of apprehending the heterogeneous practices, the long networks and the complex assemblages that constitute the nature of the studied subject?

## 1.9. Marketing intelligences: data and graphs in the heat of passions

The key role of marketing in the search for consumerist metastability was never explained more accurately than by Sloterdijk.

In Chapter 37 of *In the Interior of Capitalism*, entitled "Mutations in the Pampering Space", he strongly insists on the fact that: "That 'things' from the world of belonging do not remain untransformed in their transition to the world of options is in fact mirrored in countless nervous reflections (…). If buying, selling, renting, letting, borrowing and ending are operations that affect all aspects of life in the Great Installation, it is inevitable that the accessibility of things through monetary mediation will produce a corresponding world feeling. First of all, one experiences an immeasurable increase in accessible objects, and last of all, the convergence of the world interior and the spending power space – with consequences on the status of the devices surrounding us on a daily basis"[SLO 13].

Sloterdijk then goes on: "One can now understand why way of life that weakens allegiances and reinforces options lead to a psychopolitical rearrangement of clientele in the comfort spheres of the Western and Westernized world" [SLO 13, pp. 206–208]. This rearrangement, by the way, becomes radical when neuromarketing embodies it into its bold attempt to naturalize the "consumerist-brain". Because of such an attempt, we have to face the issue, or rather to bear the brunt of the question asked by C. Malabou: "What can we do to prevent the consciousness of the mind to coincide with the spirit of capitalism?" [MAL 04].

Bernard Stiegler also sharply criticizes capitalism. According to him, marketing's goal is to "take power on the individual's psyche in order to lead to instinctual behavior. This capture is obviously destructive. Desire is channeled to industrial means, but to accomplish it, the libidinal energy must be bypassed with all its apparatus because it is produced at a second level as it is not a primary energy. Primary energies are to be found in urges, instinctual pulsions" [STI 12].

Marketing, data-mining and geo-localization have therefore allied themselves on the basis of these core transformations. They of course come with techniques of generalized traceability, which relentlessly feed behavioral and socio-semantic traces. The recent advent of techniques to precisely geo-localize opens further possibilities of enrichment and interpretation of traces. The diversity of interfaces and associated applications ensure the structural coupling of various modes of existence, each of which is bound to a specific territory. Smartphones and other roaming interfaces are in charge of the transitions and connections from the interior of the world to the assemblages of vast relational systems.

All these new developments encourage the exploitation and evaluation of assemblages. Many such projects are seeking a kind of trace quality certification system (about judgments and user occurrences), in order to provide ever more advice services with regard to consumer choices, whether it be about products, shops, or daily facilities (localizing a shop, evaluating shops and services in the neighborhood).... These projects leverage the irresistible rise of geolocalization techniques, with its soon to come precision revolution, while in the same time progressively filling gigantic databases that, coupled with appropriate and powerful algorithms, will soon enable the development of a kind of "geo-socio-semantics" discipline. This new research field will qualitatively unveil (collective or individual) assemblages that will enrich the environment of advanced marketing policies, in line with a renewed, complex perspective on relationships with territories.

Such a technical research effort can be understood as a life-size experiment, which could lead to novel governance models. These could be of territorial nature or hybrid, coupled with decentralized and polycentered models. In other words, they could be designed according to the scales of the relational systems that determine the actants under study, and how they relate. Such assemblages, together with social-demographic and economic meters, as well even as data about other types of informational flows, could in time bring about modes of intelligibility and organization of territories that are yet unseen. Such modes would be complex and include dimensions about the subjectivities that constitute them. They could for example revive the issue of "address" in a context of the digital territorialization, which results in entangled territories. They could also foster elaborate models to striate the desire regimes that are attached to the dynamics of the previously mentioned "description – performance – prediction". Such models could be the basis of a governance similar to that of Philip K. Dick's Minority Report [BER 11][54].

So we think this movement as a threefold process: Description/ Performance/Prediction.

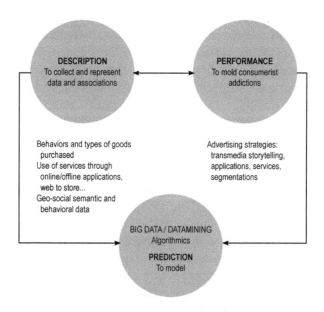

**Figure 1.2.** *The threefold description/performance/prediction process*

---

54 For the conceppt of preemption in the field of strategy, see also [HAR 10].

This trinity creates an unprecedented semiotic production and organization mechanism. It aims to elicit addiction(s) in the metastability of consumerist collectives that must (with others) sustain the political and religious order of the merchant world, ensure its continued creation, the endless pursuit of consumerist ends.

Within this framework, predictive assemblages (and their desires) are an essential apparatus, immanent in the hybrid collective metastability mechanism. As a central element, it presents itself "arched", keeping a tight grip on the "auto-fabrication" of the human – post – humans with their associated milieus.

As a nexus, the consumerist individual is threaded with the object relations that converge to or/and that leave from him or her and with the transactions he or she agrees to. The individual therefore is the expression of a relational complex written in the digital stratum. Interfaces, as we mentioned before, are an essential part of the apparatus, therefore the issues about relational technologies and applications are determinant. They support exchanges between territories, translate and redistribute digital flows of information and socio-semantic elements of any nature. These interfaces and relational technologies are the ones that enable rich existential universes as well as the emergence of new modes of existence.

In a sense, they can be seen as the "existential clutch". Marketing forces therefore increasingly obsessively edge their way into them, in order to get hold of a dominant position in their production. The new regimes of desires are being determined in this negotiation and whether there is a space, or rather which room there remains for other types of regimes is already a burning issue, the terms of a conflict with the hegemonic tendencies of marketing.

The core goal is then to ever better know the consumers to gather evermore data about their identities, behaviors, tastes, past purchasing patterns, etc. Algorithms extract knowledge in increasingly elaborate bottom-up approaches, build graphs and cartographies of the associative networks that constitute the onto-ethology of the customer, determine customer relationships, cross-check and intersect data and available information immediately or in due time. They thus enable to invent relevant adverts and enunciations, discourses that can shape and perform desires and subjectivities. In this context, the "wisdom of crowds" [ORI 09, SUR 04], the collective intelligences of usage, the complexions of passions of customers as well as the forms of trade objects are focusing most of the attention [BOU 10].

The web represents, as we pointed out before, a gigantic network of systems of hierarchical classification and evaluation of information, a network in which judgment discourses and reputation play an essential role. It is of course also an endless resource for (not only) marketing strategies. This raises several issues.

The Internet stratum, with its networks and research interfaces, help raise the profile of various emergent phenomena. Collective knowledge emerges as well as assemblages of judging discourse and utterances. These emerging semiotic elements transform with time, altered by several factors, along with their trajectories across cultural and economic worlds of varying heterogeneity and according to the networks and apparatuses through which they are expressed and circulate, a circulation that itself alters them.

Well known is the fact that this is one of the reasons why linguistic and statistical analyses were developed, in order to extract, with varying degrees of precision, semantic dynamics and semiotic regimes from large quantities of utterances, texts, documents as well as sound and images.

The history of these linguistic research developments is well known. It involves lexicometry and infometric studies, as well as works about "data mining", "opinion mining" and "sentiment analysis". These fields of research are very much appreciated by economic sectors such as e-reputation, influence networks visibility optimization, analysis of the modality of that visibility. In short, all practices that involve analyzing narratives and their inherent conflicts are attractive to marketing.

To obtain such bodies of knowledge, the main agents use a multiplicity of approaches and resources. They, for example, call on to Internet users to evaluate products, companies, organizations and services; they then evaluate the expertise of these users; they use systems of recommendations and collaboration between Internet users; they leverage crowdsourcing practices, which make humans serve computer systems, etc. [ABI 12].

More generally, "information" and "opinions" can be found on the web, not only on social networks, the various forms of microblogging and on customer experience websites etc., but also on the websites of the traditional printing press (despite their historical orientation toward factual information, "they have turned to social-based journalism since the advent Web 2.0"), on commercial and institutional websites, portals and community sites that investigate content sharing practices....

But so-called "relational" digital social networks are only a part of this sweeping movement of transformation of the "plane of immanence of the doxa". Beyond the mass networks in which communities deploy themselves, aggregate and converge via the narratives and transactions of which they are both the expressed and the expression, one can see that the expression space is progressively differentiating itself into various different subspaces. We can discern that digital networks host complex becoming minority phenomena. This is a very significant evolution. Many types of competing social networks emerge are already in operation or are being implemented. They aim to quench the emergent thirst, with ad hoc developments, for specific aggregation patterns attached to a demand for confidentiality, both in the short term and long term. We thus currently observe the convergence and reinforcement of tendencies on the basis of a common involvement in the sharing of practices, narrative modes, levels of knowledge and specific "memetic" attractors.

Beyond all these digital developments, the most important is to grasp and think the articulation between digital and non-digital. In an in-depth analysis, it must be understood as the structural coupling of the digital and non-digital milieus, in other words their co-determination. The reterritorialization mechanisms pushed by marketing tendencies via, for example, the geolocalization frenzy are increasingly powerful. They actually mean the "complication" of territories and practices, and have significant consequences on political economies, on libidinal economies and on the "complexion of passion of individuals" and their affects, across the merchandizing of objects and services.

Marketing forces, in short, aim to ever deeper influence the molecular and molar assemblages at the roots of customer relationship. To achieve this, they relentlessly increase the level of details of the description of customer relationship ecologies in order to increase the control they have on it. To do so, they use information that digital "big data" is meant to provide.

In this perspective, data mining has become a new "great narrative". It attempts at structuring and molding the world in general and specifically the regimes of desire, the pulsionnal regimes that are necessary to the continuation of consumerism. With data mining, marketing forces continuously develop new profiling techniques that feed the famous "description – prediction – performance" trinity, reaching out to the dream of "preempting" even the figures of desires and the becomings of subjectivities.

The urge to create a continuous control of an economic and consumerist reality more than ever echoes (and most certainly serves as a political apparatus terrain of experiment) the various forms of psychopower, the strategies of neuropower and even more radically what some American strategists (in another perspective) called, as soon as 1994, "neocortical war" [SZA 94].

This is the reason why marketing forces realize that they must somehow dig deeper into the analysis of the practices and transactions that social networks foster. Indeed, in these social networks: "In this context of the epochal trend towards individualistic life forms reveals its immunological significance: today [...] it is individuals who [...] break away from their group bodies as carriers of immune competencies [...] to disconnect their happiness and unhappiness form the being-in-shape of the political commune. We are now experiencing what is probably the irreversible transformation of political security collectives into groups with individualistic immune designs" [SLO 13, p. 153].

Social networks indeed provide an extraordinary milieu for experimentation, in which we play out the opposition of collective and commons against the rise, with aggregates, of "The axiom of the individualistic immune order gained currency in populations of self-centered individuals like some new vital insight: that ultimately no one would do for them what they do not do for themselves. The new immunity techniques [...] presented themselves as existential strategies to 'societies' of individuals in which the long road to flexibilization, the weakening of 'object relationships' and the general authorization of the disloyal or reversible inter-human relationships had led to the 'goal', to what Spengler rightly prophesied as the final stage of every culture: the state in which it is impossible to decide whether individuals are diligent or decadent" [SLO 13, p. 154]. On this battle field, marketing forces claim to be a reference point, a trustworthy third party, an apparatus that proposes directions in this jungle of desires, instinctual urges and addictions by means of overexposing the logics of usage and their criteria and discourses of overexposing the doxic plane of immanence. The claim that their evaluation mechanisms, viral and mimetic mechanisms and wisdom of stupidity examples can serve as landmarks.

As François Bourdoncle writes "Every time, the logic of usage prevails. The same piece of information (a comment on a blog, for example) can be structured in various ways according to how one wants to use it. Therefore, the writer of the piece of information is clearly not in position to know or predict all the uses his written production will be put to".

All this is in line with the general trend described by Sloterdijk, in which "a lighter form of subjectivity, let us say the postmodern 'user self', is beginning to replace the more ponderous form of subjectivity, the 'educated self' of the Modern Age". "The user is the agent who no longer needs to become an educatedly formed subject, as they can ransom themselves from the burden of gathering experience. The word 'ransom' refers to the relieving effect that homogeneous forms of content items of information grant their user as soon as they no longer need to be acquired through time-consuming training but can simply be 'retrieved' after a brief introduction to the corresponding techniques" [SLO 13]. Overabundance in the Crystal Palace means that access to everything that exists in the form of merchandise is greatly eased.

Marketing works as a claim to be providing valued cartographies of usages and their attached discourse utterances, as a claim to be proposing a partial reflectivity on them in order to ever revive consumerist desires and the much celebrated confidence. That confidence is a potent narcotic indeed to the point of potentially being able to bring about the pacification that some have been dreaming of.

The designers of such apparatuses thus have to negotiate with two opposing logics: "(...) a normative or 'top-down' logic, promoted by the advocates of the semantic web, which ensures interoperability and easy analysis but involves significant costs for its implementation; and a 'bottom-up' logic of emergence, promoted by business industries (Google and Exalead) and web experts, which ensure the universality of the applicative domains (including all the information, whether structured or not, and all the uses, whether anticipated or not) at the cost of the ease of implementation" [BOU 10].

He who is able to extract and exploit the graphs built on the (singular and /or collective) digital, semantic, behavioral and geo-localized traces, this one is in a dominant position within the political, libidinal and strategical economies, i.e. within the marketing field. Value extraction and graph theory are intimately related. He who is able to exploit the temporal regimes and the trajectories (the relatively complex navigational strategies and procrastination analyzed by "clickstream" research) that surround the decision to buy or not, this one is in a dominant position to predict consumerist patterns and even to achieve the performation of urges.

At the core of this marketing field of operation, we find out that the economy of attention is at stake. "The reproduction of our abundance societies is shifting its focus onto a new kind of scarcity: Up to now, material resources constituted the scarcity object that economists studied, greedy as they were in their attempts to "give" us more goods to consume; nowadays, attention time is becoming the main appropriation object, the epicenter of the conflicts that rage across our data-saturated (cultural) economies" [CIT 12].

Geolocalization and the reterritorialization of semantic and behavioral digital data are gaining momentum, despite the tale we were told of deterritorialized data that could be thought of independently from the entangled territories of the world (the well-celebrated, void riding, digital identities!). This complexifies the nature of consumerist assemblages.

In the digital fold of the world, through the interfaces and back-and-forth weaving of territories, geolocalization practices resonate with, in tight interaction, the relational geographies of the trajectories, navigations, wandering and roving on the Internet stratum. The so-called "clickstream marketing" initially worked on such cartographies. Now, coupled with other types of cartographic practices, it will enable new hermeneutics, as we have mentioned before. This ability to evermore precisely determine the geographical location of individuals or groups and of objects involved in transactions or relations is significantly affecting marketing practices and conceptions.

For the time being we can simply describe this evolution as unfolding along four interacting dimensions: geolocalization, orientation – disorientation, navigation, temporalities. The first dimension reterritorializes, the second is the expression of behaviors in the topological, relational space of the Web, the third refers to the types of progressions one can trace in the nonlinear, hypertextual and almost chaotic digital space and the fourth one refers to exploration rhythms, to ratios of speed and slowness in exploration times or decision times.

This is how an increasing number of geospatial and semantic ontologies develop. This development is a means to satisfy the need to model, analyze and visualize multimodal information, for the latter is the only type of information that can provide integrative approaches encompassing spatial, temporal and thematic dimensions as well as informational, cognitive and semantic categories. Similarly, a growing number of studies investigate the decision-making mechanisms of consumers via their online purchasing behavioral patterns. The aim is to look into how the various online decision-making mechanisms used by consumers influence the complexity of their purchasing behavior. The ends of all this, as we mentioned earlier already, is to elaborate increasingly efficient predictive models.

## 1.10. Personal data: private property as an open and unstable process

At first sight, stubbornly insisting on protecting so-called personal data seems entirely legitimate. For some, this insistence is even the central, absolute axiom of the political and democratic reflection that remains after the immersion in the digital and performative environment.

But, depending on the perspective in which it is thought of, this notion may not necessarily be relevant to democracy. Of course, upholding the notion leads to distinguishing "personal data", "private domain", "visibility and invisibility regimes", of course it implies redefining the lability or, conversely, immutability of zones of secret and the role of cryptic objects and, of course, it entails knowing who controls their production and dissemination, but these questions must be investigated in a pragmatic, differentiated, negotiated and open manner. In the perspective of industrial production, this even is an emergency. As François Bourdoncle states [BOU 14], "This law is a law of exception that dates back to 1978, when in France there were hardly more than a few dozen mainframes and, here and there, one small database. Nowadays, with the advent of 'big data', one cannot go on requesting this mandatory authorization from the National Commission on Informatics and Liberty prior to any data collection. What we need is an appropriate law whose logic enables validating a project on the basis of its industrial ends, or of the processes involved. For example: would an insurance company be allowed to take into account the speeding patterns of a driver-client, recorded by the sensors of his car, to evaluate his fees?"

We should actually endeavor into an even more pragmatic approach. In other words, we should not refrain innovation and adaptive evolutions. We should not hinder anthropological and political innovation. François Bourdoncle's example is illuminating this question because it refers to insurance policies and fees, grounding them on the concept of behavioral prediction(s) and on its supposedly natural doxic legitimation. Actual bad drivers must pay up…. This kind of principle, if applied systematically, bears with it dangerous implications that are easy to foresee.

Let us assume that "pragmatic" means "negotiation" of the validating logics of not only industrial processes. This implies that we need to be more ambitious and to bring hitherto overlooked processes on the game of Go that democracy consists of: the "processes of judicial and collective individuation", understood as the temporary agreements that grant this or that status to this or that data or dataset in the process of knowledge and value construction–circulation–transformation. In any performative society, whether "personal data are an anomaly" is a question that deserves a lot of attention. Several means of analysis, several influential forces and several strands of resistance try to elaborate, collaboratively and conflictingly, answers to that question.

*One of these means consists of imagining apparatuses that redistribute knowledge production and help the general audience appropriate data mining technologies*. The aim there is to improve the diffusion of intellectual technologies, so that various heterogeneous collectives may use them to develop distributed creative socio-cognitive activities at various levels of organization. This would foster the "bottom-up" development of "data-management" practices. In other words, the local, varied and heterogeneous agents would, too, be able to extract knowledge and data from the processes of creation, adaptation, social and environmental innovation, etc.

This would also mean that these collectives, which come in various sizes, would keep a tight grip on the processes of social and political definition and elaboration of the digital empiricist narratives. They would be in control of what this large-scale acquisition of data involves. They would maintain an intimate relationship with the narrative modes, their extension, their evocative powers and with the anthropological labyrinths they open. This is the context in which we must pay attention to the obfuscating techniques and models, because they could prove to be powerful resistance techniques to the generalized surveillance–sousveillance [NIS 11][55] paradigm.

So, we suggest thinking and acting, if not toward taking data mining and algorithmics from the hands of the great molar machines (it would be illusory to believe we could steal the tools of such masters as the scientifico-political, imperial or postimperial grabbing machines of the marketing or health systems, etc.), at least toward working on the dissemination and spreading of multiple micromachines of local data extraction, small navigation and connection machines and handcrafted writing–reading machines. In other words, we should strive to create the conditions of the emergence of molecular, techno-political counter powers.

One could also look for ways to make the great machines adaptable to the small apparatuses. The former would thus open themselves to the renegotiation of their techno-political position and status and, why not, even prepare their own dismantlement. This could actually be a strategic line that the public OD movement could further: to promote, in specific economic forms, the dissemination of applications or elements of applications that could be exploited or combined by various individuals or groups. This would entail designing formations in a manner that would be more consistent with

---

55 On the notion of sousveillance, see [MAN 03, QUE 10].

the algorithmic becoming of societies. Such a strategy would consist of creating conditions enabling basic agents to use apparatuses to resist the concentration of the means of production and extraction of knowledge to fight the curbing of cognitive ecologies. Indeed, in the status quo, cognitive ecologies are restrained by the non-dissemination of microtools for data mining, cartography, etc. We must aim to nurture all that faces, confronts, bypasses, wraps or undermines the continuation of the dominating apparatuses that promote specialization of knowledge and the consequent professional monopolies and asymmetric data access and reuse. And even if we managed to make recursive loops proliferate, loops that would breed reflexivity and open wide the possibilities of counter powers... This would be but one step in the long march ahead.

In 1972, the anti-Oedipus proposed ways of creatively resisting that go beyond disseminating relatively simple, small-scale noomachines. They consist of calling on to machinic innovation, which indeed is central to what some call noopolitik [ARQ 99], others noopolitique (Bernard Stiegler) and others even "neocortical war" (US-Army).

Agents and powers are immersed in the all-encompassing process. They are therefore irremediably confronted to the democratic, political, strategic issue of thoroughly understanding the nature of the following relationship: how does the dissemination and dispersion of new intellectual technologies relate to the genesis, within the social fabric, of novel power relations based on the knowledge-power apparatuses that emerge from the digital folding of the world?

They must understand how the differentiation and dissemination processes relate to the economic and strategic expansion enabled by the renewed transformations that collective intelligences make possible.

For example, new "socio-cognitive habitats" could be set up to host the controversies inherent to any becoming brought about by collectives to build the conditions in which we can openly be "in the milieu" of political, economical, judicial, scientific and religious narratives born by digital networks (which do not emancipate by the sole magic of their digital network nature).

One must, on the contrary, come to terms with the fact that digital networks may rather set up new forms of control and rigidity that operate at an "anonymous, non-human, a-signifying and material" level. Moreover, since there is not a strictly binary opposition between centralized and decentralized networks, we must understand that they operate as "rogue swarms" as much as "mainframe grids". This understanding should help us be aware of the constraints they impose on open systems in the perspective of democracy.

The co-functioning modes are difficult to fully understand, because we deal with complex hybrids, which can be both a-centered and centered, with norms distributed all over and with interfaces that do stimulate the required recursive loops, but with varying degrees of conviction.

The question of interfaces and software applications, as well as the possibility of access (if only partially) to the data banks, to produce new data and knowledge becomes a strategic issue. It is central to the definition of the coming democratic assemblages.

Let us now slightly shift our point of view and consider collective intelligences in the perspective of companies and more generally in organizations.

The socio-political scope of interfacing regimes is, as we have seen, essential. This specific context is not different from other environments in that the modes of actualization of control societies as well as of surveillance societies, understood against a background of transforming production relationships, force us to think the evolution of semiopolicies, which unfold and incarnate themselves into increasingly heterogeneous apparatuses. We thus have to develop a polemical stance toward the emerging means of semiotic control. We need to propose a better understanding of the processes of capitalistic seizure that, in Deleuze and Guattari's words, are now the "epitome of semiotic operation" [DEL 87].

The "machinic interfaces" are central to differentiation of the transformation of reticular economies and to the transformation of the processes of semiotic seizure. The variation of the technogenesis/ sociogenesis couplings is realized under the criteria and constraints of liberal political economies, which leverage socio-cognitive, passion-based or libidinal economies. The latter can be of various levels of complexity. Last but not least, although it is usually not sufficiently analyzed, machinic interfaces play an active role in the transformation of work temporalities as well as in the transformation of the relationship between speed and slowness, which in turn may "deteriorate our experience of time" in digital network environments.

From Koselleck to Virilio and Luhman[56], these transformations have been considered as issues raising from the compression of the present and the acceleration of sociotechnical change. The latter, in their perspective, is perceived as "an acceleration of the rhythm of experiences and action-orienting expectations, and as a shortening of the time periods that could be defined as pertaining to the present, in the various spheres of functions, values and actions" [ROS 10]. One must however be careful neither to abusively take for real nor to essentialize the notion of acceleration and deceleration, of speed and slow. One would then miss the intensive dimensions of time and events that are necessary to understand the struggles and resistance in the tensed battle field in which companies are relentlessly fabricated [GUA 81, LAT 12].

## 1.11. The figures of the network

Nowadays, we know too well, as we experience it daily, that the network is everywhere and all the time present as an intelligibility and an organization principle but also as the central black box. The figures of the network are indeed proliferating. We meet the network as a concept and encounter networks as apparatuses, as territories, as organizational modes or as politico-strategic actants on any possible substratum.

Within the networks, maps and graphs are continuously being made. One finds nodes and edges. One measures links, evaluates connectivity, stabilities, metastabilities, resilience and plasticity or on the other hand brittleness and rigidity. And, as we said already, the performativity of networks is constantly valued.

Networks can be classified according to a complex geology of underground networks and surface networks. They measure up to the "infinite mafia networks".

---

56 On this, see [ROS 77] and [VIR 86].

One details their differences, against the infinities of numbers, agents and actants. One venerates them or hates them which, at the end of the day, boils down to the same.

Omnipresent in the great change that is currently happening, the network, whether projected on an imagined reality or used to shatter essentialist discourse, is the hot bed of theoretical reflection, the new home of organizational production and the focal point of the issue of collective becomings. In the network, various lines of thought intersect. Notions like these of milieu, territory, relation, topology, or even trial meet in the concept of network. Several theoretical fields diffuse through the network idea. One finds it at the core of the Latourian associative thinking, in translational sociology, in Burt's sociology, etc. In many ways, networks reflect the "rhizome" concept of Deleuze and Guattari's philosophy. Networks also play a part in software and documentation issues, in the algorithms of corpus linguistics. All these roles imply that the network is a significant player in political and geopolitical issues.

Indeed, Guattari incidentally signals that to confront this "Hegemon" we need to know how "The means of conceiving an alternative outcome, an escape from machinic enslavement by Integrated World Capitalism, may still be nurtured. The problem is: does this mean that a-signifying[57] semiotics simply and only obey a network form and thus resistance dislodged from it

---

57 Felix Guattari: "The whole fabric of the capitalist world consists of this kind of flux of de-territorialized signs – money and economic signs, signs of prestige and so on. Significations, social values (those one can interpret, that is) can be seen at the level of power formations but, essentially, capitalism depends upon non-signifying machines. There is, for instance, no meaning in the ups and downs of the stock market; capitalist power, at the economic level produces no special discourse of its own, but imply seeks to control the non-signifying semiotic machines, to manipulate the non-signifying cogs of the system" (Molecular revolution F. Guattari 1984).
Also in Felix Guattari and Gilles Deleuze:"Unlike signifying semiotics, a-signifying semiotics recognize neither persons, roles nor subjects. While subjection concerns the global person, those highly manipulable subjective, molar representations, "machinic enslavement connects infrapersonal, infrasocial elements thanks to a molecular economy of desire". The power of this semiotics resides in the fact that they permeate the systems of representation and signification by which "individuated subjects recognize each other and are alienated from each other", in Semiotic Pluralism and the New Government of Signs, Homage to Félix Guattari, translated by Mary O'Neill, 2006.

must take its form and is, in fact, determined for the network is hegemonic (another master signifier) – for even the state is thought to be an organizational and political network [CAS 00a] – and the multitude is a distributed one [HAR 04], too?" This is a troubling issue.

We are then facing various network forms that are both differentiated from each other and hybrid. The forms vary according to the actants that constitute the network. They are expressed in two modes. The first is mainly centered, hierarchical, distributed of a fractal and even multifractal type (at the organizational and ideal – ideological level, and at the level of norms, rules, routines, interfaces and boundary objects that are immanent to production mechanisms); the other one is mainly a-centered, distributed, of a multifractal type [ROS 74]. The issue of interfaces and connecting devices is crucial in both modes but in our opinion, more so in the second case, that of a-centered, "swarm" systems.

Indeed, companies rely on assemblages of networks that the digital work environments try to exploit and manage. These assemblages are organized (to an unprecedented level) in interwoven strata, levels and territories. The rigidity versus plasticity tension that runs through these networks, although it depends on the associated milieu that constitutes their condition and substratum, is expressed by the tension between what is called the *rogue swarm* (a rough, unstable swarm) and the *mainframe grid* (a tightly structured, stable network). Thus assembled, the forms, levels and territories are linked by multiple pathways and recursive loops of varying quantity. These connections all rely on relatively elaborate information systems.[58] In this perspective, regardless of the specific figures a network is embodied in, the software question, that of connectors and interfaces, is crucial. In the case of a-centered or "swarm" systems, it is even more important. One could even consider that, in the administration of the process of work and organizational and collective networks, the network form is less essential than the "machinic interfaces" between the agents/actants of info-cognitive flux and between hypertext memories.

---

58 We study the issue of interfaces in our short analysis of the "swarm collective intelligences", in the context of our examination of the question of contemporary encyclopedism. Generally, interfaces are, in the digital fold of the world, the main synaptic population (adaptors, connectors, poinstmen-cartographers of human and non-human actants, semiotic blocs).

The scale at which we need to investigate writings has changed while, every day, new constraints have had to be deployed on the assemblages and semiotic microworlds inhabited by the actants.

The interfaces also regulate the vicinity interactions in massively topological, relational spaces. In order to exploit the complexity of collectives as efficiently as possible, we need to be able to elaborate high levels of descriptions as well as to combine, part-automatically, writings. To do so, we must rely on the diffusion (according the various techno-political and juridical criteria) of machinic interfaces endowed with efficient apparatuses to filter, index, search, contextualize, map, annotate, as well as with software to process data and create hypermedia writings. More, the networks must be endowed with mechanisms to protect and distribute data and knowledge, and we know that these mechanisms are the bone of contention of many a harsh and complex political-juridical battle.

This is why we think that the notion of "meme"[59] is useful to refer to the great variety of informational and semiotic blocs that partake to these combinations.

Writings, routines, memories, synchronization, resonance, convergence and coordination have always been central to the functioning of complex collective entities and to the process of work, including (in specific perspectives) the process of intellectual work.

## 1.12. Machinic interfaces: social subjection and enslavement

The forms of network organization are therefore based on novel "machinic interfaces" under massively distributed heavy constraints. These constraints are local and seem to apply more autonomously in strongly a-centered networks than in centered networks.

Interfaces are therefore very rich "milieus" in which, according to Lazzarato, relations between "social subjection" and "machinic subjection"

---

59 (See note 19) and [DEL 00].The term *meme* originated with Richar Dawkins' 1976 book *The Selfish Gene*. It is the "gene" sounding shortening of Ancient Greek *mimeme* (imitated thing). Dawkins also chose this word for its similarity with the French word "même" (same) also it has a different etymology. Memes were presented by Dawkins as cultural entities that could replicate similarly to the genes of biological evolution.

processes are negotiated. From this perspective, we see how interfaces regulate and define the combinations between two types of processes: On the one hand, processes of semiotic overcoding of social subjection of cerebralities on the basis of signifying semiotics (these are semiotics in so far as they are molar political operations of individuation) and, on the other hand, non-representational processes of machinic subjection on the basis of a-signifying semiotics.[60]

The notion of machinic subjection is a complex one. The issues attached to new types of reflectivity about access to the conditions of socio-cognitive practices are especially difficult to tackle.

Of course, a-signifying semiotics operate as synchronizers and modulators of the preindividual and preverbal components of subjectivity. They operate affects, perceptions, emotions, etc. like parts, components or elements of a machine (hence the machinic subjection). But, in the context of cognitive work and mass intellectuality [MAR 58], they also operate as synchronizers of conceptual fragments of cerebrality, operating memes and their assemblages like parts, components or elements of a cerebral machine.

How, then, can we rely on these new black boxes, on automatic protocols that, often long before any cognitive activity, have become the sole agents in

---

60 In "Semiotic Pluralism" and the New Government of Signs Homage to Félix Guattari", translated by Mary O'Neill, Maurizio Lazzarato writes: "The semiotic components of capital always operate in a dual register. The first is the register of "representation" and "signification" or "production of meaning", both of which are organized by signifying semiotics (language) with the purpose of producing the "subject", the "individual", the "I". The second is the machinic register organized by a-signifying semiotics (such as money, analog or digital machines that produce images, sounds and information, the equations, functions, diagrams of science, music, etc.), which "can bring into play signs which have an additional symbolic or signifying effect, but whose actual functioning is neither symbolic nor signifying". This second register is not aimed at subject constitution but at capturing and activating presubjective and preindividual elements (affects, emotions, perceptions) to make them function like components or cogs in the semiotic machine of capital" [LAZ 06].
In [GEN 08], we read "Guattari thought that miniaturization was a means for capital to endow individuals with apparatuses that could manage their perceptions by connecting them to the machinic phylum of general audience technology, which addicts them crazy to self-prescribed trips... Such a productivist dope inserts subjectivities in a-corporeal networks. To detox from them usually requires disconnection".

charge of the fundamental, primary functions of sorting and classifying? How to make informed choices or at least find a balance between what seems to be a kind of *cogitatio cacea*, a blind activity, and what we believe to be rational cognitive reflection embedded in socio-cognitive practices.

Machinic interfaces moreover give "ontological consistency to something that happens between two heterogeneous strata involved in coding or semiotic expression. These strata have protorelationships of alterity which are, on the one hand, ontogenetic, with all that surrounds them and contribute to maintaining their existence and, on the other hand, phylogenetic, with all the machinic interfaces that came before and with all the virtual protorelationships that will come after" [GUA 91].

In the digital milieus of work and organization, all this is expressed under the constraints of procedural performativity and economic performativity. This is precisely against these constraints that users can potentially desire new conditions of individuation [SIM 07, STI 04].

So, what are the leads to this capacity to reclaim autonomy, confront and actualize the machinic subjection and enslavement regimes that cognitive workers endure? This is a difficult question.

Machinic interfaces define and feed the internal and external pragmatics of the social – technical machines and organizations, in our very extensive meaning (not only that of classical writings, search engines, cartographic devices, automatic indexing, metadata production and management, publishing software, natural language and non-exclusively linguistic semiotic processing, blogs, wikis, but also that of artificial skins, biotechnical prosthetics, etc.).

They translate, filter and determine the types and numbers of possible connection and relations within the autopoietic system constituted by each specific apparatus or organization.

They also serve as mediations, such as membranes that regulate the evolution of the system – environment couplings and are involved in the filtering of the environment events that will activate specific internal states within the organization, be they beneficial or not[61]. They also define or provide consistency to interstices, zones of indetermination, motion or boundary erasure, which fill the existential territories of work. These zones and interstices continuously disrupt and upset, across molar organizations, the administrative and corporate desires of collective intelligences, desires that consumes themselves trying to always striate the libidinal energies and economies. They mediate the passage between the network's internal pragmatics or digital work environments and external pragmatics that come from other networks, other space times of work that are relatively autonomous in comparison with the growing dominance of the former. This is where resistance and social-political creation can come in full play.

These simultaneously technical, cultural, social, economic and cognitive transformations are under way. It must be said that this open situation in which the economy and society are mutating raises many issues not only about individual freedom but also about research and creativity.

## 1.13. Collective intelligences and anthropological concerns

One of the major challenges we will have to rise to in the future is the necessity to respond as creatively as possible to anthropological concerns, climate change, biodiversity issues, as well as to the novel forms of production, the new productive relationships and their industrial consequences. Challenges are also set by issues related to energy transition, bio-politics and ethics of access, by the questions of cultural diversity and the renewed definition of what "personal data" is. The challenge also consists of finding ways to disseminate intellectual technologies to serve as counter powers in a data-centric society that is based on wide socio-cognitive disparities.

We therefore need analysis models and conceptual frameworks that rise up to this challenge. We need design methods and common use principles

---

61 According to Pierre Levy: "A machine is *interfacing* and interfaced. It translates, betrays, folds and unfolds the flux produced by the upstream machine. It is itself made of translating machines that divide and multiply it, make it heterogeneous. The interface is the "foreign policy" dimension of the machine, enabling it to integrate new networks and to process new flux", in "Plissé fractal ou comment les machines de Guattari peuvent nous aider à penser le transcendantal aujourd'hui" (The fractal Fold, or how Guattari's machines can help us think the transcendental today), Revue Chimères No. 14.

that all users recognize through the establishment of collective intelligences of usage of a new type. In order to apprehend the scale of change in our modes of intelligibility, we must also reach an understanding of the various ways in which "signifying semiotics and their linear power phrases" can combine with super linear a-signifying automated processes. Indeed, this is currently happening.

In this perspective, in the context of this anthropological extension, the digitalization of the Sign, which has been ongoing for the past 50 years, makes the need to escape the imperium of signifying linguistics more pressing. Since they come with globalization, a-signifying semiotics are central to the fabric of the capitalist world and even of the world as it is. We need (and we have already explicitly insisted on this necessity) to fully apprehend the role played by these a-signifying semiotics. In line with Guattari, the mathematical sign machines, the scientific, musical and technical compounds… all "the a-signifying machines or semiotics, although they "keep" relying on signifying semiotics, only use them as devices, as instruments of semiotic deterritorialization that (then) enable semiotic flux to establish new connections with the most de-territorialized material flux. They force the signifying to work as a "tool", without co-operating with it on the same level, neither semiologically not symbolically; this way, a-signifying semiotics do not depend on the good semiological form, although they use them to communicate in the manner "required" by the dominant systems".

This anthropological process increasingly radically expresses the complex intermingling of human and non-human agents. This implies that we build ourselves a specific hyperpragmatic reflection that would be able to account for the heterogeneity of narratives and enunciation regimes, all the more that we are now immersed in the complex structures of the "Internet of Things".

Such hyperpragmatics cannot be based on linguistics or on the imperium of the linguistically signifying, as Guattari describes it [GUA 12].

We need to build ourselves a framework of intelligibility and find means to enable the emergence of such pragmatics. They are the only tools we will have at our disposal to deal with the coupling of linguistic and semiotic pluralisms with their associated micropolicies.

This is why we are so adamant about Deleuze and Guattari's notion of "collective assemblage of enunciation". The notion allows a better apprehension of the modes of communication between the linguistic and the non-linguistic. It then becomes possible to say that "an assemblage of enunciation does not speak "of" things; it speaks on the same level as states of things and states of content" (see A Thousand Plateaus). To do so, we need to be able to exploit pragmatics that are non-exclusively linguistic. Pragmatics, then, that display two components: the first could be called *generative,* since it corresponds to linguisticalization and semiotization modes, the second is the *transformational* component, non-linguistic and a-signifying.

Here, again the Guattari and Deleuze approach resonates with that of Bruno Latour: "Recently there has been a tendency to privilege language. For a long time, it was thought to be transparent and alone among actants in possessing neither density nor violence. Then, doubts began to grow about its transparency. Hope was expressed that this transparency might be restored by cleaning language as we might clean a window. Language was so privileged that its critique became the only worthy task for generations of Kants and Wittgensteins. Then, in the 1950s it was realized that language was opaque, dense and heavy. This discovery did not, however, mean that it lost its privileged status and was equated with the other forces that translate and are translated by it. On the contrary, the attempt was made to reduce all other forces to the signifier. The text was turned into "the object". This was "the swinging sixties" from Levi-Strauss to Lacan by way of Barthes and Foucault. What a fuss! Everything that is said of the signifier is right, but it must also be said of every other kind of entelechy. There is nothing special about language that allows it to be distinguished from the rest for any length of time" [LAT 88].

Latour highlights several enunciation regimes on the basis of the following definition: "enunciation, as the sending of messages and messengers, is what enables us to remain present, to be, i.e. to exist", although this definition is, according to him quite unrefined[62]. One of these enunciation regimes, then, is

---

62 Bruno Latour, Petite philosophie de l'énonciation Pour Paolo à la mémoire de notre amie commune Françoise Bastide (Small piece of philosophy of enunciation for Paolo, in memory of our common friend Françoise Bastide): "This is the only ontological postulate we will need: we set out from a continuous and risky existence – continuous because risky – and not from an essence; we set out from the act of being present, not from permanence".

of particular interest for the matter that concerns us here. Indeed, among the regimes that focus on the quasi-object (be it technical, fictional or scientific), the technical regime is an important one.

"What is a quasi-object? This is not – this is not mainly – a sign. This is the enunciator being displaced into another body, a dissimilar body that stands still even when the enunciator withdraws away, a body that speaks to the target of enunciation while holding it still. This is the main characteristic of technical enunciation", according to Bruno Latour. "The trick of the technical thus consists of shifting the milieu of interaction. The interaction that once consisted of two similar bodies grappling with each other becomes the interaction of dissimilar bodies. In the wake of this trick, in the subtle weaving of human and non-human, we find what I would call plaits, or combinations. As humans, we have been forming combinations with non-humans for a long time now, this is how we keep being present. This is probably even how we became human"[63]. And the Internet of Things world (the world of "the Internet of everything") undoubtedly creates an unprecedented complication of this weaving task[64].

This is why, in the alliances and alloys of enunciation regimes and semiotic regimes, "This very specific trick (the enunciation regime of the technical) leaves marks on the grappling mechanisms, interfaces, impacts, grasping, both of human bodies and of non-human assemblages. However, since in this regime the enunciator withdraws to let the quasi-Thing perform its signifying work alone, we (therefore) must track down the tenuous marks that enable the continuation of such an absence"[65].

This marking has now become explicit, and explaining it clearly has become the main task of analyzers of digital becomings and NBIC. This explicitation is in some ways the carving of reflectivity into the flesh of writings and mediations, thickness of skins, interfaces and plasma of data. It

---

63 Bruno Latour, Petite philosophie de l'énonciation Pour Paolo à la mémoire de notre amie commune Françoise Bastide (Small piece of philosophy of enunciation for Paolo, in memory of our common friend Françoise Bastide).

64 We are still in the limbo of a new Renaissance, in the sparkling creation of novel forms, while polycentric powers still resist, in a flurry of new collective assemblages of enunciation and of micro-noo-machine-led cerebral guerillas. Admittedly, a struggle of uncertain outcome.

65 See footnote 63, above.

also hosts renewed "differends", because the intelligence aggregates, which seamlessly thread through its framework, silently giving substance to the world surfaces, are, if not radically contingent, at least subject to a process of cerebral, neo-natural selection[66].

## 1.14. Toward a new encyclopedic state: first overview

Within the framework of the globalization processes, the great anthropological transformation under ways requires us to collectively think – in line, again, with F. Guattari [GUA 89, GUA 92] – social ecology, mental ecology, environmental ecology and to face the current bio- and psychopolitical becomings. The main lines followed by technological advances from the second half of the 20th Century are now resonating with each other.

The three aforementioned ecologies are in crisis, and the question is asked of the possibility to make new modes of existence emerge, in the context of changes that affect internal processes of differentiation within the systems or relations between beings [BAT 86, BAT 77]. This, more than ever, requires we questioned what affects the condition of a new Renaissance, on the basis of the transformation of the knowledge systems, whether that knowledge be of religious or scientific nature.

In this context, the question of the mind is essential. We need to be searching for one or several "Noopolitics"[67] that may help the setting up of new material and ideal conditions in order to prepare a specific Renaissance.

---

66 This is why we must describe cultures and intelligences in ways that enable the exhibition of parameters that vary within cultures, so that we can build, with these parameters, a space in which to configure the strict or adaptive, stable or evolutive rules of cerebrality within its productivity. This way, the adaptivity of cultures and intelligences might be able to foster ecological niches of various degrees of fertility, in which intelligence might grow. In the cognitive domain, the Internet stratum may enable both an understanding of the offsprings of cerebralities and a compass to explore the depths of virtualities, into which we are inexorably drawn. But nothing is less certain.

67 Here, we understand "Noopolitics" in Bernard Stiegler's sense. In other words, as "Politics of the mind" associated with "psycho-power" as the central locus of nowadays' political anthropology. We also understand it like John Arquilla and David Ronfeldt: "noopolitik" is a notion opposed to "Realpolitik". Here, it applies to the redefinition of power relations in the domain of geopolitics and strategy, on the basis of collective intelligences and conflicting subjectivities.

That renaissance should be specific in so far as it should enable us to face the crises and challenge mentioned above. The question of the mind is influenced throughout by the transformation of writing systems. This is not a question of a Renaissance in a technologist perspective. On the opposite, the question is how to approach it on the basis of the changes in the "cortex-silex coupling" [STI 94], in the perspective of the impacts of the adoption of new "brain–intellectual technologies coupling" [NOY 95] on the thought collectives and relational compounds. The development of the anthropological stratum is now an important part of our associated milieu, and it is as important and even more important for us to focus on creativity (in the sense developed by [WHI 79]) than to focus on innovation. The importance of this focus on creativity is steadily growing. If we are to prevent morbid symptoms from developing, thinking creativity in terms of some requisites is a pressing need. The various issues attached to the evolution of knowledge organizations, the various incarnations of the web and of its becomings as well as the transformations of the socio-cognitive systems are all inseparable from the intensive carving of thought collectives. The conditions of the development and propagation of what could become the sketch of a temporary stable form of open and processual general knowledge are emerging, if tentatively. This is of major interest for those who endeavor to outline the shape an open rationality to come, one that would both express and be expressed by cultural, philosophical or religious dissonances, which come from the "unequal development" of the specific type of rationalism one finds in the techno-scientific sphere of the west.

One possible question would be: which type of knowledge system is now developing on the basis of the scientific and technical spheres and their attached rationalities? Referring to Bertrand Saint Sernin's analysis "Will knowledge as a whole keep on being presented as an aggregate of specialized subjects whose internal relation are bound to remain vaguely defined? Or, on the contrary, is its organic unity becoming visible? In the former scenario we will at best obtain a classification of the scientific domains; in the latter, we will get a system of knowledge. Both scenarios have their promoters: in the past, Mach and Duhem advocated for the first approach; the second is supported by, for example, Cournot and Whitehead"[68].

---

68 B. Saint-Sernin, Le rationalisme qui vient, Gallimard, 2007.

Relying on our experience and on the understanding we now have of our Western Renaissance, the issue could be formulated, from a different perspective, in the following words: which conditions would enable us to overcome issues such as the explosion of knowledge or the dispersion and transformation of boundaries? To "overcome" would mean in our case to find a new way to "encyclopedize" knowledge in order to think about the intermingling of relations, writings, concepts, perspectives and translations in a way that would enable us to think, in the beautiful phrase of M. Bitbol, "within the world" and its large system of internal relations [BIT 10]. Today, memories and writings are tipping into the digital universe. Although very unequally, hypertext networked memories are developing. This could at least enable an overview of the dynamics of relational compounds and knowledge either acquired or in a process of production.

But encyclopedism is nowadays "fragmented" [JUA 07, NOY 14], and in order to think it and elaborate it we have to come out further from the discourses of essence, monovalent ontologies and bivalent logic, which are the inherited building blocks of our cultures. The new encyclopedism must now be understood as one of points of views and processes, as one of morphogeneses. It must be reflexive and multifractal, able to provide access, at least partly, to the conceptual ethologies that constitute it and to the world of internal relations that make it alive.

In this context, how to further our emancipation from the "great divide" between the two cultures: on the one side, the scientific and technical and, on the other side, the arts, humanities and social sciences?

How to think, under the constraints of creativity, the relational systems of thought and the immanent relativity of each determination? How to raise the levels of our descriptions of these relations, as these levels of description are tied to increasingly complex schemes, while simultaneously using self-simplifying mechanisms such as black boxes (writings, specific combinatorial assemblages, interfaces) in order to be able to creatively use these thought collectives as instances of their own operating?

Still, in the context of fragmented encyclopedism and in that of the heterogeneses of thought and of the world, how to conjugate complexity and simplexity… [BER 10]. Such questions are but examples of specific ways to investigate the development and the profound issues at stake in the networked digital hypertext memories, in the writing systems and their attached interfaces, in short in the new emergent conceptual onto-ethologies[69] [ALL 93, NOY 10].

The becomings of the encyclopedic question will be further detailed later on in this book.

This creates a hazy horizon that arises simultaneously from the interior of the world and from fluctuating finitudes. Through it, in any way, we observe and perceive that many lines of flight are being drawn and bring the inherited, stubborn and obsessive dialectics to their ultimate tension or breaking point.

There are concerns and creative attempts about these new conditions. They involve several fields of reflection: classifying thought (new classifying mechanisms: relational cartography), the evolution of the analogical and abductive question, the new interlacing of combinatorial semiotics that take the fragmentation of the expression substance into account, the new operating relations between speed and slowness, the new open and contextualized information retrieval devices, the new cartographic practices, the search for semiotic apparatuses that would enable a type of working on heterogeneous ontologies or onto-ethologies. These concerns and creative attempts, together with the fashionable buzz words such as Web 2.0 or Web 3.0, truly express the current reorganization of the ecology of mind and the modes of production of knowledge.

The current modes of production and circulation of knowledge raise three major issues. The first one is about the attention we must pay to the tension

---

69 More precisely, Chapter III on onto-ethologies: This non-Galilean science is the one in charge of "Bringing to light the chaos in which the brain is itself immersed as a knowledge object, (p. 203 fr) emerging along uncertain connections and rhizomatic figures causing individuations and bifurcations. Beyond cognitivism, then (because cognitive science, as a Galilean science of thought, faces the same difficulties as those plaguing the Galilean sciences of nature (p. 50, fr)), contemporary representations of thought and the latest knowledge about the brain (as an uncertain nervous system) will have to constantly cross-validate each other". The question then becomes that of an ethology of thought that would be able to trace the unknown furrows that all new creations draw in the field of the fertile brain, be they creations of concepts, of functions or of sensations: new connections, new fertilizations, new synapses… Like a material metaphor for what brain biology is itself discovering, and not without influencing the onto-ethological nature of the concept. We use "onto-ethology" in a more pragmatic sense.

between stable and metastable knowledge or even unstable knowledge, when it is produced far away from equilibriums, in zones where dissensus and indetermination are ripe.

## 1.15. Controversies and boundaries

We live in times of controversies and divergence. The second issue is about the differential relations that arise between scientific knowledge evaluation regimes, thus about the management of perspectives and cognitive practices. How do all these vary? The third issue is about the management and representation of processes and morphogeneses that express the dynamics and "conceptual ethologies" that constitute the fluctuating or stable "associated milieu" of knowledge.

This milieu propels the issue of boundaries to a critical point where they must be considered as fluctuating zones, as the intersections of trajectories, issues and concepts.

Since they enable the partial exposure of the processual dimension of research-originated documents, the new publishing apparatuses[70] should also enable the apprehension of the novel boundary zones. In this perspective, the most elaborate representation we are looking for is that of morphogeneses. Such a representation should express the dynamics and local concepts that constitute the (more or less fluctuating) associated milieu of knowledge that itself both expresses and is expressed by research documents. The increasing differentiation of the types of circulating documents in fact unveils the various fields of knowledge, the disciplines and research communities as they constitute themselves. Note that the three phrases we used are not equivalent, as they refer to assemblages that are different from one another. Their rules of operation, their normalizing and constitutive processes, as well as the way they build and constitute "boundaries as subjects" do vary.

This is why each scientific assemblage, in its discipline form, has to become reflexive when it tries to further its theorizing (and politicizing) of the question of boundaries. They sometimes consider the latter as an apparatus to filter and control knowledge, which entails the risk of erring into what could be called *autoimmune diseases of disciplinary bodies:*

---

70 See, later in this work, the notion of "documentary processuality".

*scholastics, dogmatism, lack of reflexivity.* The very conditions in which these boundaries are constituted nevertheless demand that they endorse processual aspects, which can trigger increasingly heterogeneous assemblages.

Since boundaries are omnipresent, critical research about science involves making them evolve into zones of creation and transformation. Under the pressure of the new modes of writing and digital memories, the boundary zones develop permanent and complex movements. They involve territorialization, deterritorialazation, reterritorializations, decontextualization and recontextualization.[71]

Research and thinking work must then take into account, on the basis of these zones, the fact that they progressively, increasingly acquire value as themselves, and therefore become complex actants of the reflective question.

In order to access these zones, bearing in mind the increasing fractal aspect of research fronts, the new encylopedism must face what appears as an important challenge: to increasingly clearly highlight and represent dissensus.

The boundary zones end up acquiring enough relative autonomy to establish combinatorial relationships with novel or renewed "cognitive eco-assemblages". They do not belong to what they separate anymore. They widen the gaps in which ways are paved for new imaginations, new becomings and conceptual, scientific worlds.

---

71 Here, we use Deleuzian/Guattarian concepts. They not only involve physical, geographical and historical territories, but also territories of the mind, the mental territories or territories of thought. By creating new milieus, the "digital noo-machines" trigger new processes of capture and coding... of flux of memory and informational flows, of writings. In short, territories of the intellect emerge, which are built on the basis of the new milieus. Leaning on such territories, very closely reflecting them, deterritorialization movements can deploy themselves and undo, at least partly, what the previous territorialization had elaborated. This mechanism ensures that thinking remains possible, emancipated from the stifling dough of what could become a homogenesis. "De-territorialization is a process that frees content (in the form of a multiplicity or of a flux) from total encoding (of form, function or signification) and makes it ride a line of flight". (Robert Sasso, in Vocabulaire de Gilles Deleuze, 2003). Reteeritorialization consists of making a new territory on something else "reterritorialization (is then put by Deleuze/Guattary), as an original operation, does not express a return to the territory, but rather these differential relations internal to D (Deterritorialization) itself, this multiplicity internal to the line of flight" (A Thousand Plateaus, p. 509).

We are not merely speaking, here, of studying the disagreements that can potentially develop between disciplines that would each attempt to think the other. Beyond this, we rather speak about more or less labile research fronts that emerge when "One realizes they must tackle, with their own means and to their own ends, an issue similar to one raised in another discipline" [SAS 03]. This is when communities and fields of knowledge confront each other, take risks and stage battles that are as many chances to test the resilience of disciplinary assemblages. These conflicts reveal interdisciplinary hesitations, open new ways that go beyond the internal pragmatics constitutive of the disciplinary fields and communities. So, we can expect the new encyclopedic modes to enable us to inhabit the assemblages where scientific or conceptual conflicts develop; a universe in which divergent actualization phenomena should proliferate.

This why we advocate for the digital publishing modes to be endowed with new publishing functions [NOY 05]. In our opinion, the most fundamental functions are precisely these that should enable the cartography of socio-cognitive dynamics, controversy zones and the transversal processes that not only operate at the core of scientific and research work, but also are essential to political intelligences.

This is why we undoubtedly must pay a growing attention to the intellectual technologies that tackle these issues.

Many pieces of work consider the "controversial co-construction" of knowledge as essential to provide access to the diversity of perspectives and highlight the benefits of conflicts. For example, the Center for Sociology and Innovation has been, for more than 20 years, leading research on the subject. On the basis of the sociology of translation, the research applies (among other applications) to developing software that enables the cartography of internal dynamics of scientific research fields and, with it, unveils their socio-cognitive structure [VIN 91].

We have mentioned how important this research is for the field of digital scientific publishing, in a time when a vast movement of open archives is emerging [NOY 05]. In our opinion, it must be more radically involved in the development of functionalities that will enable it to become a major player in the field of fragmented encyclopedism. This involvement must be particularly assertively expressed in fields such as the semantic or socio-semantic web, where a large part of the future of encyclopedism is currently being determined.

Novel writing modes and what happens within their development must therefore be observed in the light of these types of issues. Any memory or writing apparatus is defined by what it does or can do with what thought collectives and the cultural world make of it.

The task is then to inhabit this new ecology. According to Deleuze [DEL 88], this ecology considers variations and trajectories, considers the *concepts* as processes and events and the points of view as relations. In other words, it takes into account the relativity immanent to any point of view, according to the conditions of socio-cognitive procedures, in their material, scriptural, linguistic, semiotic, human, non-human or desiring form.

Hence, by the way, the necessity of a renewed understanding of documents whereby they are seen and processed as "relational compounds", as flux and events. Relational compounds being determined by the powers of their connectivity and by their power as attractors.

Each document is a variety of relations, associated with combinatorial capacities. It is defined by the more or less stable compound of relations of which it is both the expressed and the expression. In other words, we could say that a document is an ecology considered with its boundaries + "n points of view" that express the history of its outside, meaning the folds and unfolds that keep transforming it. It is the offspring of the coupling of its internal ecology and of its external ecology, of the mating of what converges to or is captured by it with what comes out of it. This is why the phrase "relational compound", correlated with a true intellectual energy, seems, in our opinion, to account for the transformation.

In this perspective, the extension of the analysis of the promoters of an autopoiesis [VAR 89], within the thought collectives and machinic interfaces that come with them, would also be very interesting[72] (because the specter of

---

[72] "An interface gives ontological consistency to something happening between two heterogeneous strata involved in coding or semiotic expression. These strata have proto-relationships of alterity which are, on the one hand, ontogenetic with all that surrounds them and contribute to maintaining their existence and on the other hand, phylogenetic, with all the machinic interfaces that came before and with all the virtual proto-relationships that will come after" [GUA 91].

traceability is haunting the new modes of work, the new modes of existence and the new modes of governmentality).

Let us point out that all this entails a generalized strategy of interfaces and therefore of norms. This constitutes a major principle of nowadays governmentality, especially when thought in the frameworks of the "becoming empire" as defined by Antonio Negri and Michael Hardt. We are indeed currently experiencing a general weakening of centralized control systems, in parallel with a strengthening of control and surveillance systems immanent to the distributed network system of production. Let us furthermore notice that these large multicentered networks are managed in a multifractal mode, involving many recursive loops and local rules implemented by increasingly elaborate digital machinic interfaces.

At all scales, from intranets to globalization mechanisms, forms are drastically shifting. There is the current transformation of Nation States into Market States (in the framework of the attempt to establish, forcefully and rapidly, a global market), shifts from traditional forms of sovereignty to new digital traces and avenues or to decentralized patterns and territories (in which the privatization of the most regalian functions, including that of war machines, goes unfettered). These shifts result in that the software issue is of major politico-strategic importance.

In this perspective, it is useful to recall Negri and Hardt's analysis, which they developed in "Empire", a volume which has now become a major reference.

In their work, the authors develop the idea according to which, "in the imperial framework, administration becomes fractal and aims to integrate conflicts not by imposing a coherent social apparatus but by controlling differences" (...).

Four principles are operating here. They are both the expression and the expressed of elaborate bio-psycho-politics, leveraging soaring modes of digital writing, an expanding ichnology [MER 09]. This ichno-politics is itself leveraging digital memories and the powerful intellectual technologies they are coupled with, together with multiterritorial geolocalization systems.

In other words, we speak about systems that encompass digital territories and essential territories with their subjectivation processes, their libidinal economies, at various scales. The production of digital empiricisms is of course humongous (Big Data).

> "A first principle that defines imperial administration is that in it the management of political ends tends to be separate from the management of bureaucratic means". "In the imperial regime", they write, "bureaucracies (and the administrative means in general) are considered not according to the linear logics of their functionality to goals, but according to differential and multiple instrumental logic. The problem of administration is not a problem of unity but one of instrumental multifunctionality".

The second principle is the following: "to the extent that administration is singularized and longer functions simply as the actor for centralized political and deliberative organs, it becomes increasingly autonomous and engages more closely with various social groups: business and labor groups, ethnic and religious groups, legal and criminal groups, and so forth. Instead of contributing to social integration, imperial administration acts rather as a disseminating and differentiating mechanism". The third principle states that "administrative action has become fundamentally non-strategic, and thus it is legitimated through heterogeneous and indirect means". These three principles are, according to the author themselves, rather negative.

We therefore need to understand why it functions. Negri and Hardt define the fourth principle as the "positive" aspect of imperial administration. "The unifying matrix and the most dominant value of imperial administration lie in its "local effectiveness". And "local economy is a fundamental condition, the sine qua non of the development of the imperial regime (...). Consent to the imperial regime is not something that descends from the transcendentals of the good administration, which were defined in the modern rights states. Consent, rather, is formed through the local effectiveness of the regime".

The effectiveness–performativity is incarnated in particular in the proliferation of interfaces that ensure the multiplication of recursive loops and their differentiation. Relational cartographies, variations of speed and slowness relationships, variation of "meme" combinatorics... operate at the core of the socio-political question of the modes of intelligibility and subjectivation processes. This approach, as we will see later on, resonates with swarm intelligence approaches and a-centered organizations.

## 1.16. The milieus of intelligence and knowledge

Similarly to our understanding of intelligence as "always-already machined"[73] and collective, we can consider knowledge as "always-already machined" and collective. The "milieus" in which knowledge unfolds and grows have radically changed in the past few centuries. These milieus, as we mentioned before, are collective assemblages of enunciation coupled with collective equipment of subjectivation [GUA 12], thus forming tangible assemblages that are necessarily heterogeneous. To put it in a nutshell, they are composed of increasing numbers of writing systems, storage modes, boundary objects, transmission and repetition modes and substances of expression. The numbers of actants and types of actants that constitute these milieus are increasing. This is a complex matter, which concentrates an ever-larger portion of the energies of the societies engaged in the intensive development of the technical and scientific spheres.

Knowledge (and its production) is increasingly often seen as heterogeneses and complex nomadologies. The question about the new production, circulation and consumption (hereafter PCC) modes of knowledge, which the term "organization" is meant to summarize (this is still far from being the dominant understanding in the mainstream body of reflection on organizations), is asked in its deeper dimension in that perspective: how to make livable, thinkable, the ecology of divergences, of points of view, the ecology of the double constraints that carry the weight of, on the one hand, the fragmentation and singularization of knowledge and, on

---

73 See, for example, Bernard Stiegler, Bruno Latour and Edwin Hutchins. Taking these collective dimensions to the forefront has become common after a body of major works were published in fields like anthropology of knowledge, knowledge ethnology as well as by the ever-growing part of neuroscience that is interested in the technical cortex/body/mediation coupling. Thought collectives, intelligence collectives have, since the middle of the 20th Century, entered a new era. More precisely, it started after the Second World War. These collective intelligences are co-evolving with the transformation of the process of work. Informational and communication infrastructures that can be quite elaborate, as well as new modes of memory, are immanent to these processes.

the other hand, its integration in relatively large trans-disciplinary assemblages? Researchers then tend to "become" sorts of (more or less complex) transit zones within the administrative, economico–scientific circulations of knowledge.

*Here, we need to precisely detail what we mean by knowledge, which is not the same as thought.* Their difference and relationships have to do with slowness and speed, acceleration and slowing down.[74] Let us refer here to the blazing pages of Deleuze's "What is philosophy?"[75] [DEL 94] "The image of thought retains only what thought can claim by right. Thought demands "only" movement that can be carried to infinity. What thought claims by right, what it selects is infinite movement or the movement of the infinite. It is that that constitutes the image of thought (p. 37). In a way thinking is "to give consistency without losing anything of the infinite is very different from the problem of science, which seeks to provide chaos with reference points, on condition of renouncing infinite movements and speeds".

Thought is not tree like, it rather is rhizomatic.[76] But it continuously deploys itself from narrative apparatuses and (non-exclusively linguistic) writings of machinic assemblages.[77] These assemblages slow it down and stabilize it. They are more or less complex hybrids of trees and rhizomes in very heterogeneous combinations. Among these combinatorial compounds, formal thought is but one particular case, despite its powerful quality.

The differentiation of types of memories (short and long term) and the variety of temporal intervals and interstices are determinant. Furthermore,

---

74 The question of mediation is central to the variation of the brain/world couplings. (see J. M. Noyer, la conversion topologique cerveau-monde, MEI, No. 21).

75 "The plane of immanence is not a concept that is or can be thought but rather the image of thought, the image thought gives itself of what it means to think, to make use of thought. It is not a method, since every method is concerned with concepts and presupposes such an image. Nether is a state of knowledge on the brain and its functioning (...) Nor is it opinions held about thought, about its forms, ends, and means, at a particular moment...".

76 See Rhizome, Introduction to A Thousand Plateaus (Deleuze, Guattari), tr. Massumi.

77 We refer here not only to semiotic and non-semiotic assemblages, but also to tangible collective assemblages with their "ethological and ecological (...) esthetic, fantasized (...) dimensions. In short, all the "regimes of semiotization".

the status of interfaces is essential to all the recursive processes at all scales. It is also essential to temporalities and cognitive rhythms and for the elementary processes of reading and writing. Information sciences, together with others, could be central to these issues. It could apprehend the variations of internal cerebral states (or intelligences) activated by events coming from cognitive ecologies.

Thought therefore deploys itself against that, but also adhering closely to it, and can be defined as the permanent recapturing of speed and slowness relations, of the infinite movement, of the highest speeds. "In the wild" recapturing, meaning in the interstices that both are made available to thought and dug by thought itself. Thought opens interstices with its relentless "coups de force" against the slowing down of the production of knowledge.

To try to know to which extent the currently emerging modes will accept or enable a partially augmented resonance with the infinites of thought is a very difficult quest. The question may even have no sense.

We keep wondering, however, about the effects of the changes in PCC[78] modes. Which impact will have the new speed and slowness relations between memories, reading and writing practices? How will the new relations between interstices, spaces empty or full, the cuts and links in a digital context and the infinite speeds aimed at by concepts, affect all that happens on or from the boundaries of subcognition [HOF 88] and of chaotization processes [GUA 88, DEL 91]?

## 1.17. Which criteria for writings?

Writings are evaluated and imposed on the basis of the potentials of creation and invention they open of the new combinatorial modes they bring about as so many possible hermeneutics. If we were to try to establish a number of requisites or demands from which to evaluate what the new intellectual technologies bring, one of the most interesting approaches would be to start from the renewed tension between the tree-based and the rhizomatic visions of the pragmatics that produce knowledge.

---

78 PCC: Production, Circulation, Consumption.

The ideal and material assemblages that produce knowledge must stimulate the concrete application of some fundamental cognitive practices. They must stimulate reflexivity and critical work on the conceptual reference frameworks that partly determine the structural conditions of visibility of science and the scale of its intelligibility. We then need to investigate how the latter (cognitive practices) affect the former (ideal and material assemblages). Beyond the fundamental practices, we need a detailed account of what varies or is modified in order to extract a basis for criteria. Let us review some important points that we have, at least partly, mentioned above.

First of all, there are the combinatorial constraints, the ways in which they are socially or collectively transmitted, their metastability and the substances of expression on which they operate. The number of constraints varies according to the considered semiotics.

Implied by this first point, there then is the capacity to increase and multiply the numbers of relations, in parallel with the growth of indeterminate zones and interstices. This feature is of fragile nature because, beyond some thresholds and under hyperconnectivity conditions, a tension, or even a double bind can grow. One cannot deny that increasing the associative, analogical capacity as well as the potential for potentially heterogeneous connections between data, problems, and models is essential. However, overdensifying networks of relations and connection entails the risk of transforming the would-be rhizome into a homogeneous, suffocating paste. To avoid this pitfall we need interfaces, black boxes, self-simplifying processes to create holes, lines of flight and permanently rip open the void. Conversely, we need to take care not to let emergent writings and the automatization of socio-cognitive tasks deteriorate contingency, language undeterminism, conditionality, descriptive shifts, etc.

In this context, analogy and abduction are subjected to renewed work.[79] How do the new intellectual technologies influence the power of analogies?

---

79 C.S. Peirce (1903), Lectures on Pragmatism [held from March, 26. to May, 14 at Harvard University]. MSS 300-316; EP II: 133–241; HLP; CP 5.14–212; in part in SEM I: 431–462.EP II, pp. 531f.) [PEI 97]. Pierce proposes a canonical model with the following formula: "The surprising fact C is observed; but if A was true C would be natural, unsurprising. So, there are grounds for the for the suspicion that A might be true".

For example, how do they influence the capacity to make the abstract component of a description slip from one domain to another? How do they affect this central "slippery" quality (we here walk in the footsteps of Douglas Hofstader) [HOF 79, HOF 88, HOF 95]? At the individual and collective level, what is the impact on the establishment of connections that "occur sideways, without regards to causality", although they "are also essential in so far as they enable us to situate facts in a perspective – to compare what really exists with what, in our perspective, could have happened or might even happen still"?[80]

---

Confusions

Prior to more elaboration on this matter, we would like to draw the reader's attention to some confusions that may lead to misunderstandings. In particular, we would like to insist on two misconceptions: the confusion of the various types of constraints of writings of the strata on which their productivity is at work (at scales at which they become "heterogeneous performances"), and therefore the confusion of the powers that can create empty spaces and lines of flight between their various logical levels of intervention and the full spaces of significations they produce.

This kind of confusion can make one fail to take into account the differences and their effects on the operating of combinatorial constraints and on the co-operating of various automatic behaviors. This in turn leads to exaggerating the importance granted to the notion of "loss".

There is no loss of essence in the movement of inventions of writing and form, and there is no loss of essence in the automation of cognitive functions (we have been unceasingly losing things, neural connections, artifacts, from the

---

80 Here, we can point out the growing significance, in science fiction related video games but also, more generally, in the vast domain of speculative science fiction and Uchronies , of counter-factual approaches. According to Quentin Deluermoz and Pierre Singaravélou, "the counter-factual method comes in a variety of forms: from uchronia – the telling of an alternate history by means of an imagined story, for example in a novel to econometry – a statistical reasoning method the most well-known example of which was developed by the American economist Robert Fogel: if the railroad never existed, how different would the economic growth of the US have been? There are many other examples. We were more interested in the question of possibilities: potentialities, unrealized futures, futures of the past..." In Journal Libération, 12 February 2016. On this, see also [REN 88] and [DEB 15].

dawn of times). There instead is a complication of the conditions of creativity, including the conditions of simplexity, an increasing complexity in the capacity to create void, empty spaces, interstices, lines of flight, to provide smoothness, to alter perceptive systems, to complexify analogical processes (including artifacts and semantic as well as semiotic blocs).

The current development of analogical pluralism is a good example of this trend. Analogical pluralism is currently rapidly growing. It is a process that operates in the whole spectrum of substances of expression and in all the sensualist regimes. Its metamorphoses are numerous, as well as its transformations. Furthermore, the analogies are counter produced by the relations produced by the substances of expression, their physical constraints, their grammars and modes of transmission. They therefore operate according to transformation systems in milieus that are, to various extents, heterogeneous. They cross and even dissolve, to various degrees again, what one may call the barriers of "expressive species".

Algorithmic capacities play a significant part in the reinforcement of such analogies, in the reinforcement of abductive processes, of which Peirce (followed by Bateson[81]) rightly thought they were of crucial importance, and in the exploration of the dynamics of the various perspectives. "This lateral extension of abstract components of description is called *abduction* (...) The very possibility of abduction is a little uncanny, and the phenomenon is enormously more widespread than he or she might, at first thought, have supposed. Metaphor, dream, parable, allegory, the whole of art, the whole of science, the whole of religion the whole of poetry, totemism (as already mentioned), the organization of facts in comparative anatomy – all these are instances or aggregates of instances of abduction, within the human mental sphere" (p. 142).

---

81 G. Bateson, in Mind and Nature; A Necessary Unity (1979), Charles S. Peirce made of abduction the sole element of the inferential dynamics of thought: "A mass of facts is before us. We go through them. We examine them. We find them a confused snarl, an impenetrable jungle. [...] But suddenly, while we are poring over our digest of the facts and are endeavoring to set them into order, it occurs to us that if we were to assume something to be true that we do not know to be true, these facts would arrange themselves luminously. That is abduction [Lectures on Pragmatism held from March, 26 to May, 14 at Harvard University]. MSS 300-316; EP II: 133–241; HLP; CP 5.14–212; in part in SEM I: 431–462.EP II, pp. 531f.)" [PEI 97].

Algorithmic becomings are processes that provide, in Deleuzian terms, new smooth spaces, processes that renew the cognitive conditions that are central to hybrid intelligences. Similarly, the so-called "machine learning" and "deep learning" approaches can free our minds from some cognitive tasks. At an even deeper level, algorithmics, machine learning and deep learning create the new conditions in which great varieties of data can be processed, thus opening new holes in the processes of actualization of novel internal cerebral states. They, once again, enable renewed intersticial analogical freedom.

We know that, according to Whitehead[82], "Life lurks in the interstices of each living cell and in the interstices of the brain". Following Isabelle Stengers in her essay "Thinking with Whitehead, a Free and Wild Creation of Concepts" [STE 11]. "If life lurks in the interstices of each living cell, we may say just as well that the singularity of living societies, what justifies them as such, should be called a 'culture of interstices'" [STE 11, p. 328]. The more numerous and complex the couplings brains/mediations/interfaces are, the more numerous the produced interstices are, thus augmenting the nurtured intelligences.

## 1.18. Collective intelligences of usage and doxic collective intelligences: the status of short forms

We therefore believe that we should take into account conceptual and methodological notions that arise from the research and development of a "non-exclusively linguistic general narrative practice". In the context of generally developing "digital humanities" and the implementation of algorithms appropriate to highlight the networks of actants that constitute such assemblages, such an awareness should enable a renewed thinking of multilingualism. The question of multiplicity would then be situated within each language, within each semiotic system, which would thus be seen as a substratum ceaselessly crisscrossed by complex heterogeneses: language and semiotics seen as metastable universes ridden by "variation". We briefly showed that beforehand.

In this ubiquitous perspective, to investigate linguistic and semiotic pluralism in the context of the proliferating configurations of audio, textual and musical short forms are especially useful.

---

82 A. N. Whitehead, Process and Reality, Simon and Schuster, 2010.

The status of short forms, micronarrations and their life cycle has been central to the "theologico-politico-cognitive" question of the subjectivation processes. Indeed, this question is theologico-political as well as cognitive. Knoepsel [KNO 94] reminds us that: "during the Middle-Ages and as late as the Renaissance, the Bible and classics such as the Metamorphoses of Ovid were used as compendiums of examples that were meant to be inserted into the religious meta-narrations through allegory-related hermeneutic strategies. We still have these compendiums nowadays, the only difference being that they are to be found within a much larger reservoir of electronic information".

The digital and cognitive fractures nowadays echo each other more than ever. Narratives (of languages and semiotics) and creative forces strike conflicting relationships. These generally agonistic relationships are visible in many fields, including the doxic plane of immanence, in the words of Philippe Mengue.

What we see in the Internet milieu is that "Opinion cannot be reduced to a fossilized, congealed, debased thought resembling a fallen creative thought. For there simply is no such thing as the opinion. Opinions are always multiple, they carry with them various interests and ways to tell them, as well as various affects, also related to these interests. The smaller narrations (in which languages and semiotic regimes are enjoying 'a sabbatical') are spontaneous formalizations to phrase what is happening to humans: their fears, hopes, sense of humor, disbelief... In short, their resistance to powers and propaganda. The People is rebellious, sarcastic. Despite its misfortunes and misery, it is able to tell into being the means of its struggles, victories, refusals and of what it consents to. Nothing is lost on this account, despite the common opinion of large segments of the intellectual and artistic elite" [MEN 09]. Of course, some reservations must be considered: such a doxic plane of immanence should not itself be "essentialized", or idealized; the forms of the "differend", which proliferate all the way to the extremes of reptilian languages, should be measured.

The doxic plane of immanence is both the expression and the expressed of heterogeneses that cover a wide spectrum. They range from the wisdom of crowds to their stupidity, [SUR 04, ORI 15, LIP 15], from the creative introduction of differences into the repetition to idiotic, stifling repetition and from the propagation of emancipated psychological powers to that of enslaved psychological forces.

The current proliferation of short forms is actually a very rich subject for those interested in the political metastability of collectives, and in preserving this metastability. Short forms also play a major role in the domain of knowledge circulation, in the diffusion of new models. They are central to many cognitive processes. They are the locus in which the alchemy of languages, semiotics, semantic blocs and "memes" is somehow in a wild state or even in states pertaining to witchcraft. It would be especially interesting to pay specific attention to the role the short forms play in the metastabilization and convergence of collectives.[83]

For instance, researchers commonly assume that the analysis of swarm intelligences in the context of human societies can only be based on *the modeling of undifferentiated agents* (with random variations), with models akin to those used for the behavioral analysis of insects. We think that this assumption is erroneous.

## 1.19. Collective intelligences, self-organization, "swarm" intelligences

The milieus of intelligence are becoming increasingly complex. New types of writings, mediation and intellectual technologies are developing. These transformations force us to recognize that during the past few years the efficiency of a-centered forms of organization have improved in previously unseen magnitudes. People are increasingly aware of the importance of so-called self-organization and network interaction phenomena. Let us recall the brief definition of "collective intelligence", proposed by Pierre Levy a few years ago: "An intelligence that would everywhere be distributed, constantly valued, synchronized in real time, an intelligence which would result in the effective mobilization of skills".

---

83 Amongst others: Liu Bin; Terlecky. Peter Bar-Noy. Amotz Govindan. Ramesh, Neely. Michael J. Rawitz. Dror: Optimizing Information Credibility in Social Swarming Applications. IEEE Transactions on Parallel & Distributed Systems; June 2012.

History vividly shows us that intelligence is "always-already" machined and collective. We already know of the long actualization of the structural brains/mediation/milieus couplings, which are immersed in epiphylogenetic history.

Nowadays, a very high threshold of complexity seems to have been reached. The forms of the relational, the interactive, the hybrid, which are the conditions of intelligence and which rely on a diversity of writings, on a previously unseen semiotic pluralism, on numerous regimes of perception and enunciation, on powerful external memories… are increasingly explicit. Within this stew, the relational and interactive regimes that function independently from a central instance or in an a-centered manner do hold an important position.

In their famous article entitled "Automate asocial et systèmes acentrés" [ROS 74] (asocial automaton and a-centered systems), Rosenstiehl and Petitot highlighted the importance of a-centered systems and advocated a "language of a-centerism". In their approach, they highlighted some characteristics of (organizational) tree-like structures: "In any system, an individual regulates his moves according to his or her only active "neighbors", in other words, those able to communicate directions to him. In a hierarchical system, his only active neighbor is his hierarchical superior; an individual is therefore completely unaware of the actions of any of his alter egos who dwell on the same level. In a hierarchical system, the transmission channels are preestablished: the tree-like structure precludes the individual, who must fit in a specific spot, to perform a functional role. The only exchangeable individuals are those of the same level and the transmission channels are dual: they only connect individuals whose functions are different".

They contrasted this model with that of societies qualified as "fluid", the most simple example of which being the swarm of mosquitoes: "Each individual of the group randomly moves until it sees all of his fellows in a same half-space; it then hurries back into the group. Stability, here, is ensured 'catastrophically' by a barrier, a threshold of discontinuity in the behavior of each individual". They pointed out that, in such a cloud, "Each individual regulates his moves according to his occasional neighbors, who all are his alter egos". furthermore, the neighboring relations are fluid and no network preexists individuals; all individuals are exchangeable and the regulation that ensures the stability of a system requires a certain statistical density of individuals".

More generally, we think in the permanent in-between, this zone bounded, on each side, by these two modes. Nowadays, the organizational forms as a whole increasingly rely, for their definition, on notions of hybridization whereby these modes are, to various extents of complexity and asymmetry, hybridized.

We all have seen how simplified models of insect societies can help account for the processes and conditions of emergence of structure and order independently from any central instance.

The two authors write: "We have proved that contrary to the belief that numbers generate either disorder or uniformity, that an efficient coordination can be established throughout an a-centered community of individuals with limited memory, even if they are arbitrarily many. But our article on this subject in the Communications journal aim much beyond this point. Let us look at natural a-centered systems like an anthill or a termite mound. Termites build structures with sponge shapes, ants smoothen surfaces as described by Chauvin[84]. These are undoubtedly manifestations of a-centered systems. Clearly, no single ant possesses the "plans" of the anthill, it is a construction site without an architect. But the anthill cannot be summed up in a single ant, it cannot either be recorded into any finite state automaton, whichever its complexity".

They go on: "This is where reality shines light on one of the main characteristics of a-centered systems: activities performed locally by individuals (be they words, ants, or crowds of humans) cannot be recapitulated in a central memory, because, as we often say, they are of qualitative nature".

More works about the notion of collective intelligence in insects are worth mentioning. For example, works led by Deneubourg[85] [DEN 77], or the seminal research of Brooks[86] on distributed robotics.

---

84 R. Chauvin, Traité de physiologie de l'insecte: les grandes fonctions, le comportement, écophysiologie, éd. INRA, 1949, réed. 1958 et Vie et mœurs des insectes, éd. Payot, 1956, Le monde des fourmis, éd. Plon 1969.
85 See [BON 94].

Here, recalling the importance of Rodney Brooks' work could be useful. In particular, we should remain aware of the influence it had on research about the origins of language and communication, learning processes of children and learning in general[87] [BRO 02, KAP 06, KAP 07] including in the development of video games.

As explained by Vidal in an excellent article[88] [VID 11], researchers attempt to model and study "A mode of behavior of players that is very similar [to that mode of behavior they wish to model elsewhere]. The architecture of most such games is designed to, in fact, provide the player with a succession of new environments for him to discover and adapt to in order to react as appropriately as possible to the challenges he will face. This for example means that players must learn to predict the consequences of the initiatives they take whilst playing if they want to be able to reach their expected goals. Then, when the player proved enough mastery of the environment, a new one is presented. Thus, the process of learning is similar to that of the robots that robot researchers develop. The success of these games precisely depends on the optimal degree of difficulty that designers manage to reach: the game must be difficult enough to challenge the player and stimulate his motivation but it also needs to remain doable in order not to discourage him or her, and this, at any level of player expertise. This is precisely this type of psychological economy that Luc Steels mentioned as

---

86 Rodney Brooks: Cambrian Intelligence: The Early History of the New AI, 1999; http://www.automatesintelligents.com/labo/2000/mar/brooks.html; Beyond Computation, A talk with, Rodney A. Brooks https://edge.org/conversation/rodney_a_brooks-beyond-computation  See also: Artificial Life and Robotics http://isarob.org/journal/ and Artificial Life http://www.mitpressjournals.org/loi/artl, as well as Peter N. Kluger, Robert E. Shaw, Kim J. Vicente, Jeffrey Kinselle Shaw, "The role of attractors in the Self-Organization of Intentional systems". In this article, the authors study phenomena that are referred to as self-organization in the realm of social insects: how dynamical attractors play a part in the process that leads the building of the habitat. This process involves more than 5 millions insects in the recursive movement of the several modes that partake to the construction of the habitat: "radiom depositing → pillar contruction → arch contruction → dome construction → random depositing→ ... and soon". They call "the self-organization of intentional behavior". Their work includes discussions about " the germ-determinacy which may be used to express several central concepts of ecological psychology that have proven difficult to formalize", in Cognition and the symbolic Processes Edited by Robert R. Hoffman and Davis S. Palermo.

87 See also [CSI 90].

88 http://ateliers.revues.org/8787.

particularly important in robotics. Inspired by the works of Csikszentmihalyi, he named the idea the "autotelic principle".

If we shift our focus back on human collectives, the "cultural-behavioral-artifactual memes" [DEL 00] operate as constraining apparatuses of stabilization and equilibrium (they function like the gluons of particle physics do). They enable individuals to regulate their behaviors and neighboring relationships without needing networks to preexist.

In that framework, the combinatorial productivity at work in collectives not only results from a system or a centralized body of rules and procedure, but also emerges from a decentralized process in which each meme "locally reduces" the choices during the construction of the collective as well as during the phase when the metastability of processes and becomings is maintained. *Such memes and their associated interfaces* therefore have a catastrophic correction function in the sense of René Girard. Networks are stabilized by the interplay of all the memes and their local conditions of application, which also include procedural rules. The local constraints are therefore increasingly elaborate (this is the function of the evolution and modes of selection of "memes", of social transmission according to the system–environment relationship (in the sense of Von Foerster-Varela)). If one recognizes this increase in elaboration, we understand that the a-centered, swarm mode of operating of collective intelligences cannot rely solely on undifferentiated individuals. On the contrary, it must be able to uphold the differentiation of norms, local constraints, perceptive, cognitive and behavioral singularities... Such systems are, of course, more chaotic than traditional swarm systems. At some scales, devastating emerging phenomena of instability and violence of various extents can occur frequently. But these phenomena are but the flip side of the coin, the price to pay for increased resistance to disorder, increased resilience and adaptability, and therefore for preserved, improved conditions of creativity. Of course, it entails a risk of crisis that can even degenerate into collective dementia. The past centuries are ripe with examples of such crises.

Thought collectives and collective intelligences of all sorts also are the expression and expressed of large relational and communication systems whose operation involves many actants, ever-distributed conditions and constraints and pragmatics, as well as varied interactive regimes. We have already detailed the latter in this book.

Nowadays, we pretend to be discovering the reticular, swarm aspects of collective intelligence, although they have a long and ancient history. We explicitly focus on them nowadays because the latest forms of complex intelligence and collectives require increased reflexivity. This explicating is also rooted in a school of thought that seeks to found anew the social-cognitive practices around the notion of "Commons"[89]. They seek to question and attempt to redefine the hybrid becomings of the modes of governance of populations, the contributive economy and the assemblages of knowledge production.[90]

In the framework of performative societies, there is a strong and pervasive tendency to seek to optimize such hybrid forms, to set them on their point of equilibrium or imbalance. This happens depending on the nature of such forms and on the "anaphoric instauration" in Etienne

---

89 On this, we can read: Governing the Commons: The Evolution of Institutions for Collective Action, 1990; Institutional Incentives and Sustainable Development: Infrastructure Policies in Perspective, 1993; Rules, Games, and Common Pool Resources, 1994 ; "A Behavioral Approach to the Rational Choice Theory of Collective Action: Presidential Address", American Political Science Association, 1997, in The American Political Science Review, 92(1): 1–22, 1998; Hess, Charlotte and Ostrom, Elinor (ed.), Understanding Knowledge as a Commons: From Theory to Practice, 2007; Linking the Formal and Informal Economy: Concepts and Policies, edited with Basudeb Guha-Khasnobis and Ravi Kanbur, 2006; Beyond Markets and States: Polycentric Governance of Complex Economic SystemsAmerican Economic Review, 100(3), 2010 and especially Charlotte Hesse and Elinor Ostrom, (Ed By) Understanding Knowledge as a Commons, From Theory to Practice, MIT Press, 2006 "Knowledge in digital form offers unprecedented access to information through the Internet but at the same time is subject to ever-greater restrictions through intellectual property legislation, overpatenting, licensing, overpricing, and lack of preservation. Looking at knowledge as a commons–as a shared resource–allows us to understand both its limitless possibilities and what threatens it".

90 B. Stiegler: "Les us assume that an economy of contribution is a noetic form of pollination, and that this noesis is carried by the traces we call tertiary retentions. If we remember that these are *pharmaka,* we then must understand this allegory from a pharmacological perspective. To do so, we need to concentrate on ants and their pheromones, especially in the way they were modeled in a specific cognitive science domain called artificial life, as a specific example of multi-agent model".

On "Noetic pollinization" we direct the reader to Yann Moulier Boutang's "The Bee and the Economist" p.128: "The pollination metaphor is only a specific illustration of a generalized phenomenon which we call the contributive economy of knowledge production and life in general" See B. Stiegler's comment the conclusion of "Automatic society: 1- the Future of Work. Noetic Pollination and Neganthropocene".

Soureau's words.[91] This depends on the constraints and their social transmission on the requisites of the manufacture of consent and/or divergence. This also depends on the conditions in which creativity can be renewed (for instance by various types of innovation), which itself is required to ensure the continuation and possibility of becomings. Balancing on the alternative of either the "reduplication" of a metastable state or the search for a new type of productivity, collective intelligences must therefore encompass in their thinking the conditions of a reflexivity that should be able to envision new types of emergence, whether in the ideal or material sectors. But conversely, they need to leave room for processes or recreation/alteration, while simultaneously grounding their power to maintain their own being. In that alternative, we see again how consensus and dissensus cohabit in variously conflicting manners in order to ensure the dynamics of the thought–action.

We are thus facing elaborate constructions in which the writing systems, memories, normalizing processes, the black boxes that manage the simplexity–complexity relations and the interfaces are central to the interactions in charge of the moving of ideas and concepts. They cause the weaving of trajectories and induce percolation–translation–transformation phenomena within the trajectories themselves. Within the intelligences we focus on, populations of actants (i.e., populations of human/non-human couplings) are involved in the production of forms of non-descript chains of semantic units and various grammars. To do so, they summon very varied cognitive and perceptive processes.

From this perspective, short forms and micronarrations (short "memes"), when coupled to the insomniac commentary, display several functions or characteristic. We think it useful to remind them to the reader.

In general, such forms are foremost characterized by "closure". Closure means that short forms are always localized, and respond or strive to a state that is always unique. This closure, however, remains relative. It does not determine the end of the processes of interpretations, connections or

---

91 Etienne Souriau, Les différents modes d'existence, followed by "Du mode d'existence de l'œuvre à faire". Presentation by Isabelle Stengers and Bruno Latour, Collection: MétaphysiqueS, 2009.

transformations in which the form is involved, reenacted or created. The forms can be stable and subject to repetitive uses or they can conversely be very labile, in many ways. They have a fundamental function in the propagation of psychological powers, forms (audio, visual) and semiotic energies. They are home to powerful percolations. They open to what could be called "open formations". They also have some sort of subversive power, an instability which is a cause of concern for the powers that be.

On the contrary, they can be coupled to saturated semiotics, and used as means of power and control... Saturating time by ways of stitching moments together in an ever-precarious patchwork of instants. The stitching is done by the insomniac commentary, in a relentless work of gluing.

The short forms of journalistic media are a typical example. The ceaseless, almost pathological commenting work can be seen in that case as the colonial occupation of the mind, of attention. It operates by the deprivation of lines of flight, the deprivation of silence, the deprivation of any grasp on the relations of speed and slowness as the locus of political struggle.

Silence, here, is perceived as a worrying breach, a dangerous hole in the wall-continuum of occupation, a failure of the permanent mobilizing of psyches in order to maintain the aforementioned metastability.

But collective intelligences insist on their being. They nowadays keep "becoming", under the conditions set by such short forms that constitute what we could call their "plasma".

## 1.20. Short forms, relinkage, relaunching

Micronarrations have never been as needed as they are today (not considering scaling issues). They are needed to ever-overcome the hiatuses, the holes in the relational space-times and ensure the continuity of collectives. In other words, they support the solidity of what binds together, ensures and maintains. Such short forms carry with them the tension of relinkage, anaphoric instauration, their own stability. In fact, nothing is less certain than their stabilizing, pacifying power. At the end of the day, Lyotard says, "At bottom, one in general presupposes a language. A language naturally at peace with itself. "Communicational", and perturbed for instance only by the wills, passions and intentions of humans. Anthropocentrism. In the matter of language. The revolution of relativity and of quantum theory remains to be made. No matter what its regimen".

Indeed, when we face the fear of the void, the relentless return of the issue of the "Differend" to come, the question is that of the linking, the preservation of the metastability of pulsions and energies in non-destructive zones. "How can we link it?" is a question that comes with every uttered sentence, every micronarration and even maybe any narration? How can we link in a way that prevents the disagreements from rising to extremes?

"And this question proceeds from the nothingness that 'separate' one phrase from the following. There are 'differends' because, or like, there is Ereignis.[92] But that is forgotten as much as possible: genres of discourse are modes of forgetting the nothingness or forgetting the occurrence, they fill the void between phrases. This "nothingness" is, nevertheless, what opens up the possibility of finalities proper to the genres. If the manner of linking were necessary (filled in), there would not be several possible modes, no void would leave room for that causality exerted from afar, namely, "final causality" [LYO 88].

## 1.21. Insomniac commentary as a catastrophic correction of short forms

The insomniac commentary is in charge of attempting to control the chaos inducing processes born from the short forms, between the short forms. This is a Sisyphean task because the saturating work of the commentary is essentially and radically incomplete and this incompleteness bears with it the germs of its ultimate demise. One would, however, be fully legitimate in arguing that this work of control through the proliferation of

---

92 Ereignis: "De l'événement même", see M. Heidegger. See also G. Guest's commentary, published in no. 21 (March 2005) of the Journal Ligne de risque, invited by Yannick Haenel, François Meyronnis  and re-edited in the collective volume Ligne de risque (1997-2005), Editor Yannick Haenel; François Meyronnis, in the collection "L'Infini", Gallimard, Paris 2005.

"commentaries" is a last resort condition for the practice of democracy, the worried and feverish hermeneutic activity of an open society.

This insomniac hermeneutics, which thus bears the "instauration", can become poison. It can suffocate the possibilities of freedom of operation of altering processes, the freedom of cuts and breaches to loosen the grip of what is. It can suffocate the freedom of non-ordered alteration of the reference frameworks, the freedom of becoming beyond, over the dominating oligarchies of priests and experts. Such oligarchies usually rely on financial, industrial, religious, scientific oligarchies that maneuver within the docile doxa… To end up producing a sort of sterile consumption.

In any case, in the larger perspective of digital networks, short forms augment and quicken the eventful and hazardous aspects that are inherent to any discourse or narrative form. In a digital context such as that which Twitter carved out, such questions are so-to-say brought to the burning point. The distress of control pervades the whole scale of things, from the molecular to the molar levels.

Most of the research on Twitter is very clear on this. One acutely feels the anxiety lurking around, in cargo pants as well as in evening dress. One sees a sort of generalized discourse of erethism fill up the digital stratum. It develops, assuming the shape of insomniac *mise en abymes* of polemic commentaries that attempt to control, with success ranging from uncertainty to sovereignty. In any case, the production and continuation of such commentary practices require a lot of energy and an intense semiotic productivity.

As signaled by Foucault [FOU 71], the procedures of control of discourse include the commentary, which nowadays can be subjected to the telling of its own life, of its trajectories of alteration-creation, of its insertions into specific assemblages.

"We're moving toward control societies that no longer operate by confining people but through continuous control and instant communication". And "You ask whether control or communication societies will lead to forms of resistance that might reopen the way for a communism understood as the "transversal organization of free individuals". Maybe, I don't know. But it would be nothing to do with minorities speaking out. Maybe speech and communication have been corrupted".[93]

The immense rustle of the short forms of the digital stratum captivates the marketing, socio-linguistic and mathematical linguistic fields because they always seek vast corpora from which they hope to make emerge, with the help of statistical algorithms and on the basis of the infinite variations that are inherent to languages and writings, new models to develop a deeper understanding of these very languages and regimes of signs. One of the main issue consists of differentiating the discourses "which are said in the ordinary course of days and exchanges, and which vanish as soon as they have been pronounced; and those which give rise to a certain number of new speech acts which take them up, transform them or speak of them, in short, those discourses which, over and above their formulation, are said indefinitely, remain said, and are to be said again" [FOU 71]. There is doubtlessly a permanent struggle to detect the fragments and textualities, the textures and "memes" which, bound to specific assemblages, will so-to-say open to a fertile (non-sterile, at least) commentary activity.

How to detect, within commentaries, what is properly salient or pregnant with meaning? Teaching this question could be seen as an essential task of the educational system. It is a matter of reading–writing in a such spaces, which always are in a process of saturation, with new intellectual technologies. It also is a matter of taking seriously the "bottom up" collective intelligences of usage, even if they manifest themselves irregularly and in very differentiated manners, in their interwoven strands of cognitive forces, affective and even magical energies…

The Twitter proposition therefore is an opening to a new pragmatics of networks. The writing constraints of Twitter introduce new relations of speed and slowness in the game of writing and communication practices. These new relations also concern the stability and metastability of communities (whichever their size).

---

93 Gilles Deleuze, Pourparlers 1972–1990, 2003.

## 1.22. Twitter as a Markovian Territory: a few remarks

The question of the relations of speed and slowness is a complex one. Most of the Twitter-based communications are made on a non-final mode, which is nevertheless not devoid of order. For this reason, one could say that the linguistic and semiotic interactions between Twitter actants are, to some extent, Markovian[94]. The elements of this Markovian field are themselves a-signifying, the writings deployed on them being rather "transcursive": writings that, in other words, operate "on live reality". Communication pragmatics is semirandom, "a mixture of chance and dependency that enables to think order without aligning one's thinking on a continuity or succumbing to disorder"[95].

But Twitter (since it comes inscribed in larger assemblages of writings and pragmatics) runs through territories that also run through it, discursive, narrative territories in which elements are essentially signifying.

---

94 We know that Markov studied random phenomena in which words of a linguistic chain such as a sentence depend mostly on the words coming immediately before them, not on the words at the beginning of the chain or sentence. Gilles Deleuze thought that Markov processes were very important. Markov chains are both different from absence or order and from discontinuity. In the Deleuzian understanding, in Markov chains, the order is semi-random. He wrote: " We borrow the expression 'relinking divided up' from Raymond Ruyer, who uses it to characterize the famous *Markov Chains:* these are distinguished from both determined linkages and chance distributions; they concern semi-accidental phenomena or mixtures of dependency and uncertainty. Markov was, at the beginning of the century, a pioneer of information theory. As a mathematician and a linguist, Markov wrote several articles on probability computation, which formalized his models of "chain probabilities", now called "Markov chains". Such models enable the understanding of the influence prior states have on the current state of a given system. In a nutshell, this method characterizes systems and apparatuses whose likely states depend on one or several anterior states, but not on the whole past of the system. In a linguistic framework, one can model the succession of words in this way. In a sentence, words occur in a mixture of chance and dependency, as semi-random processes. See in (*La genèse des formes vivantes,* Flammarion, ch.7). "They correspond to Markoff's scheme: they are 'partially dependent' successive draughts of semi-accidental linkages, that is, relinkages", in Chapeter 8, Cinema, Body and Brain (Note 36, p. 277, in l'Image-Temps, Editions de Minuit).

95 Gilles Deleuze et Felix Guattari, Anti-Oedipus, University of Minesota Press, 1983 (translated from the French by Robert Hurley, Mark Seem and Helen, R. Lane: L'Anti-Œdipe, p. 45–46, Editions de Minuit, 1972), Cinema 2, The Time-Image, University of Minnesota Press, 1989 (translated by Hugh Tomlinson and Robert Galeta from the French L'image temps, Edition de minuit), et Raymond Ruyer, La genèse des formes vivantes, Edition Flammarion, 1958.

Despite the writing constraints, the interacting microblocs are in constant relationship with potentially denser semiotic macroblocs (with, for instance, the use of Internet addresses). Such relationships introduce, in the heart of this type of probabilistic or semirandom pragmatics, slowing down and surging phenomena of semantic processes led by signifying chains that are endowed with strong causality and/or ends.

For example, here is how a Twitter contributor, in fact a journalist of Le Monde Diplomatique, a monthly high broad newspaper in France (http://mondediplo.com/), describes her usage and perception of Twitter: "I began tweeting about three months ago. It made me understand how this tool works and the various usages one could have of it. Some of these usages were quite far from what I was interested in. For example, I don't intend on disclosing information about my daily activities, neither the time I wake up nor the content of my meals. Nevertheless I think it is an interesting tool for three reasons: to share the reading of articles or texts that seem worthy of being spread (limiting myself mostly to articles written in English and French); to shed light on information which is not or hardly broadcast by the official press and which can sometimes interest a wide audience and sometimes only experts; to inform about the debates I am involved in, especially about themes tackled in 'Nouvelles d'Orient'[96]. Twitter uses must therefore be studied as a function of the assemblages of enunciation and the machinic apparatuses in which they are included. Thus, they must be interpreted through the lenses of the differential relationships between summoned memories, their attached social-cognitive practices and the types of interfaces involved.

From this perspective, miniaturization and therefore the mobility of interfaces are fundamental evolutions. The short forms and agile practices they support and promote are then in charge, in a distributed manner, of the preservation of the metastability of collectives. They ensure the function of linking things together like semiotic or temporal shifting in devices that operate all the way to non-digital strata and therefore widen the possibilities of adapting to neighboring actants. They thus all contribute to what could be called the "catastrophic" metastabilizing of collectives, ranging from "vanishing communities" to more stable groupings that carry on for longer timescales.

---

96 See also the very humorous article of Margaret Atwood, "Deeper into the Twungle", The New York Review of Books, March, 12, 2012.

The miniatured interfaces therefore assume a decisive role in the synchronization processes, while leaving open the processes of diachronization and the possibilities of becoming as emissions of singularities and bifurcations... This, for the powers that be, who are obsessed with the continuous control of flux and of political, anthropological and cultural reality, is a strong double bind constraint.

This is why there is some sort of Twitter obsession. We are obsessed by its potential, a might originating from the boundary zone between two processes, between the propagation of micromodels and micronarration, on the one hand, and their alteration along varying timescales, on the other hand.

In this zone, communication pragmatics and various levels of cognition and subcognition mix with each other, intermingle, are made and unmade according to all scales and substances of expression. This is also a zone in which the various abilities to introduce differences into repetition confront each other and in which the statistical emergence of mental phenomena works on signifying semiotics and opens lines of de-territorialization in assemblages that can be perceptive, cognitive, scriptural etc....

Since linguistic and semiotic pluralism unfolds in the center of this new "milieus", we need to equip ourselves with new modes of intelligibility. We believe it essential to start from the "collective assemblages of enunciation" and to think of identity as a process, and language community as an incompleteness in process of production.

# Post- and Transhumanist Horizons

## 2.1. Some bioanthropotechnical transformations

In Chapter 1, we gave information regarding the Internet's accelerated maturation and extension (the extension of its technologies and writings) to the world of objects, animals and plants. We showed that they are an essential feature of the beginning of the 21st Century. This extension, known as the Internet of Things[1], is growing at an exponential rate. On several occasions, we have given this continuous weaving the name of "digital folding of the world". This folding models and renews the definitions, under un-stabilized conditions, of the large system of internal relations that constitute the world in its very incompleteness. It provides becomings with new futures, makes new virtualities arise before us and opens a new stock of possible actualizations.

This great transformation, intensified by the convergence of Nanotechnology, Biotechnology, Information technology and Cognitive Science (NBIC)[2] and by the context of the deep environmental crisis that humanity must confront, brings several questions to the foreground. The new individual and collective pathways herald and even sometimes describe the coming forms of a great anthropological transformation.

Claude Debru, for example, states that "technologies of Life lead us into the dynamics of a neo-evolution that could end up competing with the

---

1 The IOT (see previous notes in Chapter 1).
2 See note 23.

long-established mechanisms of biological evolution". According to him, this planned artificialization of life "has the consequence of expanding the scope of the imaginable with regards to this neo-evolution, much beyond life as we know it on Earth"[3].

While we anticipate this radical evolution of life, collective intelligences, as well as the couplings between individuals in their thought collectives and intellectual technologies, evolve in an ever deeper and more manifested way. We have mentioned several instances of this profound evolutionary process.

Another dimension of the current evolutionary condition involves the following insistent question: What can a brain do? Leading research in neuroscience, cognitive science and distributed cognitive science raise the more specific question of the possibilities of many brains combined. What can be achieved by brains and their ever-renewed couplings with writings, mediations, other brains and bodies? Ever since the beginning of the long cortex–flint [STI 98] transition, these couplings have been constantly differentiating. This continuous differentiation keeps opening up spaces for the spectacular dance of creativity, with all its lushness and unpredictability.

Before investigating this subject more intensely, let us recall several cognitive science lines of work that simultaneously developed, during the past few decades, a "situated" and "distributed" approach to cognition. The aim of these approaches is to understand the conditions in which cognition unfolds in networks, the modes of circulation of information, the norms in usage and the intellectual technologies involved. These approaches branch into many varied strands and domains of investigation, and attempting to exhaustively review them would be beyond the scope of this volume. For the purpose of this book, we only need to mention that one should think of the co-determination of thinking entities and tools, of cognitive processes

---

3 Claude Debru, Le Possible et les biotechnologies: essai de philosophie dans les sciences, Paris, PUF, 2003, Dominique Lecourt, Humain, posthumain, Paris, PUF, 2003. See also "Clustered Regularly Interspaced Short Palindromic Repeats-Associated Protein 9 (Crispr-CAS9)", the enzyme that revolutionizes genetics. A bacterian immune system, CRISPR-Cas9, has become a precise, simple and universal solution to modify, at will, the genes of any cell.

and intellectual technologies as situated in the *milieu* of collective assemblages of enunciation[4], in the milieu of collective equipment of subjectivation[5], of complex and hybrid actor – networks[6].

From this perspective, the approaches developed by Hutchins are particularly illuminating. Hutchins describes the propagation of various modes of representation, from one mode to the other, as an ecology; his thinking is based on the study of the transformations of these modes. In other words, he found a kind of molecular pragmatics of such transformations. He writes, "When one applies these principles to the observation of human activity "in the wild", at least three interesting kinds of distribution of cognitive processes become apparent: cognitive processes may be distributed across the members of a social group, cognitive processes may be distributed in the sense that the operation of the cognitive system involves coordination between internal and external (material or environmental) structures, and processes may be distributed through time in such a way that the products of earlier events can transform the nature of later events. The effects of these kinds of distribution of processes are extremely important to an understanding of human cognition"[7].

As summarized by Bruno Latour, "Intellectual technologies are not (conceived as) an extension, outside of the brains' capacities. On the contrary, cognitive capacities amount to internalizing into a new medium

---

4 G. Deleuze et Felix Guattari, CAE: Collective Assemblages of Enunciation, Dialogues 1977, Kafka: Towards a Minor Literature, UMP, 1986 (translation Dana Polan form French [1975]), A Thousand Plateaus, 1987 (1980).

5 CES, Collective equipments of subjectification, Felix Guattari, schizoanalytic cartographies (2012) translated (from Cartographies Schizoanalytiques, Ed. Galilée, 1989) by Andrew Goffey.

6 Bruno Latour, Michel Callon, actor network theory (ANT).

7 Edwin Hutchins, Distributed Cognition, University of California, San Diego IESBS Distributed Cognition, 2000.

"It does not seem possible to account for the cognitive accomplishments of our species by reference to what is inside our heads alone. One must also consider the cognitive roles of the social and material world. But, how shall we understand the relationships of the social and the material to cognitive processes that take place inside individual human actors? This is the problem that distributed cognition attempts to solve". (…). "The distributed cognition perspective aspires to rebuild cognitive science from the outside in, beginning with the social and material setting of cognitive activity, so that culture, context, and history can be linked with the core concepts of cognition".

the tasks that circulate in the "groupware", tasks grabbed by the agent who then retranslates them". He continues "Hutchins proposes a new founding of cognitive anthropology because, although he remains firmly grounded in a computational approach, which makes him compatible with psychologists, he refuses to start from the group, the world or the mind. He focuses instead only on the *trajectories* of the transformations and propagations of the material forms of representation". Research on distributed cognition also leads to studying how artifacts and technologies in the most extensive meaning propose signifying resources for the action of subjects. Such is, for instance, the theory of *affordances* developed by James Gibson in the context of the psychology of perception. Some research works propose very interesting developments on this theory[8]. In short, these few examples show us that this paradigm encompasses many complex and varied trends and schools of thought.

Let us look at *distributed cognition* only. In few words, we can recall that it originates from issues investigated by the sociology of the "Outreaching Identity" (C. S. Peirce), as well as from notions of ecology of the mind (G. Bateson) and of cognitive ecology (P. Levy). It also stems from the Russian school of psychological research (Vygotsky and his historico-cultural approach to cognition, Leontiev's theory of activity …).

Bruno Latour later revived their inspirational works and expressed a program to claim the following position: "Instead of rushing directly into the mind, why not look at the hands, eyes and material context of those who know".

> "'Material', we come to realize, is not to be understood as mysterious infrastructures only known to the economist expert, nor as neural assemblages only known to the neurobiologist, nor as cognitive capacities only known to the psychologist, nor as paradigms only known to the science

---

8 See, for example, [KRU 91] "The ecological field, which couples the internal field of the organism and the external field of the environment, was proposed as providing the necessary information to guide intentional behavior lawfully. It was shown how the organization of this non stationary field (i.e. the organism–environment intersection set) depends on changes in the number and layout of the attractors within it. Theses attractors are dually specified by the affordance properties of the environment and the effectivity functions of the organism which realize them".

historian. No, the 'material' adjective refers to the simple practices by which everything is known, everything including the economy, brains, minds and paradigms".

Further on in his book, Latour specifies his argument; "The issue we are facing is not about perception, it is about mobilization. If you wish to convince a large number of people of unusual things, you first have to go out of your own usual ways; you'll then come back with a number of unforeseen allies, and you'll convince, etymologically speaking: you'll vanquish ("vince") together ("con"). But you have to be able to come back with things. If you are unable to do it, all your efforts will be wasted. The things you want to bring back also have to be able to endure the voyage without being corrupted. They must arrive in a good state, so that you can present them to the ones you want to convince and who have never been there. In short, you have to invent objects that are mobile, immutable, presentable, readable and combinable" [LAT 85]. To study the materiality of writings, mediations and transformations of the modes of representation consists of thinking and imagining better "system-environment" couplings in the sense of the second cybernetics. In other words, it consists of taking into account this massive fact: "Any system (and in our perspective any cognitive apparatus) is what it does or can do of that which the environment makes of it" [VAR 93, FOE 81]. Von Foerster [FOE 81] and Maturana thus proposed to re-establish the margin of self-determination of any cognitive system by thinking of it in the *cognitive system/environment* coupling. This corresponds to G. Simondon's notion of "associated milieu" [SIM 58].

Generally speaking, "studying situated action is not the same as studying activity in a work situation; it is characterized by strong theoretical assumptions". The ergonomic perspective, as a whole, is not essentially "situated", but it provides a very appropriate field of experimentation in which to test the hypotheses of situated cognitions studies. Beyond this practical – experimental aspect, researchers that support one form or another of situated action theory consider ergonomy as a potential source of theoretical developments and scientific knowledge on human activity, which could even lead to a general theory of activity.

The phrase "situated action" initially refers to a specific research program that was carried out by researchers in the field of ethnomethodology and conversation analysis, the most prominent of whom was Lucy Suchman[9].

Let us retrace the history of the concept by following Benoît Grison's[10] excellent synthesis, and especially his presentation of the origins of "situated action":

Initially, situated action aims to re-evaluate the notion of planification, which is central to classical cognitive psychology. This re-evaluation is achieved by re-introducing the *environment of the activity,* which was removed from the 'disembodied' vision of cognition developed by cognitivism. It was about responding to the conception of *planning* elaborated on the basis of Artificial Intelligence's GPS [NEW 58, SIM 70]. That approach relied on notions of strategies, of "ends and means analysis" or thought cognition as hierarchic sequences of operations [MIL 60].

To enrich this rapid and incomplete review, we need to also mention the works of Norman, who encourages Suchman's research, as well as the first research works in cognitive microsociology, which were carried out by Conein and his colleagues [CON 93, CON 94, CON 97]. These researchers were deeply influenced by the development of "Artificial Life" theories in the 1990s: during that decade, many successes were achieved by replacing the good-old-fashioned, knowledge representation-based autonomous planning robots with "reactive", "stimulus-response" robots [BRO 91, BRO 92].

This parenthesis into the domain of distributed cognition was necessary for us to set up the condition in which the following question can express the full tension it refers to. This is a question that not only presides over the post- and transhumanist narrations, but also raises issues about the narration of anthropological becomings, be they called narratives[11] of the

---

9 Lucy Suchman, https://en.wikipedia.org/wiki/Lucy_Suchman.
10 Des Sciences Sociales à l'Anthropologie Cognitive. Les généalogies de la Cognition Située, Benoit Grison Laboratoire Activité Motrice & Conception Ergonomique (AMCO) UFR STAPS d'Orléans, @ctivités, 1 (2), 26-34. http://www.activites.org/v1n2/grison.pdf.
11 See the works of Bruno Latour and Bernard Stiegler.

anthropocene or of the neganthropocene. This is a question borrowed from Catherine Malabou [MAL 11].

## 2.2. What to do with our brain?

From the vertiginous HBP[12] (stemming from the original Blue Brain Project) to the notion of singularity, and all the way through the performativity of the most varied organizational assemblages, our cerebral powers have always been the partially blind focus of their own Archimedes leverage point.

The Will, their only support, haunts their imagination as it haunts the sleepless nights of insomniac reason. Worse, it also haunts the wild lives of creativity, and asserts, once more as if it was necessary to insist on it, that thought is identical to the world and its variability.

The question "What to do with our brain?" goes hand in hand with the questions raised by the possible emergence of an autonomous artificial intelligence, one that would be outside the cortex – flint coupling, a potential rival. This is the prophetic position that researchers such as Ray Kurzweil support[13] [KUR 06]. In direct affiliation with Vingian thought, singularity is then defined as the moment when machines will autonomously develop the capacity to "perform" in the world on the basis of their own machine–machine coupling as well as of their own computational capacities, and thus develop abilities to interpret the world.

---

12 HBP; Human Brain Project: http://www.humanbrainproject.eu, Human Brain Project, initiated by Henry Markram (whose leadership is now a debated issue), is based on the collaboration of several European laboratories. This is a "Big Science" project, whose mode of governance is (and has always been) a debated issue. " Brain Research through Advancing Innovative Neurotechnologies". The two projects, however, do not have the exact same goals. The "Blue Brain Project" aims at understanding the brain as a whole ("The challenge consists in mapping the networks of the brain, in measuring the fluctuations of chemical and electronic activity they support. It should then lead to understanding how their interaction gives birth to our unique abilities in the cognitive as well as in the behavioral realms") and especially the functioning of all its neurons. The Human Brain Project, on the other hand, aims at building a computer simulation of the human brain on the basis of our current knowledge of its functioning. The Human Brain Project stems from the Blue Brain Project, an already ambitious research program led by Henry Markram. The Blue Brain Project consists in modeling a neural column of the rat brain.
13 Ray Kurzweil, The Singularity Is Near: When Humans Transcend Biology, 2006, The Age of Intelligent Machines, 1990 The Age of Spiritual Machines, 1999.

Which type will the system–environment relations of this new form of intelligence have? Which type of reflexivity will it develop in order to keep insisting, to persevere in being? Will this artificial intelligence fight the organic brain mediations worlds couplings to death, for the dominant position, or will we see a negotiated hybridization of the two species of intelligence? Such debates have recently flourished in the literature[14].

Science fiction has for a long time been the herald of predictions that anticipate, in the near future, the artificial elaboration of a human brain. In science fiction, non-organic cerebralities and the development of various robotic beings play a major part in narrations. To only mention some of the most famous, Isaac Asimov, Frank Herbert and before them Ambrose Pierce or Villier de l'Isle-Adam are worth reading for their artificial intelligence anticipations.

But science fiction also developed narrations that tell of our own future cerebral becomings, when we enter couplings with non-organic or even hybrid noo machines. Cinema is ripe with such projections, which we can see in, for example the "Fordidden Planet" (1956), David Cronenberg's "ExistenZ", in "2001, a Space Odyssey" (Kubrick) or more recently in "Inception" (Nolan) as well as in the whole series of movies that imagine a coming interspecies conflict between organic humans, non-organic robots as well as between humans and hybrids. Let us mention, by the way, that Samuel Butler, in his work "Erewhon; or, Over the Range"[15] (1872), and

---

14 This debate pervades even the doxic fields. When pieces of software beat chess world champions, or even champions of the game of Go, when anticipations of machinic domination are formulated by major players in the fields of robotic and digital industries as well as the main storytellers of the entertainment industries, science fiction narrators and a part of humanity indulge in fear by projecting themselves into a war against non-organic predators.

15 Samuel Butler, Erewhon, 1872 Original text (U.S. Public Domain) available on http://www.gutenberg.org/cache/epub/1906/pg1906.txt

According to Butler (we summarize), the banker has a more subtle soul than that of the member of proletariat because it is integrated in a richer "tangible machinic assemblage" ... "Those mighty organisms," he continues, "our leading bankers and merchants, speak to their congeners through the length and breadth of the land in a second of distance, instead of hearing it in a second as is done by the more highly organised classes. Who shall deny that one who can tack on a special train to his identity, and go wheresoever he will whensoever he pleases, is more highly time; their rich and subtle souls can defy all material impediment, whereas the souls of the poor are clogged and hampered by matter, which sticks fast about them as treacle to the wings of a fly, or as one struggling in a quicksand: their dull ears must take days or weeks to hear what another would tell them from an organised than he who, should he wish for the same power, might wish for the wings of a bird with an equal chance of getting them; and whose legs are his only means of locomotion? That old philosophic

more specifically in the part entitled "The Book of Machines", shows how much the human species is deeply differentiated according to the intensity and nature of its human–machine hybridizations. In a way, Butler founds a new definition of political power on the types of organic–non-organic couplings in which one engages. Class war is then based both on relations of production and integration or coupling with various states of the machine.

In their commentaries, in Anti-Oedipus, Deleuze and Guattari write: "In a word, the real difference is not between the living and the machine, vitalism and mechanism, but between two states of the machine that are two states of the living as well. The machine taken in its structural unity, the living taken in its specific and even personal unity, are mass phenomena or molar aggregates; for this reason each points to the extrinsic existence of the other. And even if they are differentiated and mutually opposed, it is merely as two paths in the same statistical direction. But in the other more profound or intrinsic direction of multiplicities there is interpenetration. There is a direct communication between the molecular phenomena and the singularities of the living, that is to say, between the small machines scattered in every machine, and the small formations dispersed in every organism: a domain of non-difference between the microphysical and the biological, there being as many living beings in the machine as there are machines in the living" [DEL 72].

On the subject of the brain, Markram tirelessly repeats that "Within ten years we will be able to know if consciousness can be simulated in a computer".[16] Later on in this book, we will return to the meaning of such Utopias and to their inscription in projects of such developments as the Internet of Things, Health, etc., with a specific attention to the software applications that come with them.

Lastly, at the roots of the thinking of those who advocate the "intelligent design"[17] approach, one finds interrogations about what could

---

enemy, matter, the inherently and essentially evil, still hangs about the neck of the poor and strangles him: but to the rich, matter is immaterial; the elaborate organisation of his extra-corporeal system has freed his soul".

16 http://markram-lab.epfl.ch/Laboratory of Neural Microcircuitry LNMC.

17 This is attached to various creationist trends: https://en.wikipedia.org/wiki/Intelligent_design et https://en.wikipedia.org/wiki/Teleological_argument, https://fr.wikipedia.org/wiki/Cr%C3%A9ationnisme.

Dominique Lecourt, L'Amérique entre la Bible et Darwin, 1992.

be called the "cerebralization of the human species". This school of thought has been edging its way in philosophy for a long time since, at least, the times of the noosphere notion. Father Teilhard de Chardin as well as Vladimir Vernadsky are the most well-known proponents of this concept. According to Teilhard de Chardin, "To explicate the true position of man in the Biosphere, one would need a *more* 'natural' classification than the one elaborated by current Systematics. According to the latter, the human group logically appears as a mere marginal subdivision ('Family'), whereas, functionally, it operates as a unique, terminal 'inflorescence' on the Tree of Life". He develops: "Man first appeared as a mere species but gradually rose up, through a process of ethno-social unification, to become a specifically new wrapping of Earth. More than a branch; more, even than a Realm; in fact, no more and no less than a sphere, the 'Noosphere': a thinking sphere co-extensively super-imposed on the Biosphere, in a much more linked and homogeneous manner".

He goes on: "We have extensively detailed how humanity tends to techno-physically converge on itself. This fact was explicated all along this chapter. However, an important point needs to be added: because of this very concentration process, the growth of the Noosphere is bound to reach a point of maturation".

Lastly, in Teilhard de Chardin's opinion: "Hominization presents itself flanked by two critical reflexive points: one is initial and individual, the other is terminal and noospheric. As Biology teaches us, the *reflected Noosphere* is the absolute, superior unit of assembled matter towards Complexity. Unless, of course, 'systems of Noopshere' manage, through chance, Time and Space, to meta-assemble themselves. This supposition may appear less fantastic if we consider that, since Life is all around us in tension (see Chapter 1, p. 44), the universe can present (successively or simultaneously) several thinking peaks".

More recently, the philosopher P. Levy developed the idea according to which a global reflexive intelligence would be emerging, thus leading humanity into a new phase of the noosphere. In the early 1990s, he highlighted several transformations of the forms of collective intelligence that were induced by networked hypertext digital memories, by digital writings that exploit digital plasticity and of new alliances between image and sound. He then furthered his research and directed his work toward the definition of semantic conditions and the design of Information Economy Meta Langage (IEML), a writing technology that should enable efficient work in these complex and heterogeneous universes. His aim can be expressed as that of producing grammars to ensure the possibility of passages between the various domains, which each have their own ontology. It is an attempt to invent new, non-exclusively linguistic[18], grammars and combinatorial methods to integrate not only hyperdocuments, but also linking graphs, the evolutions of their morphologies and plasticities, and multiple inferences. In the long term, the aim is to take charge of an extended, pluralist semiotics. All these points will be detailed later on in this book.

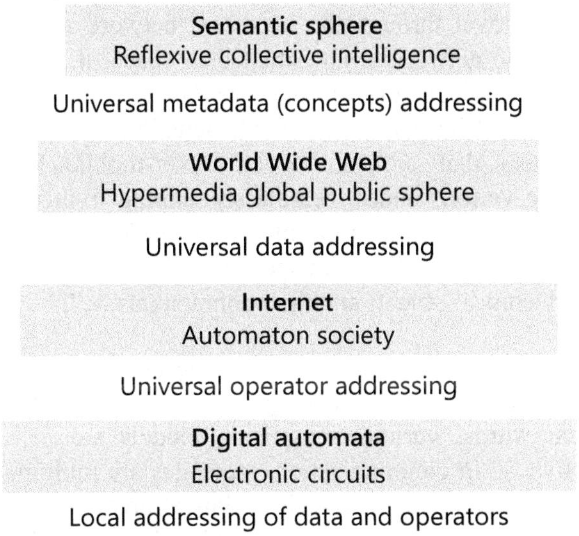

**Semantic sphere**
Reflexive collective intelligence

Universal metadata (concepts) addressing

**World Wide Web**
Hypermedia global public sphere

Universal data addressing

**Internet**
Automaton society

Universal operator addressing

**Digital automata**
Electronic circuits

Local addressing of data and operators

**Figure 2.1.** *Sketch by P. Levy, http://pierrelevyblog.com/*

---

18 See how the author opens to "Dynamic Ideography: towards artificial imagination". Dynamic Ideography is not a programming code, but a new type of interface, a language made of animated images that humans used to communicate with each other. Dynamic ideography is the writing form that the contemporaneous technical base requires. Rather than doubling the phonetic language on a visual plane like an alphabet would do, it works as an animated and figurative representation of mental models.

Beyond this scheme, P. Levy also expressed, very early in the history of the Internet, six principles to describe the cognitive and anthropotechnological stratum that was taking the shape, which he witnessed, of the Internet. The first one is the *Principle of Metamorphosis.*

"The hypertext network is in continuous construction and renegotiation. It can remain stable for a while but such a stability is itself the result of constant work. Its extensions, compositions and figures are a permanent stake for the involved actors, be they humans, microbes, X-rays, macromolecules ..."

"In hypertexts, everything works by proximity, vicinity. How phenomena occur is a matter of topology and pathways. There is no homogeneous universal space in which forces of linkage and de-connection could freely roam. Everything that moves must either travel through the hypertext network as it is or modify it. The network is not situated in space, it is space". The last principle is that of the *mobility of centers*: "The network doesn't have any center. Or actually, it always has many centers that are like several ever-mobile beacons illuminating various nodes, ceaselessly leaping from node to node and leaving behind an infinite trail of iridescent radicles, rhizomes, thin word lines, images and lines of images or contexts, technical objects and their components ...".

Then, second, there is the *principle of heterogeneity*: "2) The nodes and edges of a hypertext network are heterogeneous. In its memory, one finds images, sounds, words, various sensations, models etc. ... Edges are logically affective ... In communication, messages are multimedia, multi-modal, analogical, digital, etc. The socio-technical involves people, groups artifacts, natural forces of all scales, and all types of imaginable associations between these elements". It is followed by (3), the *principle of multiplicity and fitting of scales*: "Hypertext is organized on a 'fractal' (multifractal) mode in which any node or edge can reveal itself as being made up of a whole network whose nodes and edges can themselves be constituted of networks … In an infinite descent–ascent along the scales and degrees of precision". In some critical circumstances, the effects can propagate from one scale to another: For example, the interpretation of a single comma in a text (as an element of a documentary micronetwork), if the text is an international treaty, can have consequences on millions of people (at the scale of the social macronetwork).

The fourth and fifth principles are the *principles of exteriority and topology*: "The network does not have any organic unity. Neither has it got an internal engine. Its permanent growth, reduction, composing and recomposing depend on an indeterminate exterior: adduction of new elements, connections to other networks, exciting of terminal elements such as sensors, etc. For example, when one listens to a speech, the dynamics of activation of his/her network are triggered by the succession of words, phrases and images the external presenter utters".

The last principle is that of the *mobility of centers*: "The network doesn't have any center. Or actually, it always has many centers that are like several ever-mobile beacons illuminating various nodes, ceaselessly leaping from node to node and leaving behind an infinite trail of iridescent radicles and rhizomes, like thin white lines that sketch ephemeral maps with exquisite details then run elsewhere to outline the contours of other landscapes of meaning …"

## Structure of Emergence

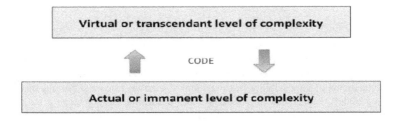

**Figure 2.2.** *Sketch by P. Levy, http://pierrelevyblog.com/*

"Emergence happens through an interdependent circulation of information between two levels of complexity. A code translates and betrays information in both directions: bottom-up and top-down".

*http://pierrelevyblog.com/*

The rise of reflexive collective intelligence develops on the basis of these characteristics.

The IEML projects cohabit and sometimes compete with the work of the proponents of the semantic and socio-semantic Web. Simultaneously, it cohabits with the heterogeneous set of works on ontologies and their complex modes of co-operation. It situates itself between, on one end of the spectrum, approaches based on predicative logic and linguistics that at the end of the day are traditional and essentialist, and, on the other end, massively statistical and probabilist approaches that rely on the pragmatics of collective assemblages of enunciation or on the enunciation regimes of actor-networks. Pierre Levy fundamentally links the emergence of reflexive intelligence to the invention of modes of writing and cognitive formalization, to specific modes of translations of perspectives and to modes of morphogeneses that are always both individual and everywhere distributed.

According to him, the IEML[19] semantic sphere "operates as a system to encode meaning. It is designed to enable the automatic computation of the largest possible number of operations on concepts and their semantic relations. (...) Far from being autarkic, opaque, closed on their own

---

19 Pierre Lévy: La sphère sémantique Tome 1 : Computation, cognition, économie de l'information; "In this book, I show that there exists no scientific, technical or ethical reason to forbid the large scale implementation of a computable symbolic system such as IEML. Akin to the theorems of impossibility that exist in mathematics (the most famous of which being that of Gödel), I think that this book provides the formal mathematical proof that a new, unforeseen by previous generations, possibility opens up to the human mind. This proof is strengthened by strong philosophical and technical arguments. *A priori*, IEML merely looks like another formal language, adding up to the plethora of formal languages that exist nowadays. Its originality resides in the fact that each of its valid expression models a semantic circuit that can canalize flows of information. The IEML semantic sphere is the immense coherent and computable graph that connects all such circuits. It thus can be used as a coordinate system for the common digital memory being constituted". "The semantic sphere can be seen as a mirror of concepts".

definition codes that would be isolated from each other, USLs (Uniform Semantic Locators), on the contrary, present themselves as points of view that are open to all other points of view, like virtual centers where multitudes of semantic perspectives meet. A USL is therefore much more than a code or a text, it is the core center of a monade whose rhizomatic spokes are generated by all the paradigmatic and syntagmatic functions that crisscross it, thus inter-weaving the semantic sphere".

Intelligences have an essential social and collective dimension. For this reason, the intrinsic computational power of computers, although important, is not the determining factor. What matters most is the dissemination of nomad interfaces and the invention of a meta-language and of integrated meta-semiotics. These are the essential conditions for the possibility of emergence of the new forms of intelligence.

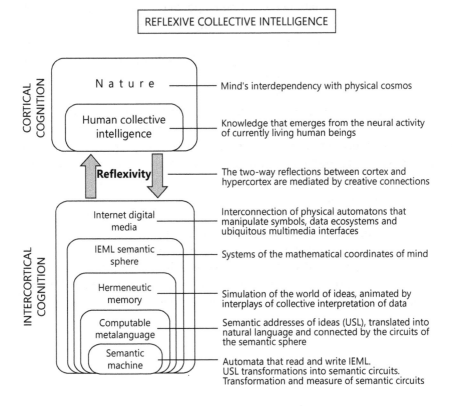

**Figure 2.3.** *(Sketch by P. Levy, http://pierrelevyblog.com/)*

We will return to this point when we investigate collectives and their distributed cognitive practices from which novel types of production, circulation and exploitation of knowledge originate and are constantly revived.

## 2.3. About transhumanism and speculative posthumanism

These movements elaborate their predictive or speculative narrations on the basis of the beliefs we mentioned earlier and on the glaring observation that the digital stratum carries with it, which is the condition for the development of a "hypercotex". This development will have massive mechanical effects and radically change our ability to understand better, maybe even solve, long-standing issues and questions about our anthropology and metaphysics. We hear the "fantastic" predictions of Kurzweil about understanding the brain and even building an artificial brain by 2040. We also hear him anticipating our capacity for "uploading" content from our brains onto no organic matter, in the form of digital encodings, in other word to transfer parts of our thoughts to an artificial medium. Such uploads could then, among other uses, be implemented on organisms (robots) who, being non-organic, would be unalterable. These movements however do not reflect upon the material and ideal conditions of the noosphere, they do not wonder about the new conditions of possibility of an ecology of mind, nor on the new conditions of "writings", interfaces, semantic grammars, although they are all deeply influenced by the great digital and algorithmic transformation. Of course, as we will later elaborate upon, they are connected to the rise of big data and to Jim Gray and Chris Anderson's correlationist paradigm.[20] Directly or indirectly, the post- and transhumanist movements are involved in the transformations of, for example, medical practice such as the development of non-invasive surgery methods. Generally, they are involved in all essential sectors of societies such as agriculture, the military and ever deeper implicated in the changes of perspectives on habitats and milieus, vital resources and urban becomings.

---

20 Jim Gray, http://research.microsoft.com/enus/collaboration/fourthparadigm/ 4th_paradigm_ book_complete_lr.pdf Chris Anderson The End of Theory: The Data Deluge Makes the Scientific Method Obsolete http://www.wired.com/2008/06/pb-theory/.

These grand narrations, between tangible Utopias and mythologies, found the new "archaea" we will come to meet. Already now, they summon the origins of the future, prepare the yet unseen forms of life, couplings and species.

These narrations grow in the boundary vortex of the great ecological crises (as we mentioned earlier) and of the vertigo inducing urbanization and artificialization of the world. Every narration related to the "augmentation" is both expression and expressed imperious desire to always open new ways of creating the world.

The issue there lies in the nature of this "augmentation". Strictly speaking, augmenting is not creating. One augments what already is. Creating is opening new ways, inventing new problems and new world games in the world, for the world, against the world and tightly pressing against the contours of the world. Creating means bringing innovation to the core of innovation itself, to the very surface of the conditions of existence of the plane of immanence. It also means bringing invention and radical innovation to the immense, extended, lush and also fragile boundary zones that ensure the comings and goings between the virtual and the actual realms. There takes place, in this process zone the very actualization and selection of becomings.

From another perspective, we will need to fully apprehend the extent of the required emergence of what could be called, in B. Stiegler [STI 98] words, "epiphylogenetic rationality", to account for the new relationships humanity will develop with its environment, or milieu. We indeed find ourselves, under the conditions set by the NBIC and the digital folding of the world in a situation in which the structural coupling between the *what* and the *who* is determinedly varying, and in which "the *what* invents the *who* as much as it is invented by it"[21].

Similarly, if we question the position of the transcendental with regards to the latest neuroscientific revolutions, Catherine Malabou signals that Kant, "here again, [he] would not necessarily have contested the assimilation of reason to the brain, since, far from being a rigidly

---

21 Idem.

programmed organ, the brain is open to the adventure of epigenetics. He would not necessarily have rejected any adaptive view of the transcendental, since he himself accepts a categorial modifiability. The epigenetic development of reason coincides with the modifiable – and modified – form of the transcendental, just as the form of a brain coincides with the modifiable development of its connections" [MAL 16].

On the epigenetic adventure, she adds, "Tomorrow, biology will prove that epigenetic modifiability is a more important evolutionary factor than genetics. Tomorrow, the order of precedence between program and its translation will be inverted" [MAL 14].

Keeping with Malabou's discourse, we know how numerous the figures of "plasticity" are. Both the tangible and ideal configurations of trans- and posthumanism are strongly related to it.[22]

Transhumanism (and especially its ideology, which is based on a neuronal ideology) is now, in a way, unable to confront or rather break in the dense block of its current, inherited political and economical tradition. This is particularly visible in contexts where the question of plasticity is asked anew, in the light of the confrontation between plasticity and flexibility, which Catherine Malabou judges fundamental. Plasticity is not a new concept. It has been through a long history in philosophy and neuroscience. One easily understands why it is so attractive to those who hope for the advent of their dreams and promises about health, immortality and the possibility to experiment on oneself under endlessly renewed conditions, under radically different anthropological conditions, including erotic and sexual ones.

---

22 See [PAP 11]. "Every epoch has its brain. The embodied brain seems to be today at the forefront of attempts to establish post-positivistic approaches in social science and social theory as well as non-reductionist conceptions of the brain and body in neuroscience, developmental science and psychology. But embodiment not only challenges prevalent epistemic and cultural assumptions in these disciplines; it also opens avenues for exploring the plasticity and the emergent epigenic nature of the brain and body. Plasticity occupies the brain-body imaginary of today's epoch. At the heart of the imaginary of plasticity lies the possibility of recombining brain-body matter and understanding the making of ecologically dependent morphologies in a non-determinist manner. But plasticity as recombination becomes not only a radical challenge to determinist assumptions about the brain-body in Western thought, it becomes also a forceful element of its own regeneration and actualization".

## 2.4. Epigenetic and epiphylogenetic plasticity[23]

The question we ask is that of plasticity when, specifically, epigenetics and epiphylogenetics are at work. We not only question plasticity at the cerebral level, but also the plasticity associated with the capacity to intervene in the cerebral milieu, as well as the influence of exterior ecologies in the form of the complex structural brain–milieu–mediations coupling.

Bernard Stiegler's work, following that of Leroi Gourhan, is central to this question, as we pointed out already. His approach also resonates with work that is presented in, for example, "Ecological Morphology, Integrative Organismal Biology"[24]. The notion of "ecomorphs" is the expression of complex phenomenas involving co-determination with the milieu[25].

The understanding of this possibility to non-genetically alter our nature is precisely what makes the notion of plasticity attractive to transhumanist trends and their doxa. If we, for example walked in the footsteps of Judith Hortsman's ideas, we should relatively soon be able to create new neurons "at will, where and when we need them"[26]. Dimitris Papadoulos displays,

---

23 *Epiphylogenesis* is a neologism created by Bernard Stiegler by combining two other terms: *phylogenesis* and *epigenesis*. *Phylogenesis* refers the genesis of the species (or more generally, of the phylum). *Epigenesis*, on the contrary, refers to all the factors influencing the development of an individual (*ontogenesis*), as long as they are not genetic (i.e. not "written" in the DNA). *Epiphylogenesis* therefore refers to the non-genetic factors of development of the human species; this hominization furthers life by other means than life itself, this is a technical externalization.
24 "Ecological Morphology, Integrative Organismal Biology" Edited by Peter C. Wainwright and Stephen M. Reilly, 1994.
25 "Ecomorphs have different phenotypes depending on the influences of contingent ecological and relational factors in which an organism is embedded".
26 J. Horstman "shows how scientific breakthroughs and amazing research are turning science fiction into science fact. She explains how partnerships between biological sciences and technology are helping the deaf hear, the blind see, and the paralyzed communicate ; how our brains can repair and improve themselves, erase traumatic memories ; how we can stay mentally alert longer and how we may be able to halt or even reverse Alzheimer's; how we can control technology with brain waves, including prosthetic devices, machinery, computers and even spaceships or clones ..." http://www.judithhorstman.com/ Judith Horstman, The Scientific American Brave New Brain: How Neuroscience, Brain-Machine Interfaces, Neuroimaging, Psychopharmacology, Epigenetics, the Internet, and Our Own Minds are Stimulating and Enhancing the Future of Mental Power, Scientific American, 2010.

in the following illustration, an overview of the various approaches of the "brain–body" problem, and creates its narration on the basis of his own plastic capacity to recombine and reconfigure. He leaves, along his progression, landmarks that help understand the processes of morphogenesis and differentiation.

| | behaviourism | cognitivism | connectionism | embodiment | autogeneric |
|---|---|---|---|---|---|
| underlying metaphor | mechanical interface | digital computer | network | animal-human-machine hybrids | autonomous machines |
| modelled on | basic animal physiological processes | controlled problem solving | distributive processes | body-environment interactions | reproduction of organic bodies |
| functioning principle | stimulus-response | universal algorithms | nodes and weights | emergent architectures | plasticity |
| organization principle | black box | centralism | decentralism | contextualism | recombination and nonhuman agency |
| supposed biological substratum | physiological processes | genes and brain modules | neural circuits | organism-environment assemblages | biotic machines |
| explanans | determinism | nativism | connectivity | relationality | epigenesis |
| dominant cultural-political conditions | Fordist state | liberal democracies | neoliberal geoculture | | postliberal enclosures |
| social movements and activism | workers movement; social liberalism | Chomskyan liberal egalitarianism; civil rights; identity politics | alter-globalization movements; situated knowledges; postmodern perspectivism; reverse engineering | | alter-ontological activism and the commoning of matter |

**Table 1.1.** *Diagram of different approaches to the brain-body*

## 2.5. Speculative uncertainties

The "trans- and post-" movements are simultaneously symptoms of the work creativity performs on itself, facing its own renewal and establishment, and their rooting into what always-already is their inheritance although it seems to be forthcoming. Hence this strange oddity between the deja-vu one feels at each new enunciation (e.g. anthropological issues) and the uncertain radicality of what we cannot enunciate in our stammering, hesitant attempts to describe these evanescent, flashing fragments of intuited novel definitions.

Astounding achievements in genomics, replication within reproductive processes themselves.... In the agoras of the convergence of NBIC and of the digital folding of the world, people speak languages that are sometimes violently rough, sometimes enchanting. Here and there, one feels the various emerging saliences signal that something is opening, tilting toward something we have not yet heard about. And that may have nothing to do with the post- and transtrends.

If we keep our task in mind, we will live these turmoiling times as the still frail expression of our unrefined attempts to find, as a species, a novel line of flight. That is, if so we wish.

As Bruno Latour writes, "This is where, in my opinion, the great religious tradition must come to help the environmentalist movements, whose current preaching can only lead to the desert. Those who are so incarnated in the created world that they may change it from top to bottom need much better teachings than 'degrow and decrease'. Since there is no 'nature' to protect, but a Creation to continue, we can re-appropriate, from the dogma of Incarnation, this fundamental teaching according to which redemption lies precisely where sin was committed". (...) "Like the Christians who had to go through pain, mourning and disappointment when they learned that the 'Coming of the Realm' did not mean the 'End of the world' at all, and that, one way or another, they would have to inhabit this 'Vale of Tears', to be in charge of an empire and soon of a whole planet, like these Christians, then, the guardians of Incarnation should understand that what is at stake in environmentalism simply is the urgent need to revive the movement of Creation: we will have to take charge of what the religious despises the most: not the Vale of Tears no, not the Empire either, but sciences, technologies, markets and the globe. Especially because we have – fortunately – made the slightest details of our existence artificial, we need to keep becoming more artificial"[27].

On his part, Peter Sloterdijk, in two small books, "Rules for the Human Zoo" and "The Operable Man" [SLO 09, SLO 10] develops several theses and details requisites for us to be able to face our condition of "lower-level engineers" in a nature perceived as a "self-constructing hypermachine".

In his opinion, one of the central tasks is to explicate our habitat as an associated milieu that must be created. This is where his theory of islands and spheres originates from, a theory in which he explains how human features are constituted by two co-dependent factors: isolation and the expression of self. He furthermore defines some criteria that will have to be applied, from now on, to the development of technology.

He writes, "To develop technologies will mean in the future: to read the scores of embodied intelligences and to pave the way for further performances of their own pieces. The most extreme states of homeotechnology are the hours of truth for co-intelligence. In them, it is revealed that the subject of the bivalent age, the former master, has become a phantom. Before this has been broadly understood, disinformed populations will partake in distorted debates led by lascivious journalists about threats that they do not understand"[28].

He then adds, "We are witnessing that with intelligent technologies a non-dominant form of operativity is emerging, for which we suggest the name homeotechnology".

In this, the author somehow agrees with a widely shared opinion according to which intelligence is accelerating, a threshold has been reached by the networking of brains and memories, the differentiation of writings and memories, even if the process is still chaotic.

---

27 Bruno Latour, "Si tu viens à perdre la Terre, à quoi te sert d'avoir sauvé ton âme"? (If you end up losing Earth, what is the point of having saved your soul?), in Conférence inaugurale du colloque Eschatologie et Morale 13th march 2008 at the Institut Catholique de Paris.
28 Peter Sloterdijk, Règles pour le parc humain: suivi de La Domestication de l'être, Mille et une nuits, 2010.

"Homeotechnic, having to deal with real-existing information, only gets ahead on the path of the not-raping of being; it acquires intelligence intelligently, thus creating new states of intelligence; (…) It must rely on co-intelligent, co-informative strategies, even where it is applied egoistically and regionally as every conventional technology is. It is characterized rather by cooperation than by domination, even in asymmetrical relationships".

However, unlike the aforementioned unrefined transhumanists, who loudly herald radiant tomorrows after each technical, nano-technological or postgenomic new feat of researchers, he (P. Sloterdijk) does not evade the possibility of polemical futures for the intelligences that differentiate within the hypercortex. Without totally buying into the strategical and military American intelligence's ideas of the emergence of neo-cortical wars[29], he mentions that "homeotechnology – the acceleration of intelligence par excellence – is also touched by the problem of evil. This however no longer presents itself as the will to enslave things and humans, but as the will to disadvantage the other in competition". For which desire to satisfy?

The transhumanist movement, associating itself with and relying on the convergence of a few great technological lines of progress (digital, postgenomic, nano-technological, artificial intelligence, neuroscience, robotics), attempts to provide a new anthropological, economical and political horizon.

This horizon is steadily taking shape, we can see it evolve daily. It is expressed through the ultra-rapid growth of the Internet of Things, which revolutionizes our cities that themselves are designed as milieus that intensify intelligence (explosion of data/Big Data, global rise of algorithmics, transformation of sciences.) This movement still lies at the meeting point of the hybrid becomings of life. Political economies emerge between the inherited political anthropology and the new political anthropology. These novel political economies favor the development of

---

29 Hacking the Human Brain: The Next Domain of Warfare, http://www.wired.com/2012/ 12/the-next-warfare-domain-is-your-brain/.

the transhumanist movement, without seeming to care about the desires and uncertainties of the democratic innovations. There is still a "resistance ritual" that insists on open communities, "commons", somewhere between a Keynesian and a Hayekian posture, but even such resistance hardly pays any attention to the anthropotechnological or to wealth inequalities, despite the few voices that vocally raise alarm about the abysmal scales of these inequalities. *We must face it. The digital folding of the world does not open any horizon in that direction, the direction of Justice, or co-immunity.*

But, as P. Sloterdijk hopes, the anthropotechnological and ecological necessities should push us into a new incarnation of the communist ideal. "Even if, from the start, communism was a conglomerate of a few correct ideas drowned in many erroneous ones, its rational aspect – the idea that the common vital interests of the highest level can only be ensured via a horizon of universal cooperative asceticism – must sooner or later regain some validity. Todays, this leads us towards a macro-structure of global immunization: *co-immunism*. Such a structure is often called a civilization. The rules of its observance must be elaborated precisely, now or never. They will serve as the code of the anthropo-technologies appropriate to existence in the context of all contexts. To wish to live under the aegis of these technologies would mean the adoption, in our daily practice, of the good habits, appropriate for the survival of the common" [SLO 11a]. Amen.

But how many private vices must we go through before we reach this virtuous new co-immunity?

Nowadays, the slogan rather goes as: "augmentation", continued!

Augmented man, accelerated hybridization, overcoming the limits are the signifying master phrases of this narration, a narration that unfolds its adventures in domains that travel between science fiction and speculative fiction, in the repeated reviving of the radiant futures of science and immortality.

But let us take a step back and re-read two positions that were proposed a few decades ago, one in the beginning of the 1970s and the other in the beginning of the 1980s. The first by Deleuze and Guattari [DEL 72], and the second by Laruelle [LAR 80].

Although 10 years passed between the two propositions, they both highlight similar changes (with all their anthropological and political radicality) that were already happening at the time. We have already mentioned the commentary of Samuel Butler's text (from Erewhon and especially from the chapters entitled "The Book of Machines") by the authors of the Anti-Oedipus. In this commentary, the authors overcome the opposition between vitalist and mechanist theses. In their opinion, what is at stake is the overcoming of such an opposition, in order to be able to fully inhabit the positive aspects of our bio-technical and bio-political becomings. That is, to think the technological complication of the world as a means to continue Life by non-organic means. In other words, they focus on the becoming complex of the body–brain–mediation–world couplings in the sense given by Leroi-Gouhran and Bernard Stiegler [STI 98].

By the way, one can legitimately say that Bruno Latour largely followed this line of thought when he developed his reflections on the "Actor-Network", on the generalized application of Bloor's symmetry principle and when he formulated his radical theories in his foundational book, "Irreductions" [LAT 84].

The second position, then, is expressed by F. Laruelle when he mentions the great Nietzschean invention: "Another body, new technical and social machines – but still, always, this compound or synthesis of human and machine, this coupling which maybe is the essence of the machine ... This is precisely the great Nietzschean invention, and his great humility. It outlines the third epoch to come, the epoch of Man-Machine: the difference from older and modern "man-machine systems" lies in the fact that the machine here is not set on one side of the relation, it fully belongs (...) to the correlation of the two terms. In the mechanist and chemico-physical metaphors of man, Nietzsche discovers the essence of the machine. In his view, this essence is the coupling itself, the pure connection, the machine-eidos, the synthesis which in fact is a transfer, the continuous transfer. He sees the machine as the metaphorical aspects of the metaphor, in other words the machine at last freed from the metaphor, man and machine becoming absolutely identical. Neither technicians nor technocrats ever managed to achieve that theory, which Nietzsche realized: that of the cog as a cog, of the node as a node ...".

He goes on: "the ultimate avatar of the Man-Machine will not be the destruction of Man and Machine, but *the annihilation of what separated them, of what differentiated one from the other*, of their "average form" which hindered the machinization of the former and the humanization of the latter. Übermensch or übermachine, this is but one concept".

Laruelle then studies the rise of "performative societies", in which one sees the triumph of means over ends (the triumph of the performativity of protocols over the ends). He notes that "The übermachine (now) corresponds to a novel type of bio-engineering which ensures the infinite, absolute, never-ending coupling of life-as-power and power-as-life, a coupling that autonomously asserts and confirms itself. The new bio-political compound ensures the coincidence, the *a priori* simultaneity of an almighty, intensive vitality which increasingly strictly subjects itself to itself and of a power that is continuous and has the ramifications of life itself, a simultaneity that one could possibly qualify as a-originated but which nevertheless is continuously becoming. And so is born the fourth realm of life, which is neither vegetal, nor animal or crystalline, which neither is a science-fiction object, but which welcomes within it the infinite vegetal patience, the animal and human aggressivity and the constant boundary-pushing growth of crystals. A realm of life which is like a project of self-domination that would exceed, in extension, intension and depth, all the micropolitical 'disciplines' and which still operates clumsily. The new avatar of the bio-political genius-engineering of humanity on herself, like a superior form of racism against the common petty racisms, much beyond racism as a superior form of life…".

Essentially, the creationist movement supported by authors such as Jim Gray or Chris Anderson somehow subscribes to the understanding of transformation proposed by Laruelle. On our part, however, we have shown how such an understanding does not correspond to the incarnated practices of science. Moreover, it does not acknowledge the theoretical and speculative practices currently at work, whereas these practices ensure the continuation of the process of Creativity.

The concept of experimentation (itself inherited), which Laruelle names "vulgar", is challenged by the rising power of the performativity of protocols as well as a "constructal" approach by means of management of resources and human collectives. It thus undergoes significant transformations and appears as "a pure bio-political engineering concept, an experimentation that the power of life carries out on itself. It may use scientific patterns or monstrous forms, which are its best allies, but it can't be reduced to them.

A policy becomes experimental and the experimentation at last takes over from the Marxist 'practice', when the distinction between objects, means, raw material and products disappears, absorbed by the differentiation of methods, within the generalization and triumphs of 'the means', when one understands that there is no contradiction left in 'things'".

He adds, "Generalized strategy creates differential relationships between – theoretical or not – processes of power, it co-determinates them as functions of each other. This is done in a continuous "machinic" chain, but this chain is outside of any ethical or scientific intention".

This seems to be the principal pattern to motivate the passion for Big Data and for the new Holy Trinity one finds at its core: description–accumulation, prediction, performation. This craze feeds upon all kinds of species of data, with all kinds of sensors. It is infinitely recursively coupled to itself via interfaces and software applications.

As early as 1981, Laruelle wrote: "The individual will become one with bio-technical data banks. But these banks will not only be abstract machines that reproduce and distribute the data. They will also be merging into the subjects. Individuals will benefit from the abstraction of these banks, and the banks will gain the subjectivity and becoming-tangible of individuals. Such a bio-engineering of evolution makes life an issue, a political and juridical problem that only life itself can solve".

Nowadays, we see how Marketing, as an experimental form of governance of individuals and populations, has deeply pervaded into these becomings. A collective intelligence of usage[30] that leans, for a good part,

---

30 François Bourdoncle "L'intelligence collective d'usage Co-founder of Exalead, Dassault", in Technologies de l'information et intelligences collectives Jean-Max Noyer, Ed. Hermes-Lavoisier 2011 and Peter Sloterdijk, Crystal Palace, In the World Interior of Capital, Polity Press, 2013, tr. From German Wiener Hoban.

on "the bio-political *a priori* that sees the human to come as ensuring the passage from traditional Ecology or environmentalism, from industrial Humanism, to an over-industrial typology". Furthermore, "the self, the I, is made of dispersed power relationships, an infinitely reflected differential I-of-I, an I relative only to self and therefore absolute, an infinite coupling... and myself ... and myself ... and myself ...".

We have shown elsewhere[31] how much the vertigoes of marketing, allied with Data Mining, the rise of algorithmics and geolocalization, is relentlessly increasing the sophistication of its methods. Consumerist practices are now mapped to unprecedented levels and semiotic production skyrockets. "Profiling" practices are now very ambitious. Marketing has truly become an experimental apparatus of new modes of governance, with strong ties with psycho-politics and new modes of psycho-power. The dream, nurtured by the so-to-say militaro-marketing compound, has become one of "hacking the brain".[32]

In their simplest, minimalist forms, Speculative posthumanism and transhumanism appear as massively antidystopic. Although they seem to acknowledge and claim uncertainties in the becomings of evolution, they hail the possibility of a major (and fortunate) bifurcation of evolution, betting on singularity to be the hypercomplex cerebral cauldron.

They urge everyone to show the greatest benevolence toward thinking patterns they judge "heretical" according to rather fuzzy criteria, but they do close the door of evolution to any other way than "Big Data Science".

Their passion, instinctual drive even, seems to be driven by the fantasies of continuous control of the anthropological, strategical and political reality, a reality that would be self-generated, self-legitimated by the regimen of predictive desire that would be granted divine status[33].

---

31 Jean-Max Noyer, Les vertiges de l'hyper-marketing: datamining et production sémiotique, in Les Débats du numérique, Edition Presses des Mines, http://books. openedition.org/ pressesmines/1662?lang=fr.
32 http://www.wired.com/2012/12/the-next-warfare-domain-is-your-brain/ and, http://www. wired.com/2012/08/movement-control/.
33 Such a desire doubtlessly leads to "the borders", the external boundaries of the interior of the world. Vertiginous labyrinth of the straight line.

In this context, needs are counter produced within the reality produced by inherited desires (expressed in rather mundane ways): to defeat illness, to extend the duration of life, to reduce moral and physical suffering, to increase security in the home of ecology and habitats. They are counter produced in regimes of individualist, hypersecuritarian becoming desires, which draw from the immuno-politics that Sloterdijk highlighted so clearly.

On that account, the example of marketing, which heavily relies on Big Data and data-mining methods, is particularly illuminating. Marketing agents, deeply aware of this characteristic, know that they must keep scrutinizing ever-deeper the practices and transactions that unfold in social networks and in which "The epochal trend towards individualistic life forms reveals its immunological significance: today [...] it is individuals who break away from their group bodies as carriers of immune competencies [...] to disconnect their happiness and unhappiness from the being-in-shape of the political commune. We are now experiencing what is probably the irreversible transformation of political security collectives into groups with individualistic immune designs" [SLO 13, p. 153].

Social networks indeed provide an extraordinary milieu for experimentation, in which to play out the opposition of collective and commons against the rise, with aggregates, of "The axiom of the individualistic immune order [which] gained currency in populations of self-centered individuals like some new vital insight: that ultimately no one would do for them what they do not do for themselves. The new immunity techniques [...] presented themselves as existential strategies to 'societies' of individuals in which the long road to flexibilization, the weakening of 'object relationships' and the general authorization of the disloyal or reversible inter-human relationships had led to the 'goal', to what Spengler rightly prophesied as the final stage of every culture: the state in which it is impossible to decide whether individuals are diligent or decadent" [SLO 13, p. 154].

In these $n$-dimensional space–times, actants are given evermore various and powerful interfaces, which however are very unequally distributed. In that context, the notion of hyperconnectivity highlights our role as mere transit points, passage entities who, shifting and metastable to various degrees, rove about the Moebius rings of the functions and services of information. This novel nature is salient in the perspective of consumerist assemblages as well as on that of cerebral and intellectual assemblages.

In there also lies a crisis, a deep-reaching transformation of the structures of perception, of its pragmatics[34] and of the processes through which things, beings and their relational systems appear to us. As Stephane Vial writes, an ontophanic revolution is under way. "The digital revolution is therefore not simply a historical event pertaining to the history of technology: it also is a philosophical event which affects our phenomenological experience of the world. It pertains to ontology, or rather to ontophany, i.e. the process by which the being (*ontos*) appears to us *(Phaino)*. However, whereas the non-Euclidian revolution or the quantic revolution were mainly intellectual revolutions which affected only those able to understand them, the digital revolution is a social revolution, which affects the whole of the population. This is a mass event, which disrupts the ontophanic experience of many hundreds of millions of people"[35] [VIA 13].

In the becomings of constructive and perceptive networks, in their turbulences and halos, we are but transit points who shape, transmit, relay and translate both simultaneously and in slowed down succession, serving a cultural, economical, aesthetic and evolutionary machinery. We sometimes end up as mere "vanishing points". But how can we be light and evanescent in such conditions? How can we avoid getting inexorably nearer the purple horizon of what could be called synaptic saturation? Or rather, how would we stop puncturing, breaching through this threat of saturation? Maybe this is where, at the end of the day, we can find the deeper meaning of this cry, of this desire to become "post-human"? These turbulences, which turmoil deep in our perceptive assemblages and in their effects at the core of intelligences, need an acute description. The need for metastable collectives as well as the risk of tetany that looms over them

---

34 Notes pour une pragmatique de la perception. Les agencements perceptifs comme pli et zone frontière in La transition du perçu A l'ère des communications Édité par Alain Mons, Ed. PUB, 2013.

35 Stéphane Vial, L'être et l'Ecran (Being and Screen), Comment le numérique change la perception, Edition PUF, 2013, http://www.etre-et-ecran.net/post/57789427357/being-and-screen.

should make us realize that we must work to maintain the conditions for such breaches and chaosmoses in the relational system. We are navigating through a proliferation of narrations, a rustling of editorial fabrications, an intensive carving of immersive space–times, a burgeoning flurry of holography, through the unfathomable erections of storytellers who, from dazzling flashes to languid fables, mesmerize a whole people into empty pursuits. How will we, then, in this unruly ocean, be able to discern the trends, the deeper swells that do affect percepts?

"We are such stuff as dreams are made on, and our little life is rounded with a sleep ..." writes Shakespeare. What are the creations that now overflow the perceptive and affective states, and where do they manifest themselves? How can we design immersive spaces that do not reduce the world to a "pure phenomenology" (i.e. to the world being nothing more than the world itself)? How, then, to immunize ourselves from immuno-politics? Beyond the question of "collaborative immersive spaces", how can we open new perspectives for our desires to produce milieus that would be means of invention and exploration, means of establishing new connections and openly seek new points of view? This is necessary in order to not exhaust becomings, in order to constantly re-open in politics and in knowledge "the breaching, or the time of the community". Is not this search the main stake of the game played nowadays, with the search for 'commons', Alterity, creation, unpredictability? How indeed car we design interfaces that do not restrain de-territorialization processes and that on the contrary, trigger chaosmoses? In D. H. Lawrence's words, "Man fixes some wonderful erection of his own between himself and the wild chaos, and gradually becomes bleached and stifled under his parasol. Then comes a poet, enemy of convention, and makes a slit in the umbrella; and lo! The glimpse of chaos is a vision, a window to the sun" Can we tear open slits in the skins of the human–machine digital coupling? Can we slit the digital immersions? Is not this question one of the lines of flight that art, in its fully bio-political and hybrid business, must embrace? In this framework, we do not question the status of the body or the critique of representation anymore, but rather the *coming neo-natural and largely holographic ecologies.* We speak about perceiving, experiencing, feeling, acting, creating and thinking while immersed in a "hologramic interface" that combines and connects things on the basis of the writing and perception heterogeneses. In this becoming holographic, what will the role ascribed to interstices and alteration processes be? That is, if we understand the becoming holographic as something other than the rise of the simulacrum, as something other than the digital, holographic representation of an outside or of an inside? Which "ontologies" (in the socio-semantic Web sense) and which combinatorial and translation systems will we need to elaborate in order for such ontologies to operate together in immersive spaces? We will need to elaborate them so that they can handle the variations of points of view, the variations of the processes we host and are surrounded with, the variations of the morphogeneses attached to the definitions of the trajectories and ethologies that make us "collective and psychic individuations" endowed with increased reflexivity and subject to an "Other" which is larger, more heterogeneous and more processual.

Where, then, are the "seers" and "becomers" actualized? Where are those who are both the expressed and the expression of new percepts, or, as Virginia Woolf would put it, of "saturated perception", involved in breaking in or creating one or several substrates to be the basis of new subjectivities? Where are those who live the transgressive movements, straddling borders until they trigger creation?

Here, "percept" is understood in a meaning slightly different from that of Deleuze in "What is Philosophy"? It is understood as a "sensation" that projects back to the plane of immanence of actions. Perceptions do not only have a knowledge function, they express a possible action. We think on the basis of our own body seen as a circular apparatus. In this circular apparatus, consciousness and body are structurally coupled so that the world and the subject emerge together through our own body. Merleau-Ponty can be a good guide on this account: "Our own body is in the world as the heart of the organism: it keeps the visible spectacle constantly alive, it breathes life into it and sustains it inwardly, and with it forms a system" [MER 12] Let us insist on the idea. He also writes, "The subject of sensation is neither a thinker who takes note of quality, nor an inert setting that is changed by it; it is a power that is born into and simultaneously with a certain existential environment, and synchronizes with it"[36].

The sensation is therefore the expression of a circularity between our own body and the perceived world. This issue of "circularity" becomes a

---

36 Idem.

"structural coupling" in the thinking of some of the founders of the second cybernetics and of the theoreticians of autopoiesis.

This well-known stance as Merleau-Ponty opens the notion of sensation to the question of the possible and of the status of "The Other". Going back to the roots of the Deleuzian genesis, we see "the Other" as a structure of the perceptive field itself. More than 20 years before the publication of "What is Philosophy?", in the postface of "Friday, or, the Other Island" Deleuze asks the following question: "What *happens* when others are lacking in the *structure* of the *world*? There only reigns the *brutal opposition* of the *sun* and the *earth*, of an insupportable light and an obscure abyss ..." [DEL 90]. In the words of Tournier, this is the brutal rule of all or nothing. Deleuze goes on: "*The known* and the *not-known*, the *perceived* and the *non-perceived* confront each other absolutely in an unconditional combat" [DEL 90].

The first effect of the Other is that "Others ensure that, around each object that I perceive or each idea that I think there is the organization of a marginal world, a mantle or background, where other objects and other ideas may come forth in accordance with laws of transition which regulate the passage from one to another".

In this perspective, "The Other is neither an object in the field of my perception nor a subject who perceives me: the other is initially a structure of the perceptual field, without which the entire field could not function as it does (...)". In short, "Thus, the *a priori* Other, as the absolute structure, establishes the relativity of others as terms actualizing the structure within each field. But what is this structure? It is the structure of the possible. (...) The other, as structure, is the expression of a possible world; it is the expressed, grasped as not yet existing outside of that which expresses it"[37].

All through the deep movement of actualization and differentiation in which life unfolds in its organic and non-organic individual and/or collective forms, the Other never ceases to transform. But what happens when the Other changes? The perceptive field transforms. Perception does not only vary at specific times, it is a continuous process. Nevertheless, when the Other undergoes great transformations that involve the anthropological basis, the modes of habitats and of writing ... the shifts

---

37 Idem.

and transformations of the perceptive field are more intense, more visible. In its essential nature, the perceptive field is stable or unstable to various extents. In its never-attainable core (what is the core of a perceptive field, anyway?) or along its boundary zones, instability is always something to consider. We have seen that mediations and interfaces are becoming ever more subtle. The propagation of psychic powers and of energetic semiotics electrify milieus that, in Sloterdijk's words, are frothy with thin membranes.

Writers, scientists, architects and movie makers create, in various places, "machineries and textures" that make byways possible, as connections to the emerging becomings of affects and percepts.

To see, listen, taste and touch are attached to evermore complex processualities. The assemblages through which these perceptive activities are experienced and felt are inhabited by new heterogeneses.

To progress, connect, write, read, memorize, translate … are affected by how mediations, interfaces and writing modes vary. They are influenced by the variations of the various sign regimes that carry within themselves such combinatorial constraints, with their attached collective modes of transmission, substances of expression and hybrids. The process of discretization, or digitalization of sign, is central to the differentiation of the world, to its becoming ever more complex, as we pointed out and repeated before.

Thus, territories transform, space–times and habitats are being carved, urban semiogriphs (where "griph" refers to enigma and network) resonate with cortical regions. Relationships of speed and slowness differentiate, new relations are created. We increasingly acutely perceive that we live on a plane where contemporaneity and co-existence of all times become salient features. This massive observation makes us feel that, here and there and especially at the limits, new becomings are being actualized. We feel that this emergence makes our anthropological plateau pulsate, that this pulsation is both the expressed and the expression of baroque assemblages, of bio-technical becomings that are sophisticated to various extents, to the point of sometimes being teratological! So, the question of the spatiotemporal becomings is of major importance.

This is, for example the case of times which, from Stanley Kubrick to Wong Kar Wai via Alain Resnais and Steven Spielberg, make us "break through" cinema. Stuff of unfolded time, but which obeys the "in-folded" orders? Here, still, contemporaneity of times. This is an important point, as it leads us to a vertiginous conception of time as "immediate relating of the heterogeneous as pure difference" [DEL 94].

This conception is pluridimensional and intensive. It grants no special status to the present and sustains a resonance and a complex conversation with the deep cerebral carving of Earth's surfaces. The explosion of substances of expression exactly instantiates this conception. Let us focus here on the sound universe, and study the proliferation of sounds and music.

Let us first point out that image proliferation is often granted more importance than the proliferation of sound, music and audio devices (Ipod, Walkman and other various nomads). In our opinion, this seems wrong because music raises, with renewed strength, the question of affects. This question forces us to grapple with what a body brain can do and with what collectives of body brains can do, when thus immersed.

The question of times, affects and of the becoming of bodies in their sound dimensions is subject to another major transformation: the transformation that occurs when the music–brain coupling rises to the frontline and comes disrupting the primacy of the linguistic signifier and of sight. Here, we refer to several seminal pieces of work, including, especially, that of Max Dorra, as expressed in the beautiful short book entitled "Quelle petite phrase bouleversante au cœur de l'être" [DOR 05] (What a moving little sentence, within the heart of being). We also refer to the concept of "ritournelle" and follow the understanding of Bruno Heuzé, who advocates taking music and sounds as "the more or less extended backside of writing: a resonating side, freed from identities even if they were remarkable, actually doubling up the identities of writing, to fuse them on the searing thread of differences and power variations" [HEU 07].

Music is central to the assertion (Music is a process and is somehow, essentially, the love of life. It even is creation of life).

Which, then, are the effects of this proliferation, when ritournelles and repetitive tunes compete and intermingle, in the milieu of the individual and collective perceptive assemblages?

Which are the new synchronization/diachronization relationships that are being actualized? What is being woven in this infinitely resonating ontology of resonances? We hear resonating sound worlds crisscrossed by heterogeneses, oscillating between harmonies and disharmonies, rocked by a multiplicity of rhythms of becoming milieus, we listen to the rise of the new economy of passion.

Echoes, rustle, more or less dense sound blocks that are, to various extents, holed up in architectures, in the fractal carving of bubbles and isolation systems [SLO 05]. The spatial aspect of music is, once again, double: one fertilizes and launches long haul modulations and resonances that act as unbound energies while the other creates and stabilizes the associated milieus of sound and music (bound energies), as individual and collective prosthetics. In this double spatial aspect dwell and *live the countless harmonics of an affect, the multitudes of associations as flashes of a kind of intensive time diagonal.* Event.

Forces are activated when the internal states of the brain–body correspond to its external states and vice versa. These forces outline the odd alliances between intense spaces and times, for better or worse. But how can we describe them?

Our relationships with our associated milieus consist of complex co-determination relations. These relations weave a sort of $n$-dimensional world, which consists of assemblages of arrangements with active boundary zones, in which, in turn, translations of various levels of wisdom happen, sometimes dashing sometimes slowly making their ways through heterogeneous milieus.

These assemblaged couplings are our "other", and our perceptive assemblages are their offspring. We think and experience these assemblages as boundary objects that ensure both the actualization of the structural brain/associated_world couplings and the interfacing of the inside/outside relationships, in which the inside is precisely the folding of the outside. Endless ends of the process. We find ourselves in the milieu of a threefold dynamics by which brain–bodies, perceptive assemblages, associated words and all the mediations co-emerge and are co-determinated. Three collectives waltz in a permanent co-differentiation, ceaselessly exchanging the outside and inside positions. Each one of the three activates internal states of the others. The question remains open, though, of the extent to which one should consider these three collectives as operationally closed systems (in Francisco Varela's sense) [VAR 89].

These are but landmarks to hint at the fields in which the transforming actants increase the richness of our environments, unsettle the sign regimes with disruptions, with the ways, in Merleau-Ponty's tradition, "our own bodies" are in the world. "In this perspective, the body is not in space like things are, it is the point or rather the void from which space radiates and around which things arrange themselves in relief" [MAD 75].

Some of these fields interest us more specifically. They involve going through territories, objects, nomad media, constellations of images, the powers of the brain .... This is where some problems and interrogations rise. For example, how do the territories of nowadays transform, constitute themselves? Which becomings are, here and now, possible? And the new territory crossings, by sedentary or nomad inhabitants, as ephemeral or repetitive progressions ... What do they create, what do they alter?

How to account for the processes of "territorialisation–de-territorialization–re-territorialization"? What are the relations between the modes of traveling, between speeds and slownesses? Which relations, which tensions between the digital and proto-digital territories? What is the nature of the membranes (borders – interfaces) that regulate the relations between connectivity and isolation?

Now, let us focus on the importance of "science/speculative fiction", both as an extension of the reflection about lateral possibles and as milieus in which perception is set as a "principle of uncertainty". What are the possibilities and abilities of a brain–body when submitted to variable bio-technical conditions or to various pathological affections? Such seems to be the main concern of "science-speculative fiction" writers.

In the early 1970s, John Brunner wrote a famous "speculative fiction" book, entitled "Stand on Zanzibar". In it, he proposed a vivid vision of the processes of globalization and bio-political becomings, of the processes of transformation of the war machines, of urbanism and of neo-natural milieus. All these processes partake to the modes of ontological self-constitution of subjects. His vision relied on the co-existence of various habitats and ecological niches, on the co-existence of affluent societies and scarcity economies, on the co-existence of very differentiated bio-technical becomings. All this was set in a world that was finite in an extensional perspective, and that had no focus other than that of finding one. Simultaneously, Philip K. Dick spread long-term visions of perceptive vertigoes.

There are also is the vertigoes of control societies and of simulations, the depths of in-differentiation. We should be questioning the various apparatuses that the "seers" we mentioned earlier summon. They create the narrations, the new sign regimes, the maps that enable us to set up connections with the coming trends and enable us foresense what is to come and to revolutionize things and events ... with yet-unknown measuring criteria. We speak here of the seers, the "becomers" who speak barbarian languages on the agoras and who brush against, barely touching them, the affects and percepts and the morphogeneses that still flutter in the limbo of perception.

Where to find the traces of these intuitions? Where are the sometimes crude, sometimes refined maps that signal a becoming underway, a becoming with a future although it is hardly perceived? Here, I think of that which came and keeps coming from the American imperial apparatus: science-speculative fiction. Speculative fiction produces narrations that take place at the frontiers of anthropology. It seems to be a perceptive and speculative machine that is dedicated to unfolding the new writings, in an attempt to define the novel neighboring zones between conceptual blocks, perceptual blocks ... "Philosophy and anthropology fiction". Is that a speculative machine set against anti-Utopia, purporting minority becomings on the fringes of a so-called "minor" literature? It is a machine, in any case, which seeks to carve lines of flight that partly detach from the pregnance of the current, inherited territories, and this, "in-between" the writings of the "science of metastability", of the morphogeneses, and the holy scriptures. A speculative narration that tries to carve its blazing way beyond the "re-duplicative science fiction", the "re-duplicative utopias" (in Butor and Eizykman sense) [EIZ 73]. In other words, science fiction is practiced as a conventional exercise about the lateral possibles, and, at the end of the day, always comes back to the metastable forms. Beyond, in short, a sort of scholastics of the future which would repeat in its sterile routine the discourse of essences, in which what is at stake is the "full", in which the target is the "meaning", "presence" is the limit, and in which intensive science always carries some sort of truth demand (Deleuze, De Landa) [DEL 87, LAN 02]. In our opinion, the true demand of "science-speculative fiction" does not exist. What is told and written in this genre is of another nature: it speaks of the reason and unreason of intensities, of the instability of anthropological bases, of experimental cerebralities. When it stubbornly tries to step in with reduplicative and pedagogical ends, when it asserts itself as the true relay and teacher of science, it collapses in a language-writing habit and submits to science's desires of control and mastership.

Conversely, speculative fiction can also become daring and steal the show when it sets out to explore the zones of tension and dissensus. Such zones are born in the coming and going between, on the one side, the more or less subtle writings of passions, affects, percepts and anthropo-bio-technical tremors and, on the other side, the holy scriptures.

This is the reason why we are interested in the "minor literature" in the Deleuze/Guattari sense [DEL 75], all the more that it is presently resonating with the novel plasticity of digital matter in all its shapes and hypertextures. This genre is becoming partially immanent to these hypertextualities, these hologram worlds that are infinitely fractal and full of holes, such as the territories of creation they are, in which the dissolution of perception is the omni-ever-present horizon. In that, it has found the recipe for a kind of reversibility between form and content. Of course, and we thought we knew it already, texts always are labyrinthine machines. They are $n$-dimensional and ceaselessly create the conditions of their own dismantlement, constantly opening an indefinite number of holes, or breaches, that are as many connexions and virtual pathways of which only a few will be actualized. Texts are never dense, full blocks. They are like Menger's cube, territories with a potentially infinite surface, home to incessant processes of de-territorialization/re-territorialization, open territories and off screen of our perceptive modes. They are hypercomplex differential architectures that create the material and ideal (psychic) conditions for a permanent tension at the heart of cuts, limits, boundary zones, holes and voids.

In this perspective, speculative fiction would be the kind of writing that attempts to lead us toward what François Laruelle (although I use his notion with some uncertainty) calls "elemental solitude". This is symbolized by space and time, but in it humans "not only are" but are rather "held, like the substance of void" [LAR 00]. In any case, in the most heretical speculative fiction, texts appear as the milieus of zones of indetermination co-inhabiting with weak combinatorial constraints.

Which are the variations, the various manners in which the perceptive assemblages are carved and co-inhabit? Which are the effects of the new artifacts, of the biological and intellectual technologies which, as mediations and interfaces, differentiate, separately or simultaneously, the worlds of seeing, hearing, touching …? Which are the worlds that become possible with the new species of technology, the proliferating populations of images and sounds, the differentiation of lights? Which are our modes of choosing the worlds that suit us, which are the modes of experimentation, which are the encounters we make?

According to how we think the "becoming bio-technical", we will indeed develop different ways of thinking the variations of the perceptive assemblages in the full account of their positivity. According to how we appreciate the non-exclusively linguistic semiotics and the various sign regimes, either under the primacy of representation or under the primacy of creation, we will tend to think the variations of perceptive assemblages sometimes as duplications or reduplications, sometimes as the continued creation of the worlds, their enriching through differentiation and uncertainty. We want to progress toward perceptive becomings, and such becomings are, in Deleuzian terms, "captures, posessions, added value", "they never are reproduction or imitation".

We precisely have to appreciate the way these assemblages create "new neighboring zones between heterogeneous perceptions, bound together in a block of becomings that transforms them" [DEL 77].

We say that the states of our associated milieus are "turbulences, distortions, both troubled and troubling states, which are our perceptions also because they do not exactly fit with us. They activate, within us, internal states that challenge the limits of what we can bear. Any perceptive assemblage thus defines a domain of changing states that suits us, a domain of destructive changes, a domain of perturbation and a domain of destructive interactions. Understood in this manner, we see them as complex, fractal frontier objects in which heterogeneous and even antagonistic forces confront each other and intermingle. Their outline, as frontier objects, is therefore labile, uneven and marked by more or less local instabilities. They are however metastable to some extent, which makes inhabiting the world possible and binds us, a priori, to transpersonal, transindividual apparatuses" [SIM 07].

When perception reaches a sufficient level of acuteness, percepts surge as saturated perceptions. This upsurge constitutes the Other, that is, the actual forms, and starts partaking to the background "which is the system of forms, or rather the shared reservoir of form tendencies which do not yet exist in their own individuality, which are not yet constituted into explicit systems"[38]. In far from equilibrium situations, when the perceptive assemblages totter, "The partaking relationships of forms and background is one that bridges over the present, diffusing an influence of the future onto the present time, of the virtual onto the actual, because the background is a system of virtualities, of potentials, of forces underway, whereas the forms are the system of the actual"[39]. The phrase "turbulences of perception" would then mean the advent of events that manifest the bumpy passages, the comings and goings that enable us to reach the system of virtualities. From these zones of indetermination would emerge the creative processes as well as other things. Creation, invention (in all their forms) "would – then – be the process in which the system of virtualities takes charge of the system of actualities (...). Forms are passive in so far as they represent actuality; they become active when they organize themselves according to the background, thus bringing into the actual that which previously was virtual"[40]. Simondon then adds: "The modalities by which *a system of forms can partake to a background of virtualities* is certainly difficult to shed light on". With regards to this process, the

---

38 Idem.
39 Idem.
40 Idem.

question then is: what is the nature, the role and the status of the becomings that roam through the perceptive assemblages? One could then suggest that perceptive instabilities and creative thought are non-local although they always emerge in a singular manner, from the relationships between protoindividual and transindividual, in Simondon terms again. In a nutshell, we speak here of all which, from the most intimate and singular perceptive fields, resonates with a larger relational assemblage. We know that, in Simondon, the transindividual "assumes a true operation of individuation on the basis of a proto-individual reality, associated with individuals and able to constitute new issues with its own metastability"[41]. The transindividual therefore is the system of individual and milieus[42] relationships as both expressed and expression of parts of the proto-individual seen as a reservoir of possibilities and potentialities. The system of relations and associations co-emerges with the multiple psychic and collective individuations, the transindividual is "an impersonal zone of subjects, which simultaneously has the molecular dimension of the intimate and of the collective itself".

Perceptive assemblages could also be approached as zone interfaces in which the resonances of morphic fields would manifest themselves, as R. Sheldrake puts it [SHE 81, SHE 98]. In J. P. Courtial's words, any perceiving entity feels, but for the (organic and/or non-organic) filters and mediation, "the large network of associations in him, of co-occurrences of psychic events (images, motor sensations, words), according to a logic of *emergence* without the a priori involvement of any anteriority. One can equate this logic of emergence to a morphic resonance phenomenon". Our subjectivities, as we saw before, are "emergences" that emerge on the basis of the structural coupling of "brains-body-mediations-associated milieus"[43]. They are the offspring of multiple translations, of a brewing alchemy of various perceptive assemblages, which bear and regulate the couplings between complex internal pragmatics and the external pragmatics of "the Outside".

Our subjectivities lie in the intersection of couplings as frontier objects. They also have a significant autopoietic aspect, which means that they

41 Idem.
42 Here, we should also refer to the actor-network of B. Latour, to the echoes of Tarde/Deleuze and of Peirce.
43 http://www.mei-info.com/wp-content/uploads/revue21/7MEI%20no%2021MEI-21.pdf.

never cease to generate and specify their own dynamics and becomings, their conditions of operation. They are what they do or can do with that which "their Outside" (associated milieu, environment) makes of them. Each assemblage thus simultaneously is a filtering, a translation, a representation, a simulation, a creation and a performance. A creation of events. The Deleuzian concept of "haecceity" is a central one. He presents it by: "There is a mode of individuation very different from that of a person, subject, thing, or substance. We reserve the name haecceity for it" [DEL 87]. "Haecceity is used to define a transcendental, impersonal and proto-individual field (...) which nevertheless neither is identical with an undifferentiated depth nor can be defined as a field of consciousness (...) that which is neither individual nor personal, on the contrary, are the emissions of singularities that preside over the genesis of individuals and persons". This is an immense production, through the creative-translating filter of perceptions. A rebellious population of "haecceities"[44] through whom the perceptions and their processes of alteration creation live and connect us to the system of virtualities via pathways of variable intensities[45].

The essential role we ascribe to mediation induces a true strategy of the "interval"[46]. Mediations indeed are central to the creation of times. In other words, they operate on the axis of time and play with the relationships of speed and slowness, which are overdetermined by the plasticity of intervals, of differences. The plasticity varies according to the substances of expression and to the types of combinatorial constraints. Life and, in A. N. Whitehead's words, thought, lurk in the interstices of each living cell, in the interstices of the brain.

---

44 This term is proposed by Gilles Deleuze and Félix Guattari in A Thousand Plateaus, (pp. 282–283) to express a mode of individuation that cannot be reduced to substance, object, or subject .... But rather is an event. (See the very clear note, in the English translation of "Dialogues" 1987: Hugh Tomilnson and Barbara Habberjam pp. 151–152).
45 Simondon, L'individuation psychique et collective (Psychic and Collective Individuation), Edition Aubier, Paris 2007. This means, by the way, that there cannot happen a radical loss of individuation because there exists, – even in the deepest of the darkest night – an individuation which is modal, intensive and singular. "Haecceities are only degrees of power that combine. They correspond to a power of affecting and being affected, to passive or active affects, to intensities" (G. Deleuze, A Thousand Plateaus).
46 We know that such interval are determinant, from the neural level already: they open to Time, difference, gap and recursivity (see Deleuze and A. N. Whitehead).

Perception, under the conditions of the variation of mediations, creates novel interstices, new labyrinths of full and empty spaces, of labile frontiers. The perceptive states are immediately metastable, processual states that co-emerge at the joints of couplings, as we mentioned already. They operate as sieves, enabling, in a fractal mode, the growth of boundary zones out of what would otherwise only be a chaos of blurry zones of sterile indeterminations. *Here, the strategy of intervals and the strategy of interfaces are equivalent.* From that point of view, the question of becomings and of the double capture, as set by Deleuze and Guattari, can, at last, unfold at all scales as the center of the question of perception.

Proposing to tackle the notion of such assemblages on the basis of the notion of autopoiesis, we naturally suspect that we need to take F. Guattari's remarks into account. He suggests that "autopoiesis deserves to be rethought in terms of evolutionary, collective entities, which maintain diverse types of relations of alterity, rather than being implacably closed in on themselves. In such a case [, he points out, ] institutions and technical appear to be allopoietic, but when one considers them in the context of the machinic assemblages they constitute with human beings, they become ipso facto autopoietic. Thus we will view autopoiesis from the perspective of the ontogenesis and phylogenesis proper to a mecanosphere superposed on the biosphere" [GUA 95]

Therefore, on the verge of one more case of solipsism, we aim to open the operational closure of Von Foerster/Maturana/Varela to associated worlds and to the other [VAR 99a, VAR 99b, MAT 72, MAT 74, FOE 74]. We seek to set the focal point of our reflection on the immanent and continuous variation that is central to perception, in the context of the frothy networks of our intelligences, in the "societies of thin walls" [SLO 13].

Venessa Miemis[47] proposes a more concrete and tangible reflection on some aspects of this notion. She details the various positions (they can superimpose on each other) that one can occupy in an elaborate, hyperconnected informational–communicational society.

---

47 Conceptual framework for online identity roles http://emergentbydesign.com/ 2010/08/04/conceptual-framework-for-online-identity-roles/.

Such a "hyperconnectivity" has significant effects on the psychic and collective processes of individuation. This doubtlessly is one of the main causes of tensions at work in the great production groups of today, which are conceived and designed as assemblages of cerebral microanthills. These tensions need to be constantly controlled, cooled. Some see in there the germs of an economy of rape and exploitation, in which a molar, partial and biased algorithmic automation could lead control societies to the collapse of reason of creativity. They see, in the emergence of novel forms of the economy of contribution, the means, as a bypassing shortcut over markets, to create the condition of an emancipation from such a bleak prospect. Bernard Stiegler, for example, supports the following understanding: "Only by going over the market (which does not mean against it) can we put automation to serve reason. By reason we mean deciding of one's own individual time as partaking to a historical and political time – that is, a time expected and collectively projected, a neganthropic time. In order to design an economy of contribution based on noetic pollinization, we need to start from this imperative encasing of the negotium into the otium, by constituting the value of value as, precisely, this imperium"[48].

---

48 Bernard Stiegler (with good reason) never stops criticizing those who miss the materiality of writings, technologies and mediations ... which are central to the movement of incarnation of the mind, of intelligence. He nevertheless chooses an *a priori* negative stance toward the algorithmic question, refusing to fully consider the entirety of its positive aspects. In our opinion, he misses the positive cognitive effects (to empty the brain, to, for example create new conditions for novel abductive and simulation regimes) of algorithms. His approach seems to be flawed by several confusions. The first confusion is due to a lack of understanding of how algorithms work on the core of thought and opening processes, on the fault lines of the intelligibility frameworks. He fails to see the new virtuals algorithms thus produce, the power of a signifying semiotics and the breaches they (potentially) tear open in, among others, signifying semiotics. Freed from the burdensome uncreative tasks, climbing up to the heart of issues is more open, easier. The becoming algorithmic, in Deleuzian terms, therefore is a process that creates new smooth spaces. It partly renews the processes of actualization of new internal cerebral states and opens new analogical freedom of interstices. This is the positive aspect of algorithms. Of course, there is also some truth in what one hears about automation and the dark powers of algorithmics. But, in our opinion, since we live in a data-centric society in which the algorithmic medium unfolds without, so far, any perceptible limit, the counter powers must also be sought in algorithmic power, but in open and disseminated forms. Rather than insisting on detailing the evil powers of algorithmics and automation, we should let power diffract, multiply and disseminate in the interstices of our societies, in order to break the monopoly of macromachines of capture and processing .... Well, *this is a possibility*.

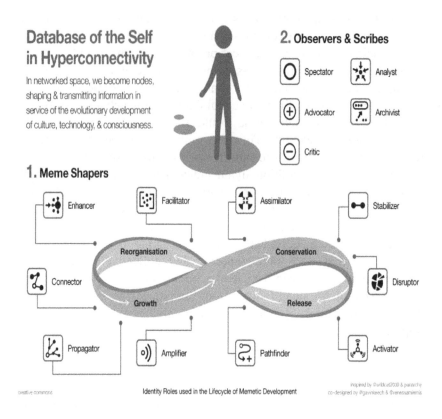

**Figure 2.4.** *(http://emergentbydesign.com/2010/08/04/*
*conceptual-framework-for-online-identity-roles/)*

Further on in this work, when we study the extension of collective and distributed practices, we will question the consequences of that, especially in the context of "swarming intelligences".

## 2.6. Trans- and posthumanism as they present themselves

These two schools of thought constitute an eschatological narration. Their content mainly consists of a declaration of faith in the radiant future of technology, which is meant to help create and master the artificialization of the world. This artificialization raises a major anthropological question, either because it necessarily leads to the re-definition of humanity and its associated milieu and to its overcoming (as an augmented humanity or even a posthumanity), or because it draws on the search for new, radically different, means of existence, on machinic innovation (in the Deleuze-Guattarian meaning), but in a perspective that goes beyond the radiant future of technical and bio-technical complication. This new stage after the bifurcation or singularity is researched and imagined in various ways and in various political paradigms (various time scales, various imagined processes of actualization of ecological becomings due to various types of ecological crisis). The variety and the asymmetry of these imagined becomings makes our apprehension of the stakes involved rather hazy. The strength of the hold we can, or imagine we can, have on them is unsure.

Transhumanism, as expressed by writers and wide audience advocates such as Vinge, Bostrom, or Kurzweil (the narrators of singularity), "promotes an interdisciplinary approach to understanding and evaluating the opportunities for enhancing the human condition and the human organism opened up by the advancement of technology", in the domains detailed above. In Nick Bostrom's words[49] [BOS 14, SAV 09], "The enhancement options being discussed include radical extension of human health-span, eradication of disease, elimination of unnecessary suffering and augmentation of human intellectual, physical, and emotional capacities. Other transhumanist themes include space colonization and the possibility of creating superintelligent machines, along with other potential developments that could profoundly alter the human condition. The ambit is not limited to gadgets and medicine, but encompasses also economic, social, institutional designs, cultural development, and psychic skills and techniques".

Very clearly, "Transhumanists view human nature as a work-in-progress, a half-baked beginning that we can learn to remold in desirable ways. Current humanity need not be the endpoint of evolution. Transhumanists hope that by responsible use of science, technology, and other rational means we shall eventually manage to become posthuman, beings with vastly greater capacities than present human beings have".

Transhumanism wishes "to refine our emotional experiences and increase our subjective sense of well-being, and generally to achieve a greater degree of control over our own lives. This affirmation of human

---

49 Nick Bostrom's home page: http://www.nickbostrom.com/, its transhumanist values: http://www.nickbostrom.com/ethics/values.html.

potential is offered as an alternative to customary injunctions against playing God, messing with nature, tampering with our human essence, or displaying punishable hubris".

The Space of Possible Modes of Being

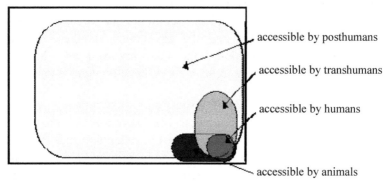

**Figure 1.** *We ain't seen nothin' yet* (not drawn to scale). The term "transhuman" denotes transitional beings, or moderately enhanced humans, whose capacities would be somewhere between those of unaugmented humans and full-blown posthumans (a transhumaniast, by contrast, is simply somebody who accepts transhumansism).

TABLE OF TRANSHMANIST VALUES

*Core Value*
- Having the opportunity to explore the transhuman and posthuman realms

*Basic Conditions*
- Global security
- Technological progress
- Wide access

*Derivative Values*
- Nothing wrong about "tampering with nature": the idea of *hubris* rejected
- Individual choice in use of enhancement technologies; morphological freedom
- Peace, international cooperation, anti-proliferation of WMDs
- Improving understanding (encouraging research and public debate; critical thinking; open-mindedness, scientific inquiry; open discussion of the future)
- Getting smarter (individually; collectively; and develop machine intelligence)
- Philosophical fallibilism; willingness to reexamine assumptions as we go along
- Pragmatism; engineering- and entrepreneur-spirit; science
- Diversity (species, races, religious creeds, sexual orientations, life styles, etc.)
- Caring about the well-being of all sentience
- Saving lives (life-extension, anti-aging research, and cryonics)

**Figure 2.** Table of transhumanist values.

**Figure 2.5.** *Transhumanist values: Nick Bostrom*
*http://www.fhi.ox.ac.uk/transhumanist-values.pdf*

For the transhumanist movement, "our human brains may cap our ability to discover philosophical and scientific truths. It is possible that failure of philosophical research to arrive at solid, generally accepted answers to many of the traditional big philosophical questions could be due to the fact that we are not smart enough to be successful in this kind of enquiry. Our cognitive limitations may be confining us in a Platonic cave, where the best we can do is theorize about 'shadows', that is, representations that are sufficiently oversimplified and dumbed-down to fit inside a human brain".

This finite aspect of our mentation could be only transitory. If we listen to the transhumanists and posthumanists, we can be convinced that the current human sensorial modalities are not "the only possible ones". In any case, "they are certainly not as highly developed as they could be"[50].

The core of transhumanism thus consists of investigating the posthuman domain; at least, it consists of spotting all that seems to make new conditions of possibility emerge for knowledge, from the most speculative indetermination zones of thought and research as well as from the most novel breakthroughs of the convergence of NBIC.

> "The conjecture that there are greater values than we can currently fathom does not imply that values are not defined in terms of our current dispositions. Take, for example, a dispositional theory of value such as the one described by David Lewis. According to Lewis's theory, something is a value for you if and only if you would want to want it if you were perfectly acquainted with it and you were thinking and deliberating as clearly as possible about it. On this view, there may be values that we do not currently want, and that we do

---

50 "Some animals have sonar, magnetic orientation, or sensors for electricity and vibration; many have a much keener sense of smell, sharper eyesight, etc. The range of possible sensory modalities is not limited to those we find in the animal kingdom. There is no fundamental block to adding say a capacity to see infrared radiation or to perceive radio signals and perhaps to add some kind of telepathic sense by augmenting our brains with suitably interfaced radio transmitters". Movies such as Lucy or the Xmen, as well as many TV series exploit this desire for another, self-constituted humanity or even for a hybrid humanity that would have pushed back the limits of the current one. These various ways of approaching this quest is key to their success.

not even currently want to want, because we may not be perfectly acquainted with them (…)"[51].

In our case, still in Bostrom's words, "Some values pertaining to certain forms of posthuman existence may well be of this sort; they may be values for us now, and they may be so in virtue of our current dispositions, and yet we may not be able to fully appreciate them with our current limited deliberative capacities …".

This is one aspect of the transhumanist stance. This is at least how it phrases its desire for a radical change and its will for another way of thinking the bio-technico-political becoming (as well as anything that could fetter its free use of abilities that are assumed to be always already forthcoming). This rupturing stance is less radical than it seems. It does not go much beyond spectacular media buzz events that almost draw from science fiction as an "enchanted" and reduplicative genre, in a practice that walks in the footsteps of our "archaea", keeping a tight hold on that which comes out of the latter. In fact, which other horizon than immortality could we conceive? What else than immortality of the body, once we have that of the soul? That would be truly stunning.

In a so-to-say "grayer" attitude, transhumanism tends to quickly confine the spectrum of possibilities sketched by its creativity. It even sometimes anticipatively condemns anything that would not fit in the framework of the intensification of technico-scientific mastership and control of the new world to come. It, for example carefully avoids focusing on inventing new

---

51 According to David Lewis' modal realism, possible worlds are as real and as concrete as ours: some have, like ours, cows, pigs, water, etc. But in some of these worlds, cows fly, Pegasuses exist, while in others there is a Leviathan, and in one other, Kennedy was never murdered. In Putnam's Twin Earth experiment, there is a world, ours, in which the chemical formula of water is $H_2O$ and another one in which the formula is XYZ, all else being equal. According to Lewis, our world is the actual world, but is only one among many others: it does not have any ontological pre-eminence over others. In other words the term *actual* in *actual world* is indexical, that is any subject can declare their world to be the actual one, much as they label the place they are "here" and the time they are "now". It does not refer to a specific ontological status. Possible worlds are causally isolated from each other: what happens in one does not influence what happens in another. Furthermore, each possible world is inclusive of the whole of its space-time: the other possible words are not remote spatially of chronologically, they simply are elsewhere, unreachable. https://en.wikipedia.org/wiki/Modal_realism, https://en.wikipedia.org/wiki/Possible_world.

modes of existence, on new collective organization modes that would not be contained by the constraints of the massively "constructal" approach of what it is. Transhumanism is relatively faint-hearted when issues related to the invention of new processes of subjectification are raised, or when the processes of alteration creation, in other words of becomings, are revived. One could even think that transhumanism thinking is haunted by a tendency to reenact the ancient witch-hunt, the persecuted notion being now the "saraband of chance"! His submission to the concept of prediction and to its structural lead weight, its will to create a constant factory of prediction is even frightening. Their perspective is that of a manic creation of concepts, skins, hybrids, interfaces and software applications that would all feed into the continuous control of the bio-politics to come and may even lead to the curbing of the assemblages of reflexive intelligence, if required for the smooth operation of that particular ecology.

Trans- and posthumanism are always already here, while not being here yet. They could be compared to the communism of the past, which was always both present and about to come, but they come with an added self-legitimation: the self-legitimation inherent to performative societies who are self-founding, haunted by their own predictions (as transcendent blind spots). So, on that account, this school of thought seems to be giving up on any Deleuzian "machinic innovation".

Trans- and posthumanism however express their thinking in multiple forms. They revolve about science and, although for the most part autonomously from it, draw on the most advanced results of physics, biology and brain science. They mostly read the scientific debates in a radiant, enchanted future perspective. There, one finds similarities – as we pointed out above – with the non-dystopic strands of science fiction and *speculative fiction*.

However, beyond the niche carved by this first stance, one finds a more radical affirmation. This affirmation is especially explicit in the "Manifesto of Speculative Posthumanism". According to such posthumanists, transhumanism still overly relies on the inheritance of the enlightenment. The former, for example criticizes the latter for their "bio-conservative" critiques: "Likewise, 'bioconservative' critics of transhumanism employ traditional frameworks such as Christian theology and Aristotelianism to argue that such developments may violate the biological integrity of species or undermine constitutive conditions for the good furnished by an unbiddable nature"[52].

According to Roden in the Manifesto of Speculative Posthumanism, for example *"speculative posthumanism"* does not deny the importance of these debates but claims that they are too regional in scope to address the potential for *ontological novelty fostered* by NBIC technologies. If it is possible for our technological activity to ultimately engender radically non-human forms of life, we must confront the possibility that our 'wide' technological descendants will be so alien as to fall outside the public ethical frameworks employed by the majority of transhumanists and bioconservatives".

Somehow the posthumanist strands, the doxa of which continuously widens their scope, resonate with the Deleuzian question: Which new forces within man are unleashed by forces from the outside? Nowadays, the new forces from the outside are, for example: the networked writings and hypertext memories, the new textures of the world woven between beings, humans and non-humans, the new interfaces and their sensualism, the genetic sculptures and the rise of epigenetics, the increasingly powerful and subtle couplings of brains and algorithms ….

When, in 1986, Deleuze publishes Foucault (translated in 1988), he writes: "The forces within man enter into a relation with forces from the outside, those of silicon which supersedes carbon, or genetic components which supersede the organism, or agrammaticalities which supersede the signifier. In each case we must study the operations of the superfold, of which the 'double helix' is the best-known example. What is the superman? It is the formal compound of the forces within man and these new forces. It is the form that results from a new relation between forces. Man tends to free life, labor and language *within himself.* The superman, in accordance with Rimbaud's formula, is the man who is even in charge of the animals (a code that can capture fragments from other codes, as in the new schemata of lateral or retrograde). It is man in charge of the very rocks, or inorganic matter (the domain of silicon). It is man in charge of the

---

52 David Roden, Humanism, Transhumanism and Posthumanism, Open University, 2013.

being of language (that formless, mute unsignifying region where language can find its freedom even from whatever it has to say. As Foucault would say, the superman is much less than the disappearance of living men, and much more than a change of concept: it is the advent of a new form that is neither god nor man and which, it is hoped, will not prove worse than its two previous forms".[53] And, in the footnotes, he points out that "Rimbaud's letter not only involves language or literature, but the two other aspects: the future man is in charge not only of the new languages, but also of animals and whatever is unformed".

*In the Manifesto of Speculative Posthumanism, David Roden writes that "Among the intellectuals to have appreciated the ontological stakes are those poststructuralists and 'critical posthumanists' who claim that the trajectory of current technoscientific change 'deconstructs' the philosophical centrality of the human subject in epistemology and politics – by, for example, leveling differences between human subjects, non-human animals, or cybernetic systems. However, while critical posthumanism has yielded important insights it is hamstrung by a default anti-realism inherited from the dominant traditions in post-Kantian continental philosophy. The deconstruction of subjectivity is an ambivalent philosophical achievement at best; one that cedes ground to potent forms of humanism while failing to address the cosmic likelihood of a posthuman dispensation".*

*Speculative posthumanism therefore rejects the post-Kantian epistemology that sets the "posthuman" as a convenient figure to highlight the intrinsic limits of thought. Its project is "speculative" in so far as it investigates the ways one could conceive the posthuman independently from its relation of human forms or cognition and from their phenomenology. It argues, on the opposite, that the posthuman, although it is not effective, actual yet, must be understood as a real state resulting from the "technological transformation of man" or its descendants.*

*Speculative posthumanism assumes that such a dispensation is metaphysically and technically possible. But this does not mean that the posthuman would result in a bettering of the human state. It does not even posits a scale of values for the comparison of these two states. In fact, if posthuman life was to become radically non-human, then there is no reason to*

53 Deleuze, Foucault, The Athlone Press, 1988 (translated by Sean Hand and Paul A. Bové from the French Foucault, Edition de Minuit, 1986).

*assume it could be evaluated with the current, human-specific ethical frameworks. This however does not mean that the posthuman is "impossible" or, like the God of negative theology, that is exceeds our epistemic capacities. It rather signals the difficulty that lies in our continuing to perceive the posthuman as a repetition, or rather as a furthering of our current technical praxis.*

*Mutant Manifesto: http://www.lesmutants.com/mutationenglish.htm*

Our forebears dreamed of a space odyssey in the year 2001, where intelligent computers could see their Australopithecus ancestors in the blink of an eye. Instead of this, they limit us more and more every day to the monotonous control of this planet. The principle of precaution has become infinitely cancerous and corrupts the spirit: more and more comfort, less and less risk, more and more security, less and less courage. We did not create anything, we did not change anything, we keep everything the same. In short, we are suffocating.

There are no ideas, no plans and no horizons. In evolutionary terms this means the following: there is no mutation or variation, thus no more choices or change. The principle is simple; those who reproduce with no change cannot adapt and will disappear in the end. Diversity is life. Uniformity is death. Do you want to end your days as a fossil, with your mouth gaping open watching in astonishment as an asteroid smashes into the blue planet? Well, we do not!

We are different. We are the first mutants.

We enjoy life, constantly changing faster and further. We want to become the beginning of the future. We want to change life, in the real sense of the word, no longer in the figurative sense. We want to create new species, use human clones, choose our genes, shape our minds and bodies, control germs, devour transgenic feasts, donate our extra cells, see in infrared, hear ultrasound, feel pheromones, cultivate our genes, replace our neurones, make love in space, converse with robots, test modified cerebral states, add new senses, last 20 years or two centuries, live on the Moon, settle on Mars, become familiar with the galaxies. Inside us, we have the most civilized and the wildest aspects, the most refined and the most barbaric, the most complex and the most uncomplicated, the most rational and the most passionate. Everything is mixed together on a clear morning and the deadly half-heartedness of time gone by is nothing more than a bad memory.

We are life's secret agents. Life does not know it yet. We, Darwin's angry grandchildren, claim the right of "non-precautionary principle". The reason is that it has led the world since it began. He who ventures nothing gains nothing. Evolution has understood this for 3.5 million years but the human primate for only 15 short decades. It is time to make up for this delay.

Do we have a choice? Some people believe so and they wish they could go back to the good old days that they never knew; so much the better for them! We feel neither hatred nor contempt. We like variety, even that of the human species yet to come. At a crossroads, each of us must choose our direction. Our ancestors did this and we follow in their footsteps. After all is said and done, the last evolutionary leap that separated us from our near relatives, the apes, has not done too badly for one or the other. Now that this story is over, we simply wish to begin another.

In complete freedom.

In total innocence.

Far away the stars that await us since the beginning of the universe are twinkling. It is midnight, Dr. Faustus. We will evolve and nobody can stop us.

These are but a few examples of the figures and narratives of transhumanism and, beyond that, of its posthumanist continuations.

These narratives serve as a Utopian reserve, a source of energy for companies such as Google, which, on several aforementioned accounts, invest huge analytical power in relation with the Flood of Data (especially in domains such as health and neuroscience)[54] [REG 14, HER 14]. In this perspective, the anthropocene leads to the obsolescence of the Human Being, but through an upwards exit. A transfiguration so magnified that it enables an emancipation from the world (posthuman, augmented man, extension of the life span). The tensions and uncertainties that traverse this subject can also be exemplified by confronting two different perspectives.

---

54 Google Brain: http://en.wikipedia.org/wiki/Google_Brain.

This first one will be that of the Breakthrough Institute[55], which develops its tangible Utopia on the basis of BIG Science, fracking, the extension and ever-improvement of nuclear power plants, great hydrological realizations, Genetically Modified Organism (GMOs), molar, monumental geo-engineering that as bases for molecular approaches, etc… The second is that of collective intelligences that rely on "Illitchian" apparatuses and on homeopathic technologies, situating invention and innovation in the milieu of the production of forms and subjectivities, of regimes of desire [SLO 10].

We know that Deleuze and Guattari were very optimistic about the mutant possibilities opened by the computer-assisted modes of thinking and creating. They saw positive potentialities in the computational capacities and in particular in that which relates to the opening of new universes, the actualization of subtle perceptive modes, of new modes of existence and of novel types of affects[56].

On our part, we favor exploring the variations that affect the structural "cortex–flint" coupling overelaborating a "processing language common to brain and computer", because the novel couplings between brains and computers ever unpredictably extend the realm of possibilities of thought. Such emergent couplings partake to the elaboration of new abstract machines.

"Speculative posthumanism", in this perspective, initiates the first moves. This is what the Manifest of Speculative Posthumanism says[57]:

"Over the last decade the possibility of innovations in areas such as artificial intelligence or biotechnology contributing to the emergence of a 'posthuman' life form has become a focal point of public debate and mainstream artistic concern. This multi-disciplinary discourse is premised on developments in the so-called 'NBIC' technologies – Nanotechnology, Biotechnology, Information Technology and Cognitive Science. The

---

55 http://thebreakthrough.org/.
56 Joseph Weissman, acceleration, becoming, control, Deleuze, machine, Nietzsche, subjectivity, technoscience and expressionism, 201 https://fractalontology.wordpress.com/2014/07/16/technoscience-andexpressionism/# more2570.
57 http://hplusmagazine.com/2013/02/06/manifesto-of-speculative-posthumanism.

transhumanist claim that human nature should be improved technologically is likewise predicated on the NBIC suite affording the necessary means for enhancement.

In philosophy, discussion of the posthuman has been dominated by concerns about the ethics of enhancement or by metaphysical issues of embodiment and mind. Transhumanists draw on Enlightenment conceptions of human nature as an improvable 'work in progress' in arguing for the moral benefits of enhancement and its political legitimacy. Likewise, 'bioconservative' critics of transhumanism employ traditional frameworks such as Christian theology and Aristotelianism to argue that such developments may violate the biological integrity of species or undermine constitutive conditions for the good furnished by an unbiddable nature".

Speculative posthumanism does not deny the importance of such debates, but "But states that they only have a regional scope, or a scope too limited with regards to the scope of the potential ontological novelties made possible by NBIC technologies. If our technical activity may eventually generate non-human forms of life, we must face the possibility that our descendants will be so alien to us that they won't fit in the scope of the standard ethical frameworks used by the majority of transhumanists and bio-conservatives"[58]

In our opinion (and in this perspective), we need to emancipate ourselves from the transhumanist horizon that is overcoded by the outdated fancies of science fiction (e.g. the "negative anti-utopia"), which themselves keep walking in the footsteps of the current political economies and positing the question of the continuous creation of value in terms that further the discourse of capitalist markets and their attached relationships of production.

---

58 See Dominique Lecourt, who, in his book "Humains, post-humains", reduces this binary opposition of two variants: catastrophism, on the one hand, and techno-prophetism, on the other, or in other word bio-conservatism, on the one hand, and techno-progressivism, on the other. According to Lecourt, these two opposed strands both stem from the same religious source, which similarly assigns to the technological project a salvation or millenarian mission. Lecourt writes: "The current debate between bio-catastrophists and techno-prophets (…) suddenly appears framed by two major theoretical Christian understandings of the situation of man in the world: an optimistic millenarianism and an apocalyptic one [LEC 11].

They insist on these outdated paradigms, even though other political economies are emerging in the interstices between inherited political anthropology and the new political anthropology, which opens to new, a-centered or polycentered modes of organization. The latter renew the question of the "commons" and of collective intelligences, of their modes of legitimization and differentiation. The narratives of this transhumanist horizon, in any case, unfold within the framework of performative societies, under the aegis of the vertiginous prediction-consensus coupling. So, leaning on the rationale of its extremely powerful self-legitimizing processes, involving a humongous production – consumption of Data, transhumanist becomings generate tangible models that seem to have no other limit than algorithm power and, henceforth, "speculative simulation".

Transhumanism, when it sets its "NBIC" veil on the covering of Earth, beings and cerebralities, dreams, as we explained before, of an intensive carving of the world. The dream displays a long lost primordial immersive apparatus, the apparatus of an infinity of data serving as the plastic material to model anew the mastership of the world.

The dream involves the becoming of the topological conversion of the brain world, within the control of epigenesis as well. This school of thought is expressed through declarations of faith in the radiant future of technology in the attempt to create and control the artificialization of the world. Such an artificialization is complex. Either it leads to the necessary re-definition of human and its associated milieu, to its overcoming in the form of an augmented humanity or of a posthumanity, or it relies on the search for new, radically different modes of existence, on machinic innovation in the Deleuze-Guattari sense, in a perspective more nuanced than that of radiant technical and biotechnological complication. This second understanding acknowledges that this can also lead us where we do not want to go. Yes, humanity might become truly obsolete, but then something worse might succeed it. Or maybe not.

Let us paraphrase Simon Leys regarding the great Maoist mystification: it may be time for us to "see through the digital's new clothes"[59]. All the more that the current conditions and becomings are perceived according to incompatible time scales. The processes of actualization of ecological

---

59 http://fr.wikipedia.org/wiki/Les_Habits_neufs_du_pr%C3%A9sident_Mao.

becomings (the types of ecological crises), in their very asymmetry, blur our understanding of the issues and perspectives involved as well as the hold we can keep on them, or at least that hold we are told we will be able to keep.

Data desires, like human, all too human desires, are at risk of decaying to be reborn as desires for control, mastership and domination, thus desires for new types of enslaving. In M. G. Dantec's words "The posthuman is this paradoxical moment when Capital becomes so concentrated it produces a non-world made of non-humans with no sovereignty other than their own. Capital, concentrated inside these non-humans in the form of fetishist neo-matricial prosthetics, totally de-concentrates them into mere peripheral devices of themselves. It truly appears as a self-reflexive sophism, a pathetic reticular cloning of technology within man, precisely when man endeavors to replicate himself like a laboratory sheep"[60] [DAN 01].

Are single anthropological bifurcations open, uncertain bifurcations, toward "other" modes of existence? The world is putting new clothes on, yes, but beyond the rising agonistic narratives, there is the interrogation of how to interweave the two sides of an alternative, instead of haplessly oscillating between its terms. On the one hand, we have the rise of differentiated artificialization, "Big Science and Big Technology" as a molar science and technology, while, on the other hand, we have the "Small Science-Technology" project of molecular science, a technology or science concerning instabilities and processes. In the middle of these oscillations dwells the desire to maintain the coexistence of boundaries that produce very differentiated articulations and translations in a complex cosmopolitan universe (which encompasses the non-human). This coexistence is required to open to a metastable world that would be able to regulate and even block the extreme rises of violence and death urges. So, such a desire has many hurdles to overcome. Let us repeat it once more, the gaping great interval opened by the desire (and its NBIC incarnation) to auto-fabricate the human and its environment … keeps widening but within it the great nuptials of chance and becomings are constantly fettered by the most archaic political motives … transhumanism!

---

60 Maurice G. Dantec, Laboratoire de catastrophe générale, Le théâtre des opérations, Editions, Gallimard, 2001.

But "the metahuman is elaborated elsewhere, secretly, in a conspiracy much better hidden because it is much more operative. It is being elaborated in the narrative process which annexes the future not as the 'likely' but as the most singular, the most ravaging, the most 'incompossible' with others" [DAN 01]. And again: "The posthuman cyborg can't, alas, be understood as the realization of 'the promise' of anthropogenesis achieved with an at last operative technology. No, it rather is the tragic flip-side of the coin of the emergence of the future. 'Tragi-comical' would actually be a more appropriate qualification, because we will often see the old worn out figures of humanism repeat their refrains in the rags of their pseudo-experimental, pseudo-critical framework …".

The "trans and post humanist" horizon is therefore partly (and only partly) the symptom of the desires and uncertainties of the "machinic" and democratic innovations. The data are inseparable from the hesitations of the new abstract machine while the politics of relentless, continuous control keep, in our opinion, missing the question of 'machinic innovation'.

Ironically, one can note that this(these) movement(s) close(s) up the creativity of modes of existence and anticipatively condemn(s) anything that would not fit in the paradigm of the intensification of control over the new world that comes, on the basis of already existing political models, precisely in the same move as it(they) express(es) its(their) longing for a rupture and demand(s) another way of thinking the bio-technico-political becomings, rejecting any fetter to the free use of faculties. It (they) already worry(ies) about the powers of alterity and becomings, of the radical contingency of things and of the movements of alteration–creation. They look for "Mastership" in the compulsive accumulation of data and its insomniac exploratory processing. A new world that is always already here, but has not yet arrived, both a tangible and speculative model. A promise that is still inset in the grounds and peat bogs of ancient imaginations. A tangible Utopia that worries about the saturation of economical models, and falls to their vertigo. Like communism formerly, they enforce an always present Utopia that forever remains to come and, as such, is insurmountable. But they come with an added self-legitimation, the self-legitimation inherent to performative societies who are self-founding but haunted by their own predictions.

Transhumanism fabricates a singularity horizon, an explosion of intelligence, but misses the political question of the co-intelligence and of desires. Let us listen once again to Peter Sloterdijk: "To develop technologies will mean in the future: to read the scores of embodied intelligences and to pave the way for further performances of their own pieces" [SLO 00].

> "The most extreme states of homeotechnology are the hours of truth for co-intelligence. In them, it is revealed that the subject of the bivalent age, the former master, has become a phantom". And if "biotechnologies and nootechnologies nurture by their very nature a subject that is refined, cooperative, and prone to playing with itself[, if] this subject shapes itself through intercourse with complex texts and hypercomplex texts [...] In the inter-intelligently condensed net-world, masters and rapists have hardly any long term chances of success left, while cooperators, promoters and enrichers fit into more numerous and more adequate slots".

But "what stands against such a brightened view of things is the mentioned predicament that the inheritance of bivalence and of the strategic polemological paranoia casts its shadow far on to that which is to come". "When capital and empire grab for information, the course of the world turns increasingly into a kind of divine judgment that antagonistic intelligences pass upon themselves" [SLO 00].

Which intelligences will prevail? Which regimes of desires will they bring along? Which new polemologies will they arouse?

# Fragmented Encyclopedism

## 3.1. Collective intelligences and the encyclopedic problem

In the face of that vast reticular transformation of collective intelligences, the extension of cerebralities and intellectual writing and technology, and the considerable transformation of the ways we produce and spread knowledge, the question of navigating and using it is crucial. On the horizons that we are chasing, this question is even more significant because the questions are huge regarding the future place of the heterogeneses of thought and research, the controversies under the conditions of a "constructal" and "transhumanist" approach, "optimal" for ecological futures, an approach itself under the norms and constraints of an expanding neoliberal economy. It is worth giving some points of reference here and lending evidence to one of the visionary figures of 20th Century encyclopedism, namely Paul Otlet.

It is not by chance that Paul Otlet has come out of the attic[1] [OTL 34] where he was confined during the upsurge of the Internet. Still trembling all

---

1 In the 1980s and 1990s, Otlet was practically no longer taught in France, just mentioned in passing, and with the exception of a few researchers (e.g. Sylvie Fayet Scribe, Arlette Boulogne, Isabelle Rieusset-Lemarié), his thought was inert. See P. Otlet's Mundaneum and the international perspective in the history of documentation and information science Isabelle Rieusset-Lemarié, Article first published online: 7 Dec 1998 Issue Journal of the American Society for Information Science, vol. 48, no. 4, pp. 301–309, April 1997, Paul Otlet's book and the writing of social space Ron Day, Article first published online: 7 Dec 1998 Issue Journal of the American Society for Information Science, vol. 48, no. 4, pp. 310–317, April 1997. Also see Emanuel Goldberg, electronic document retrieval, and Vannevar Bush's Memex. Michael K. Buckland, Article first published online: 4 Jan 1999 Issue Journal of the

over from the major disruption brought about by this new anthropological stratum, the information world found in Paul Otlet a gratifying figure, a humanistic vision associated with an inherited progressive utopia. He also found some important concepts for himself (among them, the hyperdocument concept), allowing it to regain its footing and not succumb to the digital and hypertextual breaking wave conceived and incarnated by communities of thought and research, forged directly at the center of ever-more complex, heterogeneous and dynamic knowledge-generating devices.

These communities thought about information problems not through and under the constraints of scholastics by the same name (and when this was the case, this was conservative, in their most creative – sometimes very old – margins), but through a liberty and an informational experimentation immanent to new intellectual ecologies[2]. The emerging classificatory school of thought was shaking up the hegemony of essentialist documentation to make way for new information practices that would quickly be considered procedural and seriously considering the encyclopedist project expressed by Leibniz for a perspective encyclopedism. These communities thought (and very quickly equipped themselves with the necessary tools) of the information question not as an access problem, but as a knowledge-generating and navigation problem. The orientation, association, analogous processes, abductive processes, mapping practices, extension of the document spectrum, etc. showed up on the scene once again.

## 3.2. The political utopia in store

Let us go further: in Paul Otlet and through his political engagement, the information world was given, at the center of its deepest distress, in the wrinkle of its fear of dispossession, brand new habits supporting a revived humanist vision, a political project for access to knowledge, reaffirming

American Society for Information Science, vol. 43, no. 4, pp. 284–294, May 1992, H.G. Wells's idea of a World Brain: A critical reassessment W. Boyd Rayward Article first published online: 22 Apr 1999 Issue Journal of the American Society for Information Science, vol. 50, no. 7, pp. 557–573, 1999.
2 On these well-known points, see [BUS 45].

the encyclopedia project on the glowing horizon of the new anthropo-technological stratum. The Net "was from Paul Otlet plus the Digital"!

The 1930s, with the release of the "Book of books", the invention of Bush and Goldberg's Memex and the rising international tension, the transformation of power relations, had seen the projects of large, ambitious Information Politics mix with the spread of forces and drives bringing strategies and ends contrary to the desires of the League of Nations' founders, who tended to underestimate, or at least not "see", the effects of the diabolical dance of sleepless and besieged reason. Universalistic goals of those who believed in the pacifistic virtues of education, the benevolent desires of technoscience, the convergence of passions for a shared democratic desire. The Internet had one goal. It had already been thought of by Otlet, before Nelson, and before Berners Lee. Utopia could become concrete.

The essential points[3] [RAY 94, RAY 06, BUC 09] have been made about Paul Otlet and the greatness of his work, and we think that the problems we faced, the creativity movement in which we are trapped, could have, beyond a shred of doubt, partly stimulated it, provoked it.

The Internet stratum dragging up the issue, taking fresh pains, of what storing and classing, writing and reading, repeating and copying, mapping and indexing, memorizing and associating, etc. mean, the extremely fast development of digital network memories, hypertextual writings and the

---

3 From Paul Otlet to Internet passing through HYPERTEXT (http://www.uhb.fr/urfist/SerreDEF.htm ). "A Story" and some convolutions of networks are suggested here. Some markers and fragments (work in progress) (under the direction of Alexandre Serres and Jean-Max Noyer, URFIST Rennes, Brittany). This work has been largely expanded by Alexandre Serres. "History of tools and information networks". See also Pierre Mounier's comment. http://cyberspace.homo-numericus.net/2010/09/01/histoire-des-outils-et-reseaux-information-par-alexandre-serres/ as well as Serres' thesis – At Internet sources: the emergence of ARPANET. Exploration of the emergence process of an informational infrastructure. Descriptions of the trajectories of actors and agents, channels and networks are the constituent of the birth of ARPANET. Critical and epistemological problems posed by the history of innovations.

emergence of a new "Images, Texts, Sounds" alliance have indeed deeply shaken intelligence communities. The same is true for the famous "hyperdocument" notion that is going to suffer radical treatment and leave the "essentialized" world to become an information "event" (at extremely different times), a complex environment where the distinctions, the orders between texts, images, sounds and computer programs, algorithms, etc. come to be erased, ultimately, an environment of data, of linked data and metadata, signals, etc.

Digital encyclopedism is thus as a vast domain open to internal relations, a domain where the very notion of digital information objects seen from the substance point of view can no longer operate, and where trajectories and morphogeneses of relations, transformations and deformations of relations are at the root of all semiotics, between meta-stability and fluidity, between emergence and erasure, and between attraction and evanescence. From knots and ties, more and more powerful and supple beacon languages to ontologies ("all the way down") fabricated from specific relations and their procession of translations and boundaries, interstices and cracks for mapping practices opening both the creation of new connections and infinitely variable time gaps, making analogical freedoms explode.

But this assessment is not enough, as the digital information object, the digital object enters presently and very quickly in more and more powerful mixtures with objects made up of other materials and textures. (Technical, animal, etc. objects, crossed with sensors that enter into new relationships, including those with humans.) Thus, more complex encyclopedism, made up of all the relationships, the current weaving and all those to come, caught by the vortex of those expanding digital skins covering the world. Encyclopedism is thus "full of holes" from all shapes and substances of expression.

The digital squinting of the world and new intellectual techniques strongly affect the ecologies of the mind, the conditions of thought, in resonance with growing semiotic pluralism. And the problem of access to knowledge distributed at the planet's surface is no longer the central problem (next to geopolitical, socioeconomic and legal conditions).

These ecologies compounding and continuing to compound in a radical way, the question of writings and memory (memories), of the "hands of intellect"[4] under the conditions of digital content, its plasticity combinatories and particularly rich semiotic environments.

In his famous text from 1945, Vennevar Bush[5] noted that "knowledge" had undergone at least two major transformations, which manifested themselves as an exponential growth in the number of documents and their heterogeneity, on the one hand, and by the complication of the conceptual and material devices, the more or less heterogeneous communities producing them, on the other hand.

The ways in which encyclopedisms connected to political economies of inherited knowledge and to non-digital external writings and memories think up and create the necessary conditions for the exercise of intellectual activities are thus no longer satisfactory in the face of that which we have just quickly described, in the face of those (local encyclopedisms) that have been spreading for approximately 30 years.

Collective assemblage of enunciation producing knowledge, particularly scientific and technical knowledge, with the "hands of intellect" that accompany and cross-cut them, have taken on very diverse shapes in this digital context, and sciences confronted with new, immense, digital empirical data are cross-cut; we have already stated this through the irresistible growth of algorithms [CAR 14a].

The differentiation of knowledge production and circulation methods (PC), the shifting of disciplinary borders, and the often increasingly hybrid character of research fields has led to the emergence of a certain number of questions and problems concerning the sociocognitive devices at work. The question of encyclopedism is thus not "that of an impossible totalization". It is that of orientation in the ways of linking, associating, interpreting knowledge, it is that of setting this knowledge, its grammars, syntaxes and semantics in motion in an $n$-dimensional, not exclusively linguistic

---

4 Christian Jacob, Lieux de Savoir 2. Les Mains de L'Intellect. Albin Michel, Paris 2011..
5 Vannevar Bush, "As we may think" *The Atlantic Monthly*, 1945, http://www.theatlantic. com/magazine/archive/1945/07/as-we-may-think/303881/.

information space-time, woven by relations and trajectories in a potentially infinite number.

Among other things, it is a matter of understanding how research communities, a collection of devices allowing the comprehension and exploration of the information space of its heterogeneous and open corpora to be accessed, can be put in place through the activity and products of a certain number of laboratories. (This collection of devices, found on intellectual technology, and algorithms then aims to develop means of co-operative work functioning independently of a central instance.) The transformation in progress is thus characterized by a consideration of the procedural and collective dimensions of intellectual work. The stakes tied to hypertextual memory in networks and the systems of writing and reading that are associated with them, as well as new techniques, are considerable, particularly the exploitation of the sometimes uncertain productivity of "border zones".

Fragmented encyclopedism expects considerable attention to be paid to intellectual technology/cognitive device interactions, the constituent morphogeneses of disciplines, communities, fields (these expressions are not the same), the shifting of boundaries and the heterogeneses in progress at the center of knowledge. Finally, we examine their epistemological and institutional effects, and their cognitive implications.

## 3.3. Encyclopedism and digital publishing modes

It is in this framework that the question of new digital publishing methods is significant. By allowing greater visibility in the products of research and a better consideration of texts at stages more differentiated than their *production-circulation-validation-legitimization* mode, these publishing modes indeed open the path to better access to networks, devices, collective statement arrangements, constituents of disciplines, communities, fields. The hypercortex is in fact a dense and noisy aggregate, made up of more or less dense zones, shaken as much (even more) by chaos as by logical and mathematical inferences, made up of heterogeneous combinatories and more or less unstable, analogical tribes.

This associationist hyperbricolage, which brings a sort of endless finality, calls on new equipment for uncertain, though locally oriented explorations, but without transparency of itself for itself. In short, "*cogitatio caeca*".

Yet, at present, the progress accomplished in the last 30 years in the domain of automatic digital trace processing, in the sectors of indexing, filtering, linguistics, information engineering and ergonomics is sufficiently advanced for the associative, analogous etc. abilities of complex man–machine systems called in during the intellectual work process now to be affected in a very visible way in a large number of sectors.

By forcing ourselves to bring and spread, further than in the past, the notion of a "heterogeneous and dynamic collective" along levels of agent chains, the expression and, expressed in various sociocognitive activities, the digitization process makes the establishment of tools allowing the orientation of texts, hypertexts, textures and heterogeneous research hypertextures in complex space-times more necessary than ever, as we have previously indicated.

Therefore, bringing the question to the level of the make-up of corpora themselves, learning to use them and exploit them to access new visibilities concerning agent networks and their dynamics, the constraints and combinatories at work during the emergence, stabilization convergence, or even the disaggregation transformation of this or that field, this or that problematic, this or that discipline, constitutes one of the major stakes. Following the "percolation" of concepts such as multiplicity, shifts in assemblages and the deformations of the former in their shifts themselves are central tasks.

"New visibilities" mean being able to represent the associations, association networks, aggregation and selection modes, social modes of transmission selection of constraints that are at work in the heterogeneous search arrangements, laboratories, texts, journals, themes, concepts. "New visibilities" still mean being able to update the search fronts, the networks of influence and the systems of translation, overlapping of notions, concepts, subjects, etc.

Networks of actors, citation networks[6], co-citation networks, etc.; modes of repetition-alteration for texts and the associated contexts; conceptual graphs must be all represented in order to offer new forms of orientation and thus to lead a better management navigation of perspectives, to increase the associationist abilities that make up our structural visibility conditions and any case still singular and marked. Herein lies the meaning of what are called new mapping practices.

The make-up of these digital memories, using various documents produced by actors in each discipline, community or field of research must, therefore, also be used to bring to light these collective statement arrangements to move quickly, for example from laboratory networks to the overview of concept components. The aim is to give, through these new cartographies, writing–reading tools, encouraging the emergence of hermeneutic abilities adapted to the growing heterogeneity of the textures and semiotics of research activities, etc., giving access to a sort of conceptual ethology is vital.

Thus, the task is to go back to Whitehead's expression of thinking, inhabiting the community with works such as "incompleteness in the production process" and to progressively put in place adapted intellectual techniques. Herein lies one of the fundamental dimensions of what are called "digital humanities".

## 3.4. A new documentary process

The publishing question is, fundamentally, also and still, the question of reading, of what is given to be read, of the critical work of reading. In what way can new publishing models, like that of overlay journals[7], creatively affect this reading task?

---

6 The questions raised as a result of this quote are complex. I of course refer to [DER 90]. See also [COM 79, VAN 01, CAS 00b, WOU 99, CRO 98, LEY 98, SMA 73, SMA 95, STA 89] It would also be necessary to study how the followers of memetic theories tackle the question as a particular case of replicative theories. In that same vein, this research should dig deeper through works on the notion of borders.

7 A type of open access academic journal that does not produce its own content, but selects from texts that are already freely available online (source: Wikipedia).

In this task of reading, a search that is carried out offered to an intake or to an appropriation that immediately segues into a new production, which in turn, and immediately, is a way to make the former circulate – from writing to writing, from book to book, from article to article, from work to article...all by immediately joining the production of production, that is to say, this primary production in which the objective transformation of a space of knowledge is immediately a subjective transformation of its immediate producers; in other words, where self-transformation goes into and through the formation of new knowledge, new perceptions, and through these, new possibilities (...) new powers of being affected and acting [SIB 09].

In what way can the experience of the reading task in the writing and rewriting process environment be affected? How can the worlds of digital exhibition that overlay journals try to explore pertain, if only in part, to a vaster textual machine that "would suspend reading in a system; neither finite nor infinite, labyrinth abyss" [BEN 91], though still singular? How will this task of reading "through an initial linearity or platitude, (as) an act of tearing apart, crumpling, twisting, restitching the text to open a living environment where the meaning can unfold" be encouraged by these publishing devices through which these processes are written? If "the space of meaning does not pre-exist reading (and if) it is by scouring it, by mapping it that we make it, that we update it" [LEV 98], the more we allow, locally and according to constraints blocking the risk of too great a complexity[8], the bringing to light of the writing process of the search, of thought, the more we will offer, thus, the chance to make high levels of perception fuse with more numerous abstract processes, the more the labyrinths of writings will be open as active territories of creativity. It would then become possible to experience scientific and critical textuality more intensely as an event[9].

From this perspective, it would be necessary to consider joining software to this device capable of generating associations toward, if only fragments of

---

8 When hyperconnectivity, precision, on the one hand, and meaning, on the other hand, become mutually exclusive, when this becomes counterproductive in cognitive terms.
9 See, for example, [TES 09] and more essentially on these matters [WOL 08] ABD [ZUN 12].

conceptual ethology[10] whose texts are both the expression and the expressed, to express cartographies according to varying scales, software capable of offering combinatories between the theoretical and practical assemblages using this writing–reading task in motion. Encyclopedism is available for law and, in fact, for perspectives and processes.

Placing variation at the center of the publishing process and not leaving it in the margins is strategic, but we note that there is much left to be done in the invention of software, invention dedicated to facing populations that are ever more differentiated from textualities in progress. And yet this machine, as Bennington [BEN 91] notes, is already in place, "it is the 'already' itself. There, we are at the written advance, promise of hazardous memory, in the monstrous future…". But we think the challenges that must be faced today, critical thought, even research activities, in the context of this information spread, in the framework of a complex alliance between texts/images/ sounds, and between forms of information and constraints of extremely differentiated scientific writings, are campaigning for experiments aggravating the question of writings through current or possible digital publishing arrangements, and this too at varying and open levels.

These transformations in the scientific publishing sphere have, in fact, been fiercely at work since the start of the 1990s and they are far from being stabilized. The passage from a "bleached under the paper" publishing mode with creation devices (their sociology), of financing, legitimization (criteriology of scientific selection) and distribution, toward a complex hypertextual digital publishing mode has been accelerating for about a decade.

The first phase of this passage is currently well on its way and the saturation of inherited paper forms, always present at the center of the first digital achievements, is in action. A second phase is unfolding. It consists of putting the question of digital publishing *"in the middle"* or, to put it another way, under the constraints of a critical reflection concerning the conditions of production/circulation/consumption of scientific knowledge, all while developing the experimentation of publishing devices that make the expression of the research task, its processes, uncertainties and hesitations possible.

---

10 We mean by conceptual ethology, the field, the diagrams from which concepts emerge like singularities woven from other concepts, perceptions, effects, more or less heterogeneous writing, of a combination of diverse constraints.

In an interview with Didier Eribon [ERI 85], Michel Foucault stated, "do you know what I dream of? It would be to create a research publishing company. I am desperately in search of these possibilities to bring about the work in its movement, in its problematic form. A place where research could be presented in its hypothetical and provisional character". It is in this sense that we maintain efforts in order to pursue and widen the path opened by Paul Ginsparg[11] and the global movement of open archives by presenting a publishing device attempting to respond in part to the desire expressed above.

In short, faced with an ever stronger exhibition of procedural dimensions and communities of scientific textualities through the memory setting of a growing number of traces produced by researchers, scientific publishing must rethink the way in which it has founded its efficiency and its legitimacy on a relatively simple selection of finite publishing objects such as hypostases of scientific knowledge, relative deletion (of the process of scientific production itself) and the expression of the egalitarian fantasy of the redistribution of knowledge.

Let us go further: owing to the plasticity that digital hypertextual associationism brings today, it seems easier to conceive means of exposing research, publishing modes, writing modes working much more richly than in the past toward their production conditions. More than ever, new publishing modes should have the supplementary goal to ensure that a work can say and show how it is made. Today, while, from a certain point of view, reason is besieged, to return to the title of a work by Al Gore, *The Assault on Reason* [GOR 07], it seems particularly important to us to test out what, from within scientific writings, writings on critical thought, allows the recording of part of the conditions having presided upon elaborating texts and documents.

How can writings and emerging textualities ensure that "the theoretical content (can) ideally present in itself the trace of its mode of production (and be able to) record in itself, we will say, pushing things to the limit, its complex relationship with the whole process of restricted economy of knowledge" [SIB 09].

---

11 http://en.wikipedia.org/wiki/Paul_Ginsparg.

The ongoing transformations in publishing can thus be thought up and tested out, keeping in mind the trinity production-circulation-consumption of knowledge[12] and as we have already expressed before, *hyperdocuments as relational facilities including n-perspectives on the mentioned facilities or "condensed" ecologies.*

Scientific publishing today should allow itself to inhabit communities of works, arrangements that produce and circulate documents, like incompletion in process of production[13]. In fact, it must take into account the complex dimensions of the processes of scientific writings and encourage the task of research, particularly by describing in detail the conceptual ethologies at the center of practices. It is still a matter of allowing the establishment of pertinent paths, of connections, between the information heterogeneses and fragments, and the most unstable short forms to stabilized and canonized texts going through "working papers", any corpus of data...that are called forth in the course of the research task.

Scientific publishing therefore must consider general transformations of scientific knowledge production and assume its needs for increased reflexivity. Today, it seems to us that these modes of knowledge production and circulation make a quadruple question rise toward it. The questions concerning the tension between stable and meta-stable, even instable, knowledge when the latter emerges far from balance in zones of indetermination or lacking consensus are the following: the question concerning the variation of differential relationships between the systems of evaluation of scientific knowledge; the question concerning the management of perspectives and cognitive practices; finally, the question concerning the

---

12 (1) Moment of production, that is to say, the production of the producer subjects (theoretical producer forces) and means of production: on the one hand, the theoretical prime matter, which poses the problem, for example, of statutory and material conditions of access to sources, books, debates, necessary information, etc., and on the other hand, the theoretical instruments, which poses the problem of access to methodologies and their use; (2) moment of circulation, that is to say, the concrete production of modes of knowledge circulation and knowledge producers, thus also explicit or tacit criteriologies that determine the conditions of that circulation that can be published? And in what conditions? And by whom? And under what conditions will this be read?, etc.; (3) moment of consumption, that is to say, the production of means of consumption and of knowledge consumers, as well as their mode of consumption, for example their specific and socially conditioned reading habits ....
13 We borrow this expression from A.N. Whitehead [WHI 79].

management representation of processes and morphogeneses that express the conceptual dynamics and ethologies forming the related environment, moving more or less from this knowledge, in short, the immense and endless work of comments, critical reduction and expansion and dissemination of knowledge. The last question lends even more importance to the problem of borders, their variability and their "shapes". Rather fluctuating zones, principles of translation, cross-roads of problem and concept trajectories, rather zones of differentiation and/or integration than boundary line. And this against a backdrop of the great "hinge"[14] (scientific, economic, political and bureaucratic all at the same time) between the arrangements of the elite and their legitimization procedures, self-legitimization through power (Saint Matthew Effect) and the arrangements of research people (Ortega y Gasset Hypothesis)[15]. Yet, this hinge is relatively complex. The new publishing methods, by making the precise analysis of these arrangements possible (due to the wealth and heterogeneity of traces and analysis of software processing large information corpora with the view to follow the trajectories of concepts, citations, co-citations…), allow the nuancing and better understanding of what Bailon Moreno defined as "The pulsing structure of science"[16] [BAI 07]. Particularly when we are far from equilibrium of Kuhn paradigms.

---

14 *Brisure*: Bennington also refers to Derrida and the idea of the hinge (*la brisure*) as developped in 'De la Grammatologie'.

15 By a new fractal/transfractal geometry of the unified scientometric model, it is possible to demonstrate that science presents an oscillating or pulsing dynamic. Science presents an oscillating or pulsing dynamic. It goes alternatively through two types of phases. Some phases are fractal, with crystalline networks, where the Matthew effect clearly manifests itself with regard to the most notable actors and those that provide the best contributions. The other phases are transfractal, with deformed, amorphous networks, in which the actors, considered mediocre, present greater capacity to restructure the network than the more renowned actors. The result after any transfractal deformation is a new crystalline fractal network. Behind this vision lies the Kuhn paradigms.

16 The pulsing structure of science: "This paper shows that finally the two opposing traditional proposals that have been used to explain the behaviour of scientists – the Saint Matthew Effect and Ortega's Hypothesis – may constitute successive phases of the same process of continual renewal in which scientific activity unfolds. This activity undergoes periods of predominance by the Matthew Effect, characterized by the domination of the élite, who defend a certain paradigm which they manifest when, in mathematical terms, or fractality index tends to 1. These periods alternate with phases of controversy or struggle of paradigms, during which the scientific structure loses coherence and there are no authors that accumulate all the scientific capital, whereupon the fractality index becomes negative and the term transfractality applies".

It is acceptable to ask oneself what scientific ingenuity means today. The appearance of brand new ideas of concepts, of innovative techniques, is a sort of molecular epiphany, slow and blind, for a large collective part. This is why collective intelligences must be coddled and protected; this is the reason why, more than ever, the emergence conditions of reflexive and lively collective intelligences are decisive.

Maintaining the intelligibilities of intelligences, that is to say, the intelligibilities that exude from within them and project themselves forwards and outwards, is difficult. And this even more so, as Kipling said, when "darkness is always under the lamp"[17].

This work, the productive ability to be heretic and the ability to speak barbaric in the agoras of research at the risk of unproductiveness and sterile consumption of enjoyment energies, is complex to supply.

There is a whole libidinal economy, a whole passionate constitution of researchers at work, busy sometimes in the snares of bureaucratic nets, sometimes in specific and uncertain assemblages for the free and wild creation of concepts, for pyrotechnic fabrications at the center of thought or the living, or even for teratological man–machine constructions.

For Jean-François Lyotard, "the modern scientist no longer exists as a scholar, that is to say, as a subject, but as a small region of transit in a process of extremely refined energizing metamorphosis; he only exists as a researcher, which on the one hand of course means as part of a bureaucratic machine of scientific power, but on the other hand inseparably as a tireless experimenter not enslaved by new junctions and combinations of energy; the utterances that he makes are only valuable for their intensity. And in this, in his anonymity and wandering, he is no less the man of capital than of power in the subordination of his works in charge"[LYO 73].

From one perspective, studies are completed, more empirically, seeking to bring about sociocognitive zones, more or less dense in creativity, or in other words, zones that carry the movements and weight of invention, innovation, between reduced collective arrangement and vast arrangement, using models of sociology, sciences and scientometric methods (analysis of citation and

---

17 "I am only a beginner at the Game, that is sure. I could not have leaped into safety as did the Saddhu. He knew it was darkest under the lamp" [KIP 01].

co-citation networks, analysis of sociocognitive structures using co-words analysis, etc.), consensus and lack thereof in their border zones[18]. There, we do not have in mind the connections between minor and major science, as defined by Deleuze and Guattari in 1,000 Plateaus.

It would, however, be very productive to take back the evolution of science and technique of this perspective and to reflect on ways to bring to light cartographies of the heterogeneses that result from the comings and goings between the two types of scientific models and thus to try to see what we do and not do to the other and vice versa.

Therefore, according to Deleuze and Guattari, "two scientific models (…) the one would be called Compars and the other Dispars. The compars (they write) is the legal or legalist model employed by royal science. The search for laws consists of extracting constants, even if these constants are only relations between variables. An invariable form of variables, a variable matter of the invariant is foundation of the hylemorphic schema. But for, the dispars, as an element of nomadic science, the relevant distinction is material-force rather than matter form. Here, it is not

---

18 See [BOR 10]: "In contrast to Newton's well-known aphorism that he had been able "to see further only by standing on the shoulders of giants," one attributes to the Spanish philosopher Ortega y Gasset the hypothesis saying that top-level research cannot be successful without a mass of medium researchers on which the top rests comparable to an iceberg. A third possibility offered by Turner and Chubin is the so-called Ecclesiastes hypothesis: these authors argue that scientific advancements can be considered as the result of chance processes or fortune using an evolutionary model of science. These findings support the Newton hypothesis and call into question the Ortega and Ecclesiastes hypotheses (given our usage of citation counts as a proxy for impact). Our results also suggest that medium-impact research plays a different role in the four fields: whereas in the social sciences and physical sciences scholars cite this underlying research, in the life sciences and health sciences the subtop is less important".
See also [BAI 07] "By a new fractal/transfractal geometry of the Unified Scientometric Model, it is possible to demonstrate that science presents an oscillating or pulsing dynamic. It goes alternatively through two types of phases. Some phases are fractal, with crystalline networks, where the Matthew effect clearly manifests itself with regard to the most notable actors and those that provide the best contributions. The other phases are transfractal, with deformed, amorphous networks, in which the actors, considered mediocre, present greater capacity to restructure the network than the more renowned actors. The result after any transfractal deformation is a new crystalline fractal network. Behind this vision lies the Kuhn paradigms".

exactly a question of extracting constants from variables but of placing the variables them selves in a state of continuous variation" [DEL 87][19].

This would be a more groundbreaking work than producing such cartographies of these heterogeneses. This would be a supplementary step (admittedly, it may not be a decisive one) to overcome the bifurcation of nature (Whitehead) not conceived as dualism [DEB 15]. A step to access "the *modus operandi* of division (…) the constitution gesture of division and not the expression of its consequences in a dual vision of nature". This would be another supplementary movement to go towards what could be a truly reflexive science.

Proposing publishing modes that take into account and offer the possibility of an analysis that constitutes one of the major stakes of Open Archives and Open Access in all their forms.

Indeed, if online accessibility of documents is generalized and made commonplace, particularly through different forms of devices (specialized motors for bibliographical reference research, equipment for digitalizing/putting articles or works online, platforms dedicated to the publication of electronic journals or to archiving digital documents), the diversity and creativity of publishing forms seem to remain.

Since the advent and near-saturation of the first digital publishing model, the experimentations of overlay journals are on the rise. The aim of these new publication forms consists of grasping the writing, which is no longer in the form of finite publishing objects, but open; open on "the current incompleteness of production", which is, as we have seen, the characteristic of communities of works today. The goal is thus to explore another aspect of Open Archives (the making visible of researchers' works and new publishing criteriologies), which bring to light the complex dimensions of the writing process and of creation.

These publishing pathways are not new. The Overlay Journal has been considered by Ginsparg, the founder of ArXiv, since 1996: "he discusses the possibility of information services provided as an 'overlay' within the Physics e-print archive" [SMI 99]. Let us cite "Geometry and Topology"[20] as an example of an overlay journal that is built on ArXiv, the initiative by the

---

19 Translated from French by B. Massumi.
20 http://www.maths.warwick.ac.uk/gt/.

University of California using the "funds" of articles as their own deposits[21], Boston College's initiative that proceeds in the same way[22], or even the virtual journals in Science and Technology[23] published by the American Institute of Physics and the American Physical Society.

Peter Suber defines the overlay journal in the following way: "An open-access journal that takes submissions from the preprints deposited in an archive (perhaps at the authors initiative), and subjects them to peer review. If approved (perhaps after revision), the postprints are also deposited in an archive with some indication that they have been approved. One such indication would be a new citation that included the name of the journal. Another could be a link from the journals online table of contents. A third could be new metadata associated with the file. An overlay journal might be associated with just one archive or with many. Because an overlay journal doesnt have its own apparatus for disseminating accepted papers, but uses the preexisting system of interoperable archives, it is a minimalist journal that only performs peer review. It is important to FOS (Free Online Scholarship) as an especially low-investment, easily launched form of open-access journal"[24].

The dimensions proposed in this definition and in the examples above are nonetheless too minimalist, as P. Suber indicates, and seem to come down to a compilation/selection of texts. In fact, the overlay journal model, which in its initial form [GIN 96] consists of selecting e-prints (pre- or postprints) to make a singular publishing object, seems too cold to us.

Yet, this conception is improved today not only by the Web 2.0, notably by the arrangement possibility of heterogeneous information units (video, screencast, podcast, blog note, tag, etc. [cf. Post-Genomics, ResearchGate, Open Social Scholarship, etc.[25]]), but also by the progress realized in the processing of information corpora, the development of relatively complex associative and cartographic approaches. If open peer commentary and open peer review are associated with this process, it is then a matter of making the

---

21 http://repositories.cdlib.org/peerreview/overview.html.
22 http://escholarship.bc.edu/peer_review_list.html.
23 http://www.virtualjournals.org/vjs/.
24 Guide to the Open Access Movement, http://www.earlham.edu/~peters/fos/guide.htm#o.
25 http://postgenomic.com/.

traces of a cognitive record visible or even taking into account the structures' agents, sociocognitive dynamics making up a domain, a field of research, a publishing object always necessarily being taken in a process, as well as putting forward the principle of percolation. From this point of view, we situate ourselves in the framework of a weak deconstructionist perspective of the notion of a journal [DER 87].

In "The deconstructed journal – a new model for academic publishing", Smith [SMI 99] insists upon the essential functions of a journal. Notably, he shows how they can be found or developed in a Deconstructed Journal (DJ). The main center of this new model is entitled Subject Focal Point. It is a matter of pointing, filtering, fixing, associating texts coming from different sources and putting them to use through a publishing entity. We return to this perspective, but we hope to widen it, particularly by developing the publishing function and all the technical artifacts that could bring to light the "writing process" in action at the center of a scientific community[26]. To better grasp our project and to register it in the continuity of research on scientific publication models, we are departing from a text by Pinfield [PIN 09] that lists, through three models, the different relationships between reviews and information repositories (i.e. Open Archives). Models 1 and 2 finally illustrate the conventional processes of text circulation between journals and open archives with the question of the preprint, postprint, copyright, etc. in inscription [GAL 05]. Model 3, entitled "repository to overlay journal", schematizes Suber's definition cited above and carries the mark of software projects such as RIOJA (Repository Interface for Overlaid Journal Archives)[27]. If the model that we have developed (Figure 3.1) is inspired by a classical overlay journal (model 3 by Pinfield [PIN 09]), we put greater emphasis on the "writing/reading" process. In fact, the work engaged upon the coming and going between information repositories and journals (but intrinsically whenever putting it into writing) must be recorded and thus made partially visible in such a way that this inscription encourages both the reflexive task and the critical function.

---

26 On this point, see the exchanges between Smith and Harnad, http://users.ecs.soton.ac.uk/harnad/Hypermail/Amsci/0216.html, sic_00688414, version April 1–17, 2012.
27 http://www.ucl.ac.uk/ls/rioja/about/ and http://arxivjournal.org/rioja/sic_00688414, version April 1–17, 2012.

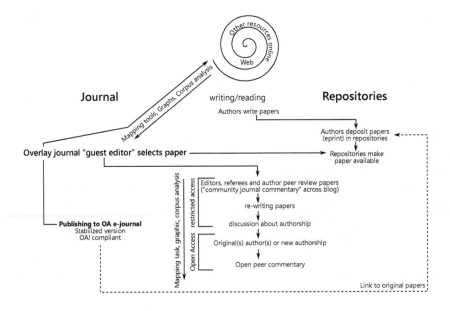

**Figure 3.1.** *Toward procedural research editing*

This model echoes the project expressed above and pursues several goals:

– to give an added value to open archives (from green to gold);

– to give visibility to the different ways and statuses of texts coming from diverse writing and publishing processes from varied selection modes;

– to assemble complementary, but scattered texts likely to enrich the debate;

– to test out "postediting", which would not only be a hybrid between the open peer postcommentary model (repository of comments after the acceptance of the publication) and the customary task of reviewers, but a device demonstrating the relative instability and the more or less conflicting dimensions of scientific practices;

– to bring to light the concept of "document as a relational complex";

– to be attentive to the questioning of current publishing variations that, even within digitization, remain confined within the limits of exposition and science circulation constraints at the height of their certainty, transparency, and own mythology, outside the exposition of their elaboration, patch-up jobs.

In Figure 3.1, the term "repositories" thus indicates that the selection of texts can be realized for the totality of the world's open archives. A guest editor (one or two people) responsible for a themed edition after having selected the texts (with or without the help of mapping tools, graphs, corpus analysis) surrounds himself with proofreaders who will comment on the texts using a blog-style platform. On this blog, whose access is, in this phase, restricted, exchanges will take place with the authors (of all the texts selected). According to the content of these exchanges, the "auctorat" can be discussed and "budding" texts can appear. This infers three possible types of texts: (1) a revised original text, corrected, but the mastery of whose content remains the primary author's; (2) an original text thoroughly improved by community journal commentary, the auctorat (at the request of the original author) is then shared with the commenters; (3) an "autonomized" text that comes to complete the primary text. A stabilized version (but still likely to be taken back, under conditions to be determined) of the texts will constitute an issue of an open access journal.

Each of the texts (except the "buds") will bear the mark of its process (links to the primary texts) and access to the comments will be open to the readers of the texts on the blog..., thus following the writing/reading process. Likewise, after the release of some issues, an endogenous and exogenous mapping of the journal's micro corpus (it is here a matter of processing the internal and external links of the texts) can be realized.... There, too, the opening up to the Web in the direction of greater, more heterogeneous resources would, in our opinion, allow the consideration of conceptual ethologies through, but also against, all against which, research and critical thought open up their pathways. What is thus affected are both conceptions and practices associated with an essentialist, not reflexive and unpragmatic approach to the sciences and thus of publishing objects as the blind presentation of research and critical thought, outside their writing and production conditions. Research publishing brings to light a part of the arrangements that texts come from to form a sort of onto-phylogeny, of onto-ethology of intellectual practices, of concepts. From this perspective, the notion of documentary ontophylogenesis can possibly be brought up, in the sense where digital plasticity, the evolving digital modes and textures reinforce the reversibility of the relationship between forms of content and of expression, in Hjelmslev's sense.

It would then be possible to further develop an immanent theory of documentation as a flow [HJE 71a, HJE 71b, DEL 72], or, and in a more prosaic way, to catch up to what Web theoreticians today call "Web streaming" or "Web of data". It would be a matter of better grasping not the content/documents, but the content/data, that is to say, a finer level of granularity where the notions of information and process traces and their incidences on the creation (creativity) of knowledge will lie more than ever at the center of the question of scientific writing.

It is under the pressure of these general transformations that the model of "liquid journals" has emerged. This model aims to provide custom-made shapes according to researchers' reading and connection needs. Here, we are following Marcos Baez, Fabio Casati[28] [BAE 10]:

1) it allows researchers to have a tailored journal to read what they care about;

2) it allows real-time dissemination, that is, it exposes new ideas and brainstorming-like thoughts besides validated/reviewed research. It also exposes papers as soon as they "appear" on the Web;

3) it combines breadth and depth: it combines personalization with awareness to new ideas as the journal selection model allows combining relevance, novelty and interest as search criteria (so a reader may learn about very relevant research, but also about research less related but more novel or considered interesting by the community);

4) it exploits the filtering power of the community to help select interesting contributions. It also observes behaviors in the sense of reading/tagging/forwarding contributions to determine, also in real time, how interesting a contribution may be. In essence, the journal contains contributions that members of the community believe to be "worth reading". It is like a mechanical turk for finding good contributions;

---

28 On these matters, see also: http://www.peerevaluation.org/, http://www.liquidinformation. org/index-fr.html, http://www.liquidinformation.org/index-fr.html.

5) rewards creativity, early sharing of ideas, and collaboration: by considering (and therefore rewarding) blogs and in general non-reviewed thoughts as contributions, it encourages scientists to share their ideas. This is key as collaboration is a great catalyst to innovation. Today, ideas are not shared early as they can be taken by others and turned into a paper, but if an appropriate reward is given to seed thoughts, then the obstacles to sharing will be reduced;

6) provides a complete, lightweight and real-time assessment: evaluation is a necessary aspect of research.

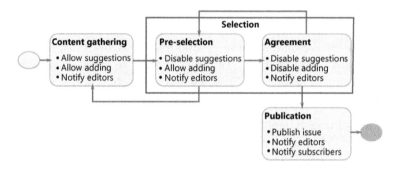

**Figure 3.2.** *Example of the selection and publication lifecycle for a liquid journal*

It should be noted that what we indicate here can be extended to other activities and communities, under certain conditions, to companies or state organizations. The stakes are the same and the general process, which management teams call "mapping in the making", is the expression of identical constraints. The complication of knowledge flows, of communicational pragmatics, makes knowledge of places and environments necessary, a skill increased for the amount, to define its position, if only as a more or less stable point of transit in the interfacing of trajectories and heterogeneous announcements that make up the framework of activities in these communities.

## 3.5. Fragmented encyclopedism: education/interfaces

What shapes research, training and education under the new conditions and the conditions of the crisis of knowledge incapable of "considering the new situation and thus the flaw of analysis and synthetic theorem criteria allowing the constitution of an appropriate epistemic retention device, and as a resulting inability to create the developer foundations of a WE, that is, of a desired future vision in its nondetermination itself, in its factual improbability, in the uncertainty of its borders, and in its idealism, in both the Kantian and Husserlian senses of the word", is crucial [STI 01].

The development of a strategic approach of hypertextual–hypermedia interfaces in a constantly changing co-operative context is no longer necessary. We have noted this several times. The definition of an interface strategy is vital (it should even be able to differ as an opposing force) in order to have hold in a critical way of the tsunami of applications attached to the Internet of Things or hybrids and to the analytical powers of Big Data, such as those of Marketing, Big Science, Insurance, monopolizing the definition of value, its quantification.

On another level, the elaboration of new intellectual organizational forms connected to a better understanding of our a-centrical and decentralized sociocognitive abilities is also a key stake. We examined this in the first section. If our goal and desire are to produce new states of intelligence, then it is necessary to learn how to shape, train and educate using "dynamic and strongly connected contexts" that currently serve us with *milieu associé* (associated environments). In a connected world where the quantitative growth of information, knowledge and ignorance, the differentiation of production conditions in general, and the need to increase the size of each thinking entity's cognitive ecologies live alongside one another, the question takes on a new dimension.

From a political perspective, this implies better grasping the nature of the relationship existing between the dissemination spread of new intellectual technology and the genesis at the center of the social training of an ulterior ability to expand economically, strategically, culturally, connected to an increased ability of collective intelligences. Therein lies one of the major transformations of the encyclopedic question, a shifting of its political character.

It is expressed strongly in the bonds that tie Big Data/Data Mining/Internet of Hybrids as robotization gains in strength, with a more and more hegemonic character of prediction.

## 3.6. Encyclopedism and correlations

### 3.6.1. *"Correlation is enough": the Anderson controversy and the J. Gray paradigm and their limits*

It is thus in the context of profound transformation that, for example, Chris Anderson's text [AND 08] draws attention. From a certain perspective, that of sociology/anthropology, science and the philosophy of science, it really must be recognized, this text seems relatively cursory[29]. In fact, what Anderson tells us: "at the petabyte scale, information is not a matter of simple three- and four-dimensional taxonomy and order but of dimensionally agnostic statistics. It calls for an entirely different approach, one that requires us to lose the tether of data as something that can be visualized in its totality. It forces us to view data mathematically first and establish a context for it later". "There is now a better way. Petabytes allow us to say: 'Correlation is enough.' We can stop looking for models. We can analyze the data without hypotheses about what it might show. We can throw the numbers into the biggest computing clusters the world has ever seen and let statistical algorithms find patterns where science cannot".

For Anderson, the primacy of data has a taste of revenge on what he calls models. Science and its theories take the attire of transcendence by replacing it with empiricism flirting with positivism: only what is deduced from these direct observations, namely data, would exist and the algorithmic method would be presented as the royal pathway toward knowledge. Statistics speak in the name of beings (dixit) and are made up of sufficiently "pure" shapes to free themselves from any plot and all conceptual equipment (even those of scientists themselves!).

---

29 Please see [HEY 09] for Jim Gray's position. Data-intensive science consists of three basic activities: capture, curation, and analysis. Data comes in all scales and shapes, covering large international experiments; cross-laboratory, single-laboratory, and individual observations; and potentially individuals' lives. "We must create a generic set of tools that covers the full range of activities–from capture and data validation through curation, analysis, and ultimately permanent archiving". And "Curation covers a wide range of activities, starting with finding the right data structures to map into various stores. It includes the schema and the necessary metadata for longevity and for integration across instruments, experiments, and laboratories. Without such explicit schema and metadata, the interpretation is only implicit and depends strongly on the particular programs used to analyze it. Ultimately, such uncurated data is guaranteed to be lost." "Data analysis covers a whole range of activities throughout the workflow pipeline, including the use of databases (versus a collection of flat files that a database can access), analysis and modeling, and then data visualization".

The critique that is brought against him is first epistemological. Forgetting the entire history of science, the heterogeneity of its methods and the pluralism of its intelligibilities and their histories, passing by the vast material and conceptual constructions of science and the rationalisms that accompany it, the variations that affect the coming and going between speculative and empirical propositions and the increasingly complex construction of the "acquisitions", Anderson grossly simplifies the heterogeneses of the job of science. In the brief controversy that followed, as Kelly and others stress, *this emerging method will be one additional tool in the evolution of the scientific method. It will not replace any current methods (sorry, no end of science!) but will complement established theory-driven science.* Furthermore, for the case of astrophysics, Smolin [SMO 08] explains that this has long been equipped with supercomputers, *but has at every stage been guided by theoretical knowledge and analytical approximations.* Gloria Orrigi indicates again that *science has always taken advantage of correlations in order to gain predictive power. Social science more than other sciences*[30]. The controversy has not actually taken on a wide scale, despite how long the transformations in the hard sciences have been happening and how decisive the work (done for a century now) in sociology and philosophy of the sciences has been[31].

On the other hand, where the controversy persists are in the social sciences, the overwhelming power of the digital empirical data/numerics couple presenting itself as the means of their re-enchantment (supposing that they need it) through the systematic mobilization of ethnographic and statistic approaches. These approaches have to be "a-theoretical" for Anderson: *Out with every hour of human behavior, from linguistics to sociology. Forget taxonomy, ontology and psychology.*

It is not without use to recall that before him, the ethnographic approaches and a whole collection of works on the anthropology of science and technology called for the study of the "social" as it is in the process of

---

30 For the discussion of Chris Anderson's (Editor-in-Chief of Wired magazine) theses, see [AND 08] and [DYS 08]. See also [BER 12] by Gerard Berry, Research Director at Inria and a member of the French Academy of Sciences.

31 For the essentials on these points see also, from a general point of view, the works of Karl Popper, Michael Polanyi, Paul Feyreabend and Bruno Latour.

being made (not as he thinks to himself) and this, by doing away with the previous categories, with the magma of collective representations, with structures, psycho-sociologisms, symbols…. For all that, the project of an immanentist social science (sociology of translation) by Latour is not that of Anderson and depends on a collection of speculative and strong theoretical propositions.

As such, the third political critique focuses on the naturalization and *essentialization* of statistics, clear-sighted omniscience in the ether of data. Anderson suggests that the creators of algorithms would never create their operations instructions using research and knowledge, for example from information/computer science, mathematics, etc., and that Google would be born in two brains outside of history.

But Anderson himself reminds us that Sergey Brin and Larry Page possessed a model posing *a minima,* that is "the organization of information", "useful information", and thus "a user-usage model of information (on a global scale)". In fact, the creators of Google are recorded in the history of database constitution and that of their search engines, in the massively essentialist history of documentation, of information engineering and of inherited classification school of thought. The famous algorithm of the *Page Rank* being recording at the same time against and right against this history. Against because it introduces the motion of "quantified usage" as a filtering and classification criterion. Thus, it is a matter of a fundamentally anthropological and political choice recorded in the historical movement of critiquing *top-down* criteriologies, for the rising strength of *bottom-up* criteriologies suffering the fluctuation of interpretations and readings, uses and controversies…when the more or less sophisticated doxas create meaning and are operators of semantics' lines of force [BOU 10, JUA 10][32]. Google's algorithm is fundamentally inserted into a model of political economy…of knowledge. Others, it since has become known, are possible, such as those of Exalead or Autonomy… that propose other criteriologies and other explorations based on the bringing to light of sociosemantic networks and the procedural nature of knowledge and their arrangements. The attempt to describe Google and the algorithm as a-theoretical and a-

---

32 "While the subject of historical was necessarily a searching, indeed a living, collecting point for experience, the current search engines and storage methods now give it a sign that it can rest from its time-honoured labors. The present gesture which expresses the transition into the post-experiental age most perfectly is that of downloading. It exemplifies liberation from the imposition of gathering experience" [SLO 11b, p. 315].

political is in reality a purely political posture, even an imposture. It is a matter of "setting outside of history" by expelling the work of the forces at hand, of passions, out of all normative, economic, financial, political, etc. plans. By denying the heterogeneity of these applications, it is the critical strength with respect to certain governmentalities being created (and state, bank, marketing instances that manipulate them) that is weakened. Catherine Malabou's critical question about the brain must be followed (and its weight borne), namely the following: "what to do so that mathematics and its algorithms do not coincide purely and simply with the spirit of capitalism" [MAL 04]?

It is known that Data Mining is found at the center of the description-performance-prediction loop. By releasing it from the entire chain of mediations, translations, updates, ratios of force (including scientific ones) and various types of technological solution (that themselves convey a whole series of program transformations); from constraints and interests that create its various application environments, Data Mining can appear as a self-founder (and even freed from all business models). Self-legitimization through power (and its strategies and tactics), especially highlighted since the end of the 1970s by Jean-François Lyotard [LYO 79], today finds blossoming conditions...imperial ones.

Pierre Levy [LEV 13] did a great job of bringing to light the limits of this statistical positivism[33]. Here, too, it is worth stating that the establishment of

---

33 P. Levy: "How to transform the torrents of data into rivers of knowledge? The solution to this problem will determine the next step in the evolution of the algorithmic medium. Certain enthusiastic observers of the statistical processing of "big data", like Chris Anderson, the editor-in-chief of Wired, have hurried to state that scientific theories (in general!) were henceforth obsolete. We would no longer need anything but massive floods of data and statistical algorithms. It seems that the numbers speak for themselves. But this is obviously forgetting that, before any calculation, the pertinent data must be obtained, it must be precisely known what is being counted, and a name must be given – that is to say, categorization – to the emerging patterns. Moreover, no statistical correlation delivers causal relationships immediately. These necessarily raise hypotheses that explain the correlations brought to light by powerful statistical calculations operating in the "clouds" of the Internet: the theories – and thus the hypotheses that they propose and the reflection that they come from – would belong to a revolution stage in the scientific method (...). Chris Anderson and his emulators revive the old positivist and empiricist epistemology popular in the 19th Century according to which only inductive reasoning (that is, those based solely on data) is scientific. This position comes back to drive back or silence the theories – and thus the risky hypotheses based on personal thought – that are necessarily at work in any process of data

cause and effect relationships using statistical data is a complicated matter. How to go from the updating of correlations, statistical links, to the determinations of these cause and effect relationships lies at the center of the scientific practice and general reflection on this notion of causality. In a recent popular science article, Isabelle Drouet reminds readers, for example that there are correlations without causal links, based on research done by Nancy Cartwright [CAR 79][34]. "However", notes Isabelle Drouet, "this analysis of causality has its limits. In fact, it is impossible to directly transpose probability theories of causality to the domain of scientific methodology (...) Why? First of all, because these theories are circular (...) then because probability theories do not define, *a priori*, closing principles that would come to define the set of possible causes for a given effect" [DRO 14].

Moreover, a quick test shows that the production conditions for scientific knowledge are not affected in the same way by this increase. What strongly appears is the persistence of an intertwining and a co-determination between methodologies and "acquisitions", correlations (in their variety itself), intelligibility principles, construction of proof, etc., and theoretical research and "empirical" programs. To name a few examples, the relationships between computer science and mathematics that renew the latter, research concerning postgenomics and the understanding of "protein association modes" all of these express the ways in which computer science and numerics shape entire sections of research.

But things can take an even more troubling turn. It is worthwhile to bring to the fore the larger complication of the relationships between theory/modeling and digital empirical data, and to stress that the expected productivity of the research of creative correlations should not be separated from the reflexive frameworks and the work of and on models, even the most speculative. It is known, for example (to stay in the realm of biology) that Jean-Jacques Kupiec, in his work *L'origine des individus* [KUP 08], tries to draw a line between genetic determinism and theories of self-organization by proposing a new theory of biological individuation. This so-

analysis and that manifest themselves as selection, identification, and categorization decisions. Statistical processing cannot be initiated nor its results interpreted without a theory".
34 See also What are randomised controlled trials good for? 2009 (Open access at Springerlink.com) http://link.springer. com/article/10.1007/s11098-009-9450-2.

called theory of "hetero-organization" reestablishes the link between Darwin's theory of natural selection and Bernard's theory of interior milieu. It also allows us to go beyond reductionism and holism, which, in his opinion, have imprisoned biological thought since Antiquity. This proposition precedes the Encode Encyclopedia of DNA Elements[35] program. That is to say, the equivalent of 3,000 DVD (data) on the human genome taken as a whole, and thus well beyond single genes. This program (encode) is carried out by an international consortium that brings together more than 400 scientists under the direction of the main American universities (Harvard, Sanford, MIT, etc.) and National Health Institutes (NHI) and biomedical research institutions in the United States. Launched in 2003, it is gaining in power.

*Nature* published an exceptional series of articles relating these results. These "acquisitions" represent a gigantic volume of information. In a recent interview, Jean-Jacques Kupiec accounts the inherent difficulties of the reductionist program and the dogmas of molecular biology. He recalls the belief that had prevailed in the 1990s, according to which "it would be enough to analyze the consequences of DNA – which is written in the genes, in some way – to decipher that supposed genetic information". In fact, he writes, "DNA alone is nothing, or rather, it never exists in isolation, except in the test tubes of chemists. A cell's DNA is always interacting with other proteins in a structure called chromatin. These interactions are indispensible; they decide if certain proteins are produced or not".

According to Kupiec, the Encode program allows "the detailed study of these very numerous interactions. It aims to identify systematically, at the level of entire genomes, all the DNA sequences and all the proteins interacting together in a cell in order to activate certain genes". It is because of the "automated molecular biology techniques (that) have seen extraordinary development, (it has been possible) to obtain an immense amount of data on entire animal and plant species genomes and those of microorganisms" [KUP 12]. The examples of such interweaving could be multiplied limitlessly.

---

35 http://encodeproject.org/ENCODE/ and http://en.wikipedia.org/wiki/ENCODE.

## 3.7. "Perplication" in knowledge

We find this detour necessary, as it indicates that a widened context of fragmentation and differentiation of the sciences (and knowledge) are simultaneously and necessarily "at the crossing" relative to one another and are in a sort of "perplication" [DEL 68][36] in the sense where they must be seen as in more or less transitory states, meta-stable of arrangement problems, with their multiplicities, repetitions and digital empirical data, their methods, their algorithms and models, their specific evidence construction zones, evidence in turn wrapped in other zones, those of indetermination, from where the "coming events" spread and which feed the analogous freedoms of the interstices that research (to various degrees) and thought carry along, interstices and "inessentiality" immanent   to their processes.

### 3.7.1. *Doxic tension in fragmented encyclopedism and format accordingly*

If the main interrogations posed by the current knowledge production, circulation and use modes (scientific or not) are quickly summarized, the first contributes to the tension between stable and meta-stable knowledge – even instable when it emerges far from balance, in zones of disaccord and indetermination. The second contributes to the variation of the differential relationships between scientific knowledge evaluation regimes, knowledge legitimization regimes in general and thus the management of perspectives. The third question concerns the management representation of the processes and morphogeneses that express dynamics, "conceptual ethologies" and collective termination arrangements, with the unprecedented multiplication of recursive loops, forming the associated, more or less moving environment of knowledge. This is one of the reasons why the question of controversies in general both in scientific and sociotechnical domains in particular has taken on such great importance. Last but not least, the final point concerns

---

36 For "perplication" see [DEL 68]. To overcome the 'bifurcation of nature', we must go towards a science conceptualized as Idea: "Ideas are by no means essences. In so far they are the objects of Ideas, problems belong on the side of events, affections, or accidents rather on that of theorematic essences. Idesa are developed in the auxiliaries and the adjunct fields by which their synthetic power is measured. Consequently, the domain of Ideas is that of the inessential. They proclaim their affinity with the inessential in a manner as deliberate and as fiercely obstinate as that in which rationalism proclaimed its possession and comprehension of essences".

writing technology (including interfaces) participating in sociocognitive innovation.

## 3.8. Networks of the digital environment

In the same way that intelligence is "always-already-machinated"[37] and collective, it can be said that knowledge and learning are "always-already-machinated" and collective.

There is a wide variety of intelligences, knowledge and learning. The "*milieux*"[38] from which knowledge spreads and lives have been evolving profoundly in the last centuries. We have said that these environments, as a collective assemblage of enunciation  coupled with collective equipment of subjectivation [GUA 89] for the subjectification of necessarily heterogeneous, concrete arrangements, contain an ever-higher number of writing systems, storage modes, border objects, transmission and repetition modes, expression substances and bring into play a large number of methodologies, algorithms [CAR 14a].

And the figures of the network, at the center of fragmented encyclopedism, are closely linked to the types of recursive loops, of interfaces-synapses proposed. Therefore, proliferation of the network's figure as a concept, devices, territories, organizational modes...facilitate learning. And there is no end to the making of maps, the making of graphs out of these networks. There are nodes and edges. The links are measured, the connectivity, stability, meta-stability, repetition, resistance, or on the other hand, the fragility of the learning networks are studied. Their performativity is also measured. They are divided up according to a complex geology.

In a general way, the shapes of learning networks are a function of the types of agents that make them up. They are expressed between two modes, the one displaying a centered, hierarchized, distributed dominant feature of a fractal or even multifractal type (at the organizational and conceptual ideological level, at the level of norms, rules, routines, interfaces and border

---

37 On this theoretical point, see the works of Bernard Stiegler, Bruno Latour, Edwin Hutchins.
38 In Georges Simondon's sense.

objects, immanent to the production processes) and the other with an a-centered, distributed dominant feature of a multifractal type.

But whatever the mode associated with the techno-political dimensions of protocols may be, the question of interfaces and connectors, the software question haunts (or should haunt) fragmented encyclopedism.

In fact the assemblage that serves us today to produce learning and knowledge is organized (as they never have been before) in tangled strata, levels, territories, these levels and territories being linked by multiple paths, more or less numerous recursive loops that depend on software, more or less sophisticated intellectual techniques and new mapping practices.

And the possibility of using these collectives' complexity in the best way requires both the ability to develop levels of higher description combined with combinatories and partially automated writings. All of this depends upon the spread (according to various techno-political and juridical criteria) of machinated interfaces equipped with filtering, indexing, research, contextualization, mapping devices, annotation, data processing software and efficient hypermedia writing systems.

*In the framework of networks and collectives that produce knowledge, it is less the shape of the network that is strategic than those of protocols and those of "machinated interfaces" among hypertextual memories, among the actors that are implicated in the final recursive loops.*

### 3.8.1. *Variations of speed and slowness at the center of encyclopedic pragmatics*

The variation of speed and slowness connections is decisive here. We will return to this point later. This reserve of "variations" through the differentiation of textualities as spaces of encoding and decoding, the differentiation of relationships between order and "random", begins to resonate with the variation of relationships between synchronization constraints and constraints on guarantees that the processes of diachronization will remain open. This is useful for every collective assemblage in general and all the more so for the collective assemblage of enunciation that produces and circulates knowledge.

Writings, routines, memories, synchronization, resonance, convergence and coordination have always been at the center of complex collective entities' functioning and of the work process, including the intellectual work process. And the speed and slowness relationships are also at the center of multiple analogue processes. They also cross the whole system of relations among the various retention types[39].

## 3.9. Knowledge and thought in fragmented encyclopedism

At this stage, it is necessary to specify what we understand as knowledge, which should not be confused with thought. There again, their differences and relations deal with speed and slowness, with acceleration slowing down. Here, we return to the extraordinary pages of *What is Philosophy?* [DEL 94][40].

"Thought demands 'only' movement that can be carried to infinity. What thought claims by right, what it selects, is infinite movement or the movement of the infinite. It is this that constitutes the image of thought". In a certain way to think is "to give consistency without losing anything of the

---

39 We choose here the representation by [STI 04] "... The 'I' is also a consistant conscience in a flow of primary retention (...) which the conscience retains in the flow's now that makes it up... my conscious life is essentially made up of such retentions Yet these retentions are selections... you do not retain everything that can be retained". (Note from Bernard Stiegler: What can be retained as relations: primary retentions are in fact relations.) "... these selections are made through filters of which the secondary retentions consist, those that that your memory conserves and that make up your experience. And I pose that the life of the conscience is made up of such primary retention arrangements, written R1, filtered by secondary retentions, written R2, while the relations of primary and secondary retentions are overridden by what I call tertiary retentions, R3 – those R3 rising as much from the technical individuation as from the grammatization process that crosses it. It obviously must not be believed that such a flow is a regular line. It is less a line than a tissue or a weaving, which I have called fabric of my time, such as motifs and drawings design it, where primary retention is also the recurrence, return, refrain, coming again of what insists. Ultimately, the flow is a whirlpool where events can be produced...".
40 The plane of immanence is not a concept that is or can be thought but rather the image of thought, the image thought gives itself of what it means to think, to make use of thought, to find one's bearings in thought. It is not a method, since every method is concerned with concepts and presupposes such an image. Neither is it a state of knowledge on the brain and its functioning, since thought here is not related to the slow brain as to the scientifically determinable state of affairs in which, whatever its use and orientation, thought is only brought about. Nor is it opinions held about thought, about its forms, ends, and means, at a particular moment" [DEL 94].

infinite is very different from the problem of which seeks to provide chaos with reference points, on condition of renouncing infinite movements ..." [DEL 94]. Thought is not arborescent, it is rather rhizomatic. But it spreads endlessly from narrative devices and (not exclusively linguistic) writings of machinated arrangements that slow it down and stabilize it and are more or less complex hybrids of arborescence and rhizome, under very heterogeneous combinatories, among which formal thought is a particular, powerful case, but a particular case.

Thus, it spreads against but also close to that and can be defined as a permanent re-conquest of new speed and slowness relations, of the infinite movement, of the highest speeds. Re-conquest "in the world", that is to say, in the interstices that are both proposed to it and that it creates, too, by permanent forceful blows against the slowing down of the production of knowledge and learning. But to what degree do emerging modes accept a partially increased entry into resonance with the infinite movements of thought is a very difficult question, possibly devoid of all sense.

However, we continue to think that it is more necessary than ever to ask questions about the effects of Production, Circulation, Consumption (PCC) mode variations, of new speed and slowness relations between memories, reading and writing practices. We must remain in the new productivity of interstices, those that are empty and those that are filled, of disconnections and links. We must approach further approach than in the past above all what happens to or from borders of sub-cognition [HOF 79] and processes of chaotization [DEL 94].

## 3.10. What criteriology for encyclopedic writings?

Writings are evaluated and imposed, among others, from what creativities and inventions they open, from what new combinatory modes they bring, as hermeneutical as possible.

If an attempt were made to establish a certain number of requisites or demands from which the contribution of new intellectual technologies could be evaluated, for an fragmented encyclopedism, from the renewed tension between an arborescent, essentialist, rhizomatic and procedural vision of the pragmatics that produce knowledge, it would be of greater interest.

The conceptual and material arrangements that produce knowledge must encourage the exercising of a certain number of fundamental cognitive practices, including those of reflexivity (the critical work on conceptual reference frameworks that partially determine the structural visibility conditions of the sciences, their intelligibility strength), from which the necessary examination of a certain number of points, processes and constraints that new digital technologies are apt to influence. First of all, combinatory constraints, the social or collective transmissions of these constraints, the meta-stability of these constraints, and the expression substances on which they operate. These constraints are more or less numerous according to the semiotics in question.

Connected to the previous point, the constraints have the ability to increase and multiply the number of relations and simultaneously the growth of indecision zones and interstices. This is a delicate point, as there can be a tension, even a double constraint, under certain thresholds and conditions of hyperconnectivity. Certainly the growth of associative, analogue abilities is central and the possibilities to establish a connection between data, problems, models and the heterogeneity of these connections are central. But in order to prevent densification of these networks of relations, connections, etc. from turning into a more or less homogenous and stifling confection, there must be interstices, black boxes, self-simplifying processes that create gaps, escape lines and interstices that open the space permanently.

Attention must be paid so that emerging writings and the automation of certain sociocognitive tasks do not change the contingence, the indecisiveness of languages, the conditionality, the sliding of descriptions.... Then the question of analogy and abduction is dealt with, as is the removal. How do new intellectual technologies influence the analogical power, the ability, for example to slide the abstract components of a description from one domain to another? How do they affect the central character of this sliding, following here Douglas Hofstader [HOF 79, HOF 95][41]? On the individual and collective level, what is the impact on the establishment of connections *"that are made by the set,* owing nothing to causality", connections that "are just as essential in that they allow us to situate facts in

41 See also [HOF 88]. That central characteristic that is sliding is also tied to writing modes, to collective arrangements that call upon "multiplicities of individuals, technological, machinated, economic multiplicities ...". Sliding has to do with the constitutions of subjectivities and is thus located directly like them on a transindividual level (Guattari), and a preindividual level (Simondon).

one perspective – to compare what really exists with what, according to how we consider things, *could have been produced* or could even come to be"[42]?

How do repetition, synchronization and diachronization modes affect the work at the center of knowledge production and circulation devices at any level? How does this shape the diverse ways of introducing differences into the repetition?

How do new intellectual technologies increase the quality of description of collective statement arrangements (that are themselves immanent to concrete machinated arrangements)? In this case, what are the tools that promote the emergence of new mapping practices and with them new sociocognitive territories?

In the world of "fragmented encyclopedism", the consideration of changes in information levels associated with a multifractal vision of knowledge is decisive if only for the conception of a political economy of reflexivity. In passing, that is also valuable for new organizational forms, for the question of the mastery, for example of information systems, communication systems in enterprises and administration where (we have previously noted) the constraint of "mapping in the making" is very strong.

In the universe of digital memories, encyclopedism then takes the shape of a meta-language allowing navigation in the heterogeneous space of ontologies or "onto-ethologies" that describe specific knowledge making up general processes of scientific knowledge available on the Web. For, rather than ontologies, it must be possible to access the definition of "onto-ethologies": they express the sociocognitive structures brought by the corpora, the translations and processes at work at the very heart of communities. The "structuration" (formalization) of texts and documents,

---

42 The importance currently given to the notion of serendipity is the expression, the symptom that the changing of level also affects the relations and there is tremendous temptation to consider cognitive ecology as a vast arrangement of interconnected graphs. It is also the index that if the probability of establishing connections or networks of connections encouraging creativity seems to have risen, making serendipity (under all forms) more central demands the elaboration of better thought out intellectual technologies. This is particularly visible in the case of new generation search engines, engines that propose logicians of open information searches, proposing more intuitive search and association practices. These approaches, by leaning on the production of new maps and the complex processing of information corpora, offer renewed conditions adapted to the changing of level for serendipity.

even of their filtering, must be considered in their technical aspects, under a double constraint.

It must be possible to process populations of digital texts, suitable for being permanently recomposed and transformed, on the one hand; on the other, exploration and intellectual exploitation tools must be made from these populations, tools for the representation of their constituent processes that promote analogical, associationist and combinatory abilities, according to multiple organization levels.

## 3.11. Borders in fragmented encyclopedism: autoimmune disorders and disagreement

In this general context, the question of borders is found to be taken to a new critical point, having to be considered as fluctuating zones or crossing of problem or concept trajectories. By allowing the partial exhibition of the procedural dimensions of documents stemming from research, new publishing devices should, we have already said, be able to allow the grasp of these border zones. From this perspective, the representation that must be researched is that of those morphogeneses and must express the dynamics and the local concepts that make up the *milieu associé*, with more or less movement, of learnings, represented by documents stemming from research. The make up of fields of learning, disciplines and research communities in fact spread progressively through the growing differentiation of the types of documents in circulation. It is necessary to note that the three expressions used are not equivalents and cover different arrangements. Their functioning rules and their constitution and normalization processes, as well as their ways of making and forming these boundaries in subjects, are variable.

This is because each scientific arrangement, in the form of discipline, wants to be reflexive at the very moment when it tries to theorize (and politicize) further the question of borders, the latter being considered a filtering device for controlling knowledge, *with, consequently, possible drifts that could be labeled as auto-immune (scholastics, dogmatisms, lack of reflexivity, etc.)*. However, the production conditions of these boundaries themselves lead them to take on procedural aspects likely to give rise to more and more heterogeneous arrangements. Boundaries being omnipresent, critical scientific work consists of making them evolve towards transformation and creation zones.

Under the pressure of new writing and digital memory modes, these border zones raise complex and permanent movements of territorialization, deterritorialization and decontextualization–recontextualization. The task of research (and thought) from these zones must consider the fact that the latter, with their internal and external margins, their spread, are progressively beginning to be valued for themselves.

To access these zones, taking into account the increasingly fractal character of research fronts, the bringing to light and clearer representation of the disagreements appear as one of the challenges of the new encyclopedism. These boundary zones end up acquiring a relative autonomy that allows them to enter into combinatory relationships with unedited or renewed "eco-cognitive assemblages". No longer belonging to what they separate, they gradually cross gaps that will open the path to new imaginaries, conceptual and scientific.

There, it is not so much a matter of measuring the disagreements likely to arise between different disciplines that begin to reflect on one another, but rather the research fronts, more or less unstable, that develop when "one realizes that it must resolve for its sake and with its own means a problem similar to the one that is asked in another" [DEL 03]. It is then that the fields of learning and the communities in the midst of risk-taking and struggles that are the chance to prove the resistance of disciplinary arrangements face one another. These conflicts reveal interdisciplinary uncertainties and openings that appear through internal pragmatics constituting these fields, disciplines and communities. The new encyclopedic modes therefore must allow us to inhabit the arrangements where conceptual or scientific confrontations are created and develop, in a cultural universe where divergent updating phenomena are certainly going to proliferate.

One of the decisive tasks today consists of rising back up toward the problems themselves. Rising up toward the problems means evaluating the interest and the strength of problems, their productivity. What strength do they give to the path of thought, the way in which the matters are built and the drilling into these same matters. Rising up toward the problems is also less building on the interlacing of disciplines than penetrating into the spaces full of holes between these disciplines. This does not necessarily mean finding common problems with different disciplines. It means that a new problem is emerging, which will redefine the morphology of the interactions between disciplines, or else make another appear or once again gather fragmented disciplines[43].

This is the reason why we have pleaded for new functions to be associated with digital publishing modes. In our eyes, the essential functions are precisely those that make the mapping of sociocognitive dynamics, areas of controversy and interdisciplinary processes that operate at the center of scientific activity.

## 3.12. Fragmented encyclopedism: a habitat for controversies?

In the framework that we all share, giving the means "to occupy" the coexistence of perspectives and the work of controversies is thus an important task. What does it mean to describe or study a controversy? A controversy is expressed according to very differentiated modes and narrations and through various actors. It is rarely symmetric (that is to say that the actors or groups of actors that provide for it are not only heterogeneous, but occupy positions of strength that can be quite variable). And this as a result of the networks of actors that are united and come together for such a position, discourse, etc. Describing a controversy is thus not only a matter of identifying the actors' different positions (from their own discourse), but describing the forces that... precisely give strength to their own narrations and to their arguments, the way in which they create proof, of which they sometimes form, if not un-natural, in any case very complex alliances, as we have learned from the great anthropologist

---

43 http://joi.ito.com/weblog/2014/10/02/antidisciplinar.html. "An antidisciplinary project isn't a sum of a bunch of disciplines but something entirely new – the word defies easy definition. But what it means to me is someone or something that doesn't fit within traditional academic discipline – a field of study with its own particular words, frameworks, and methods. Most academics are judged by how many times they have published in prestigious, peer-reviewed journals. Peer review usually consists of the influential members of your field reviewing your work and deciding whether it is important and unique. This architecture often leads to a dynamic where researchers focus more on impressing a small number of experts in their own field than on taking the high risk of an unconventional approach. This dynamic reinforces the cliché of academics learning more and more about less and less. It causes a hyper-specialization where people in different areas have a very difficult time collaborating – or even communicating – with people in different fields. For me, antidisciplinary research is akin to mathematician Stanislaw Ulam's famous observation that the study of non-linear physics is like the study of 'non-elephant animals'. Antidisciplinary is all about the non-elephant animals".

Machiavelli, as the great science ethnologist Latour showed us in his currently canonical analysis of the Pouchet/Pasteur controversy. Describing a controversy is therefore crudely describing the alliances and chains of actors that give strength to the statements of each other. It is not only a matter of listing points of agreement and disagreement, but of showing the strengths that support them and build them up. Describing a controversy therefore supposes being the narrator and cartographer of many narrations and discourses, being able to make more or less long "translation" chains appear that are going to move and crash into one another and therefore interlace and make up the place or places where the "*dossoi logoi*" are going to try to take control or be able to negotiate. Controversies manifest this massive fact, that discourses and narrations are bearers (ultimately and firstly) of disagreements and conflicts.

The controversy is on the side of the Agon, even when it is policed in the garb of the sciences, of "reasons and interests" that collide with one another. Describing a controversy is describing each actor or network of actors as a heterogeneous group of forces fighting against another actor or group of actors with different strengths.

This is the reason why the constitution of corpora is central. These corpora must be large and they must be made up of all the documents or in any case of the greatest number of documents left by the actors throughout their practices. All of these documents being both behavioral traces, traces of the actors' trajectories and transformations, semantic traces, semantic social environments, traces of narrative genres, semiotics used, etc. The analyses of corpora for controversies therefore consists of producing cartographies to express the morphology of the interactions between the actors (or the agents in the Latourian sense) and in this way qualifying the interacting actors, each of the actors or groups of actors being themselves at the crossing of more or less complex assemblages of their own networks. The tensioning in a controversy leads to hybridizations and transformations of each one's positions (partially) at the center of the controversy.

Therefore, there are two kinds of transformations (or heterogeneses) when there is a controversy: (1) those that affect the operational closure of a camp (of an actor or group of actors) and a field when there are events activating such a state in themselves and (2) those that express the general deformation of the field of confrontation where the disagreements are expressed.

Mapping a controversy is therefore, by playing with the analysis modes, the types of traces and, if not permanent, in any case regular levels and redefinition of black boxes, making several maps. To get to the real fact of the matter, the "essentialist" and molar map of actors detected in the controversy, the maps of the network(s), the internal dynamics, etc. that make up the actors, the maps of the border zones and the hybridizations that are manifested or not, when a controversy arises. Furthermore, there are still other ways to devise maps: *be this as more or less static representations of these dynamics, interactions and transformations, or as intelligibility and filtering devices giving access to the strengths and actors* as they are expressed, for example through more or less heterogeneous documents, showing the constituent networks of proof and of discourse genres. In other words, maps to allow the establishment of new connections within the arrangements in controversy, between these arrangements. Describing a controversy is therefore showing the more or less complex networks (with their relative deformation) of actors that are fighting and form the controversy itself. Cartography is thus an active element of controversies: who creates and imposes the best maps misrepresents the controversy in his own favor. The goal, when the decision is made to chart a controversy, to provide various intelligibility modes, are the means to understand how each actor in a controversy can transform and does transform from what his environment (which is partially made up of other competing or conflicting actors) makes of him, and himself making changes to varying degrees to the assembly of the controversy itself....

The data mining methods applied to controversies must aim at the heterogeneous co-differentiation of actors and thus make visible the process of individualization of the controversy itself, that is the "controversial co-construction" of learning (particularly scientific learning) in order to give access to the diversity of perspectives and the necessity for conflicts.

### 3.13. Encyclopedism according to the semantic and sociosemantic web (ontologies and web): mapping(s) and semantic levels

The efforts of defenders of the semantic web, such as it has been formulated in its principles by T. Berners Lee, are mainly based on the means of a logical formalism. It is practical and it allows the automation of a certain number of intellectual tasks. Such a concept is based on a certain number of postulates. The main idea therefore depends upon the possibility of developing formal semantics, founded on a logicist and inspired approach, among others, of the hard program of Artificial Intelligence in its beginning stages, which describes the documents in order to facilitate the automatic processing of functions and tasks. It is in the continuity of inherited predictive logic. This semantic approach, outside all pragmatics, would allow the description of both the data and rules – formal and logical – of reasoning on these data. It aims toward simple general interactions and functions. It depends upon an essentialist base of documents and a reduction of the sociocognitive mechanisms implied in the production of learning, an erasure of the tangled mechanisms.

The semantic web proposes logical information coding norms. Its goal is to make up a store of Web data exploitation system that would mainly be at the service of search engines and "intelligent agents". In short, the semantic Web depends on a certain number of tools, of markup languages. The XML language (eXtended Mark-up Language), derived from Charles Goldfarb's SGML language, authorizes the description of the structure of data (RDF, Resource Description Framework) and allows the cataloguing of Web data. The OWL language (Ontology Web Language) is used to describe "ontologies", that is to say, the conceptual structure of various domains of knowledge. These tools – descriptors and markers – aim to promote the automatization of processing in data searches and the execution of operations entrusted to intelligent agents or software robots.

The semantic web is thus specialized in the consensual definition of normes encouraging online interoperability. Its efficiency mainly depends upon a closed, reductive vision of cognitive practices, translation exchange situations, real work processes and differentiations in essential research, navigation or reading – writing phenomena. Another idea tries to take into account the communicational practices "associated with the behavior of fleeting interactions between distant users through the offer of representations, often of a graphic nature, of thusly built social networks", which opposes itself to the software approach of the formal semantic web. It defends a pragmatic conception of the informational and communicational processes, while more openly considering linguistics and semiotics. "According to this vision, the web is grasped firstly as an instrument of information management facilitating interpersonal cooperative transactions, possibly very asynchronous and distributed amongst individual actors and collectives engaged in exchanges, debates, controversies within very diverse domains. According to this vision of the Web, the methods and tools for document management must be partly thought up by the actors engaged in active cooperation. Among these tools, the sociosemantic web encourages theme cards or description networks that can be considered to fall under semiotic ontologies" [ZAC 05][44].

In the perspective of spreading new encyclopedisms associated with the creative exploitation of hypertextual logic, we think, therefore, that there is a large interest in not leaving the field free to the only formalism evoked by Berners-Lee's "cake"[45]. In fact, its efficiency is subject to a "semiotic lockdown", that is to say, to a reduction and standardization of behaviors and practices. The inverse position, which we defend, takes radical consideration of the actual sociology of practices and usages, as well as the phenomena of knowledge co-construction, so that "syntactically formal languages" may be precisely efficient. The problem lies in thinking up methods that can represent such semiotic and sociocognitive structures in such a way that a weak formalism can make a strong pragmatic approach possible through new writings.

To us, this seems to be one of the main goals of the Information Economy Metalanguage (IEML) project being developed under the direction of Pierre Lévy[46] in Canada, who is seeking an "encyclopedism without

---

44 http://archivesic.ccsd.cnrs.fr/sic_00001479.

45 The infrastructure dedicated to the semantic web is often presented in the form of a "cake", says Tim Berners-Lee.

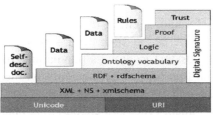

46 "… I propose the construction of a sixth layer – based on IEML – above the semantic web. IEML proposes a semantic coordinate system independent of natural languages, capable of addressing an infinite number of different subjects and suitable for serving as a basis for calculating the relationships between concepts. IEML was conceived to translate the most varied ontologies into others and to interconnect divergent disciplines and perspectives at the heart of the same addressing system. The language IEML uses XML and translates ontologies. Therefore, it is not the rival of a semantic web on which it rests, at least in technical terms. IEML aims to resolve communication problems between ontologies and compatibility problems between local information architectures that the semantic web has

totality", conceived as a *"ideography combinatory (... tempered) by a complementary principle of conceptual economy according to which the maximum semantic surface is covered by a minimum of symbols"* [LEV 13].

In our opinion, the logicist approach of the semantic web should be brought out, or rather complicated, this type of formalization depending on overly reductionist logical linguistic schemata regarding the consideration of community uses. This is the reason why we find it important to discuss, critically, the elaboration of these new alphabets, their combinatory constraints and their grammars. We should also reflect on new, "non-informational" ways to produce open and dynamic "onto-ethologies" [ALL 93], and this is in order to remember that writings are evaluated and imposed according to what they open in terms of creativity and inventions and what they bring in terms of new combinatory modes among possible hermeneutics.

## 3.14. From ontologies to "onto-ethologies" and assemblages

In the universe of digital memories, encyclopedism then takes the form of a meta-language or a geo-graphical grammar, allowing the navigation of the heterogeneous space of ontologies or "onto-ethologies" that describe specific learnings constituent of general scientific and procedural knowledge available on the Web. This allows the establishment of new connections. For, rather than ontologies, there must be access to the definition of "onto-ethologies": they express the sociocognitive structures brought by corpora, the translations and the processes at work at the very heart of communities.

The "structuring" (formalization) of texts and documents, as well as their filtering, must be considered, in their technical aspects, under a double constraint. It must be possible to process populations of digital texts, likely to be re-composed and transformed permanently on the one hand; tools for intellectually exploring and exploiting these populations must be made, tools to represent their constituent processes encouraging analogue, associationist

---

allowed to be posed but cannot regulate on the level it is situated on. In short, the language IEML, with the collective intelligence protocol (CIP) that organizes its digital addressing, wants to create a new cyberspace software layer, opening the way to renewed cognitive informatics (semantic and pragmatic calculations), as well as to new uses of the Internet oriented towards the development of collective intelligence, the distributed control of the information economy, and the self-organizing governance of multifactorial and interdependent human development".

and combinatorial capacities, according to multiple levels of organization, on the other hand.

This implies continuing down the trail blazed by the founders of Scientometry and works engaged by the sociology of science following Bruno Latour, for example. But this also leads to a reliance on a radical conception of linguistics according to which "the language function (...) is neither informative nor communicative; it refers neither to significant information nor to intersubjective communication. And it would do no good to isolate a meaning outside information or a subjectivity outside communication. For it is the process of subjectification and the movement of meaning that refer to systems of signs or collective arrangements. Linguistics is nothing without the pragmatics (semiotical or political) to define the effectuation of the condition of possibility of langage and the usage of linguistic elements" [DEL 87]. By bringing the notion of arrangement to the foreground starting in 1972 [DEL 77], Deleuze and Guattari defend that there is *"primacy of a machinic assemblage of bodies over tools and goods, primacy of a collective assemblage of enunciation over language and words"*. For them, in the linguistic context, *"an arrangement comprises neither infrastructure and superstructure, nor deep structure and superficial structure, but flattens all of its dimensions into a single consistency level where reciprocal presuppositions and mutual insertions compete"*. In a more general way, if the external pragmatics of the non-linguistic factors must be considered, "If the external pragmatics of non linguistic factors must be taken into consideration, it is because linguistic itself inseparable from an internal pragmatic involving tis own factor" [DEL 87]:

> "The minimum real unit is not the word, the idea, the concept or the signifier, but the assemblage. It is always an assemblage which produces utterances. Utterances do not have as their cause a subject which would act as a subject of enunciation, any more than they are related to subjects as subjects of utterance. The utterance is the product of an assemblage - which is always collective, which brings into play within us and outside us populations, multiplicities, territories, becomings, affects, events" [DEL 07].

Understanding and describing the arrangements inside which we are included is therefore essential. It should be noted that software stemming, for example, from the philosophy of analyzing associated words and that embody, if such can be said, the Latourian[47] principle of calculability [LAT 95], in a certain way return to the notions of "Grid" and "Group" for Mary Douglas through the notions of centrality (an assemblage's place in a rhizome network) and density (an assemblage's solidity/stability as it differentiates itself from others).

### 3.15. Fragmented encyclopedism in the digital age: metalanguage and combinatorial

Even if it is restrained to scientific knowledge, fragmented encyclopedism thus poses a major problem of navigation in the heterogeneous space of ontologies (or "onto-ethologies"), which describe the arrangements of specific knowledge constituent of the general scientific and procedural knowledge available.

The linking of this knowledge is done through variable differential relationships, always open and singular, that imply progressions, associations, translations…. It can therefore take the form of a meta-language and a combinatorial one making the continuous creation of problem cartographies possible at various levels. Such a meta-language must also allow the mastery of what P. Lévy identifies as a "metalinguistic fragmentation", which is one of the "main hindrances to the collaboration of searches in science (…)". According to him, this supposes that this meta-language is "*a formal notation writing* of the phenomena and ideas of the sciences. In order to fill this roll usefully, this scientific writing must respond to two principal constraints. Firstly, it must be able to address an open

---

47 See [TEI 95]: "The robustness of structured relations does not depend on qualities inherent to those relations but on the network of associations that form its context The principle we started from in constructing the Hume machine is a *principle of calculability* different from that of Turing machines, but one which occupies the same strategic position for our project as his did for his project. The reasoning is as follows:
- any form is a relationship of force;
- any relationship of force is defined in a trial;
- any trial may be expressed as a list of modifications of a network;
- any network is resolvable into a list of associations of specific and contingent actants;
- this list is calculable.
Thus, there is no formal concept richer in information than that of a simple list of specific and contingent actants".

infinity of 'subjects' of discourse and relationships between these subjects in a distinct way. Secondly, it must encourage the power and variety of the automatic interpretation of addresses and their relationships as much as possible". It is a matter of "making the mingling of data, the description, simulation and exchange of models, the rapid tracking of ideas and new observations easier"[48].

This is not an easy task. However, the encyclopedic project demands the development of intellectual technologies capable of providing the new cartographies of conceptual territories, both complex and hybrid, in the midst of which we work, search and sometimes think. *The increased reflexivity of scientific knowledge under the constraints of creativity is the price we pay.*

Digital scientific publishing could thus avoid confinement in the confrontations determined by the declining hegemony of former political economies of scientific publishing, which lead it into relatively unoriginal debates – such as those of a generalist encyclopedia such as *Wikipedia*. Although this has opened the way to innovative research on the use of differentiated processes of article co-construction and on the means of summoning the heterogeneous and contradictory work brought about by communities of thought through the singular expressions of one contributor, it is no less pervaded by the schemata constituent of inherited encyclopedias.

Nonetheless, it renews the criteriologies of evaluation and legitimization, all the while weakly using the knowledge (scientific and not) of the Web via hypertextual links. As P. Lévy notes, it does not offer any *"possibility of automatic link generation between documents bearing upon the same topics"*. And *"the situation is even worse if these documents are written in different languages. There are also no calculations of semantic distances that would allow, for example, users to be directed to information 'close' to the question that they have asked if these questions do not find exact equivalents"*. In the same line of thinking, publishing modes (particularly

---

48 "The translation of documentary languages and ontologies in IEML would have three direct advantages: first, all indexing and cataloguing work already done would be saved (it should not be redone); secondly, ontologies and documentary systems would become mutually compatible on the logical level, that is to say, automatic inferences and calculations of semantic distances can be executed from one ontology to another. Thirdly, once it is translated into IEML, a terminology or ontology would automatically see itself interpreted in all the natural languages supported by the IEML dictionary".

"Open") face similar problems, or in any case problems of the same nature [NOY 10].

### 3.15.1. *Encyclopedism and doxic immanence field: the proliferation of short forms*

We have already handled this point through a reflection on the so-called "swarm" intelligences and pointed out their decisive importance in the digital era. We will not return to these points.

Whoever can extract and exploit the corresponding graphs using digital traces (singular and/or collective) holds a position of superiority at the center of political, libidinal and strategic economies.

Whoever can exploit the variations in speed and slowness of relationships between writing systems, the variations in combinatorials among "memes"…operating at the center of the sociopolitical questions of intelligibility modes and subjectification processes would acquire a dominant position in the production, circulation and consumption of knowledge.

We have mentioned data mining elsewhere [NOY 13][49] as a great story of performative societies of watch companies. We have quickly seen how much the constitution of immense digital memories associated with an increasingly and more combative algorithm made it possible to increase the visibility of what we call individual and collective onto-ethologies.

In this framework, the renewed interest in short narrative forms, all the attention given to their proliferation and to everything of which they are the utterance and uttered is easily understood.

The advent of Twitter as the latest incarnation of the deeper analysis of writing modes and text weaving modes, as modes of short form exchange, confirms the deeper analysis of writings, the exploration of the constraints that are associated with them. "Constraint" being taken here in its whole and utter positivity, that is to say, as a "condition of productivity". Twitter thus relates fundamentally to the transformation of communicational pragmatics, their components, to the transformation of inexhaustible rewriting and commenting processes.

---

49 http://rfsic.revues.org/377.

But it must be remembered that we would be missing the essential point if we thought we could isolate the associated pragmatics, establish a *cordon sanitaire* that would let this device float freely, anthropological stratum in its solitude. What is given to us and serves as our environment is a convolution of combinatories and combinatory constraints.

## 3.16. From fragmented encyclopedism to gaseous encyclopedism

We are looking at the inside of the world of the fragments of the topological conversion brain world whose documentary universes are the utterance and the uttered, under variable conditions of writing systems and multiple expression substance systems, systems of cerebralities in ever more cobwebby and plastic networks. And we are looking at the inside of the world through "singularizing perspectives" that we are able to extract from the encyclopedic brouhaha and the bustling of data (of the different types of data at work).

We fold and unfold ourselves in what, in the end, is but a gigantic digital veil assuring the sometimes near and sometimes far manifestation of an endless reserve of potentials, which endlessly engages itself and us in the updating processes serving our projected fantasies.

These engagements are updated under the powers of the writings and their expression substances, in the immensely numerous forms, bringers of the possible, opening up to the consideration of an endless finality in the game of creativity's conditions, in an always singular manner. Encyclopedism is, maybe, like *"Empire du Milieu"*, between virtual and actual.

# Bibliography

[ABI 12] ABITEBOUL S., "Sciences des données : de la Logique du premier ordre à la Toile", available at: http://www.college-de-france.fr/site/serge-abiteboul/inaugural-lecture-2012-03-08-18h00.htm, 2012.

[ALL 93] ALLIEZ E., *La signature du monde ou Qu'est-ce que la philosophie de Deleuze-Guattari*, Éditions du Cerf, Paris, 1993.

[AND 08] ANDERSON C., "The End of Theory: The Data Deluge Makes the Scientific Method Obsolete", *Wired*, August 2008.

[AND 12] ANDERSON C., *Makers: La nouvelle révolution industrielle*, Pearson, 2012.

[BAE 10] BAEZ M., CASATI F., BIRUKU A. *et al.*, Liquid Journals: Knowledge Dissemination in the Web Era (Position Paper), DISI Department of Information Engineering and Computer Science, Technical Report DISI-10-028, 2010.

[BAI 07] BAILÓN-MORENO R., JURADO-ALAMEDA E., RUIZ-BAÑOS R. *et al.*, "The pulsing structure of science: Ortega y Gasset, Saint Matthew, fractality and transfractality", *Scientometrics*, vol. 71, no. 1, pp. 3–24, 2007.

[BAT 77] BATESON G., *Vers une écologie de l'esprit*, vol.1, Seuil, Paris, 1977.

[BAT 80] BATESON G., *Vers une écologie de l'esprit*, vol. 2, Seuil, Paris, 1980.

[BEN 91] BENNINGTON G., DERRIDA J., *Circonfession*, Seuil, Paris, 1991.

[BER 10] BERTHOZ A., *La simplexité*, O. Jacob, 2010.

[BER 11] BERNS T., "L'efficacité comme norme", *Revue de Philosophie Politique de l'ULg*, no. 4, pp. 150–163, 2011.

[BER 12] BERRY G., "L'informatique renouvelle les mathématiques", *Les Dossiers de la Recherche*, 2012.

[BIT 10] BITBOL M., *De l'intérieur du monde : Pour une philosophie et une science des relations*, Flammarion, 2010.

[BON 94] BONABEAU E., THERAULAZ G., *Intelligence collective*, Hermès, 1994.

[BOR 10] BORNMANN L., DE MOYA ANEGÓN F., LEYDESDORFF L., "Do scientific advancements lean on the shoulders of giants? A bibliometric investigation of the ortega hypothesis", *PLoS ONE*, vol. 5, no. 10, 2010.

[BOS 14] BOSTROM N., *Superintelligence: Paths, Dangers, Strategies*, Oxford University Press, 2014.

[BOU 10] BOURDONCLE F., "L'intelligence collective d'usage", in NOYER J-.M., JUANALS B., *Technologies de l'Information et intelligences collectives*, Hermès Lavoisier, Paris, 2010.

[BOU 14] BOURDONCLE F., "Big Data: la France peut gagner, si...", Le Monde.fr, 2 October 2014.

[BRO 91] BROOKS R.A., Artificial Life and Real Robots, MIT Artificial Intelligence Laboratory, 1991.

[BRO 99] BROOKS R., *Cambrian Intelligence: The Early History of the New AI*, MIT Press, 1999.

[BRO 02] BROOKS R.A., STEELS L., *Robot: The Future of Flesh and Machines*, Allen Lane, 2002.

[BUC 09] BUCKLAND M., DOUSA T. M., SHAW R., "Narratives, facts, and events in the foundations of information science", *Proceedings of the American Society for Information Science and Technology*, vol. 46, pp. 1–6, 2009.

[CAR 79] CARTWRIGHT N., "Causal laws and effective strategies", *Noûs*, vol. 13, no. 4, 1979.

[CAR 13] CARMES M., "Territorialisations socio-numériques et sémio-politiques organisationnelles", in CARMES M., NOYER J-.M. (eds), *Les débats du numérique*, Presses des Mines, Paris, 2013.

[CAR 14a] CARMES M., NOYER J-.M., "L'irrésistible montée de l'algorithmique, méthodes et concepts en SHS", *Les Cahiers du Numérique*, vol. 10, Lavoisier, 2014.

[CAR 14b] CARMES M., NOYER J-.M. (eds), *Devenirs Urbains*, Presses des Mines, Paris, 2014.

[CAR 14c] CARMES M., "La ville intelligente vue par ses chefs de projets", in *Devenirs Urbains*, Presses des Mines, 2014.

[CAR 14d] CARR N., "The limits of social engineering", *MIT Technology Review*, April 16, 2014.

[CAR 15] CARMES M., NOYER J-.M., "Désirs de data", in SEVERO M., ROMELE A. (eds), *Traces Numériques et Territoires*, Presses des Mines, Paris, 2015.

[CAS 00a] CASTELLS M., *End of Millennium*, Blackwell, Oxford, 2000.

[CAS 00b] CASE D.O, HIGGINS G.M., "How can we investigate citation behavior? A study of reasons for citing literature in communication", *Journal of the American Society for Information Science*, 51, 2000.

[CIT 12] CITTON Y., "Traiter les données : entre économie de l'attention et mycélium de la signification", *Multitudes* vol. 2, pp. 143–149, 2012.

[COM 79] COMPAGNON A., *La seconde main ou le travail de la citation*, Seuil, Paris, 1979.

[CON 93] CONEIN B., DODIER N., THEVENOT L., *Les objets dans l'action. De la maison au laboratoire*, Éditions de l'École des hautes études en sciences sociales, Paris, 1993.

[CON 94] CONEIN B., JACOPIN E., "Action située et cognition: le savoir en place", *Sociologie du Travail*, vol. 36, no. 4, 1994.

[CON 97] CONEIN B., *Cognition Distribuée, Groupe social et Technologie cognitives*, La Découverte, 2004.

[COU 90] COURTIAL J.-P., PENAN H., CALLON M., *Introduction à la Scientométrie*, PUF, 1990.

[CRO 98] CRONIN B., "Metatheorizing Citation", *Scientometrics*, vol. 43, 1998.

[CSI 90] CSIKSZENTMIHALYI M., *Flow: The Psychology of Optimal Experience*, Harper, 1990.

[DAN 01] DANTEC M.G., *Le théâtre des opérations 200-2001. Laboratoire de catastrophe générale*, Gallimard, Paris, 2001.

[DAV 07] DAVIS M., *Le stade Dubaï du capitalisme*, Les Prairies Ordinaires, 2007.

[DEB 15] DEBAISE D., *L'appât des possibles*, Whitehead, 2015.

[DEL 68] DELEUZE G., *Différence et Répétition*, PUF, Paris 1968.

[DEL 72] DELEUZE G., GUATTARI F., *Anti-Oedipe*, Éditions de Minuit, 1972.

[DEL 75] DELEUZE G., GUATTARI F., *Kafka, Pour une littérature mineure*, Éditions de Minuit, Paris, 1975.

[DEL 77] DELEUZE G., PARNET C., *Dialogues*, Flammarion, 1977.

[DEL 87] DELEUZE G., GUATTARI F., *A Thousand Plateaus*, University of Minnesota Press, 1987.

[DEL 90a] DELEUZE G., "Postscript on the societies of control", *JSTOR*, vol. 59, pp. 3–7, 1990.

[DEL 90b] DELEUZE G., *The Logic of Sense*, Columbia University Press, 1990.

[DEL 91] DELEUZE G., *Qu'est-ce que la philosophie ?*, Éditions de Minuit, Paris, 1991.

[DEL 94] DELEUZE G., *Qu'est-ce que la philosophie*, Éditions de Minuit, 1994.

[DEL 00] DE LANDA M., *A Thousand Years of Nonlinear History*, Swerve Editions, MIT Press, 2000.

[DEL 03] DELEUZE G., *Deux régimes de fous*, Éditions de Minuit, Paris, 2003.

[DEL 07] DELEUZE G., PARNET C., *Dialogues*, Columbia University Press, New York, 2007.

[DEN 77] DENEUBOURG J.-L., "Applications de l'ordre par fluctuations à la description de certaines étapes de la construction du nid chez les termites", *Insectes Sociaux*, vol. 24, pp. 117–130, 1977.

[DER 10] DESROSIERES A., *La politique des grands nombres: Histoire de la raison statistique*, La Découverte/Poche, 2010.

[DER 87] DERRIDA J., *Ulysse gramophone, Deux mots pour Joyce*, Galilée, 1987.

[DER 90] DERRIDA J., *Limited Inc.*, Galilée, 1990.

[DES 10] DESROSIERES A., *La politique des grands nombres Histoire de la raison statistique*, La Découverte, 2010.

[DRO 14] DROUET I., "Des coorélations à la causalité", *Pour la Science*, June 2014.

[DYS 08] DYSON G., KELLY K., BRAND S. *et al.*, "On Chris Anderson's the end of theory", *Edge*, June 2008.

[EIZ 73] EIZYKMAN R.D., *Science-Fiction et Capitalisme*, Repères Mame, Paris, 1973.

[ERI 85] ERIBON D., "Pour en finir avec le mensonge", *Le Nouvel Observateur*, 1985.

[FAR 11] MCFARLANE C., "The city as a machine for learning", *Transactions of the Institute of British Geographers*, vol. 36, no. 3, 2011.

[FAY 72] FAYE J.P., *Théorie du récit, Introduction aux "langages totalitaires" , La raison critique de l'économie narrative*, Hermann, Paris, 1972.

[FLE 05] FLECK L., *Genesis and Development of a Scientific Fact*, University of Chicago Press, 1979.

[FOE 74] VON FOERSTER H., "Notes pour une épistémologie des objets vivants", *l'Unité de l'homme*, Centre de Royaumont, 1974.

[FOE 81] VON FOERSTER H., *Observing Systems (Systems Inquiry Series)*, Intersystems Publications, 1981.

[FOU 71] FOUCAULT M., *L'ordre du discours*, Gallimard, 1971.

[GAL 10] GALLOWAY A.R., *French Theory Today, An Introduction to Possible Futures*, Public School, New York, 2010.

[GAL 12] GALLOWAY A., *Les nouveaux réalistes, philosophie et postfordisme*, Éditions Léo Scheer, 2012.

[GEN 08] GENOSKO G., *Banco sur Félix. Signes partiels a-signifiants et technologie de l'information*, Multitudes, 2008.

[GIN 96] GINSPARG P., "Winners and losers in the global research village", *Joint ICSU Press/UNESCO Expert Conference on Electronic Publishing In Science*, Paris, 19-23 February 1996.

[GOO 77] GOODY J., *The Domestication of the Savage Mind*, Cambridge University Press, 1977.

[GOR 07] GORE A., *The Assault on Reason*, Penguin, 2007.

[GRA 12] GRAHAM S., "When life itself is war: on the urbanization of military and security coctrine", *International Journal of Urban and Regional Research*, vol. 36, 2012.

[GUA 81] GUATTARI F., ALLIEZ E., "Le capital en fin de compte, systèmes, structures et processus capitalistiques", *Change International 1* (Autumn), pp. 100–106, 1981.

[GUA 83] GUATTARI F., ALLIEZ E., "Le capital en fin de compte: systemes, structures et processus capitalistiques", *Change international 1*, pp. 100–106, 1983.

[GUA 89] GUATTARI F., *Cartographies Schizoanalytiques*, Galilée, Paris, 1989.

[GUA 91] GUATTARI F., "Les systèmes d'interface machinique", available at: http://www.revue-chimeres.fr/drupal_chimeres/files/termin52.pdf, 1991.

[GUA 92] GUATTARI F., *Chaosmoses*, Galilée, Paris, 1992.

[GUA 95] GUATTARI F., *Chaosmosis: An Ethico-aesthetic Paradigm*, Indiana University Press, 1995

[GUA 11] GUATTARI F., *Lignes de fuites, Pour un autre monde de possibles*, Éditions de l'Aube, 2011.

[GUA 12] GUATTARI F., *Schizoanalytic Cartographies*, Bloomsbury, 2012.

[GUR 11] GURSTEIN M., "Open data: Empowering the empowered or effective data use for everyone", *First Monday*, available at: http://firstmonday.org/article/view/3316/2764, 2011.

[HAR 04] HARDT M., NEGRI A., *Multitude: War and Democracy in the Age of Empire*, Penguin Books, 2004.

[HAR 10] HARCOURT B.E., *Against Prediction. Profiling, Policing, and Punishing in an Actuarial Age*, University of Chicago Press, 2010.

[HER 07] HERRENSCHMIDT C., *Les trois écritures : Langue, nombre, code*, Gallimard, 2007.

[HER 14] HERNADEZ D., "Microsoft Challenges Google's Artificial Brain With 'Project Adam'", *Wired*, 2014.

[HEY 09] HEY T., TANSLEY S., TOLLE K., "Jim Gray on eScience: a transformed scientific method", in HEY T. (ed.), *The Fourth Paradigm: Data-Intensive Scientific Discovery*, Microsoft Research, 2009.

[HIG 00] HIGGINS G.M., "How can we investigate citation behavior? a study of reasons for citing literature in communication", *Journal of the American Society for Information Science*, vol. 51, 2000.

[HJE 71a] HJELMSLEV L., *Prolégomènes à une théorie du langage*, Éditions de Minuit, 1971.

[HJE 71b] HJELMSLEV L., *Essais linguistiques*, Éditions de Minuit, Paris, 1971.

[HOF 79] HOFSTADTER D., *Gödel, Escher, Bach. Les Brins d'une Guirlande Eternelle*, Dunod, 1979.

[HOF 88] HOFSTADTER D., *Ma Thémagie*, Interéditions, Paris, 1988.

[HOF 95] HOFSTADTER D., *Fluid Concepts and Creative Analogies: Computer Models of the Fundamental Mechanisms of Thought*, Basic Books, 1995.

[JOX 12] JOXE A., *Les guerres de l'Empire global, spéculations financières, guerres robotiques, résistance démocratique*, La Découverte, Paris, 2012.

[JUA 07] JUANALS B., NOYER J.-M., "La stratégie américaine du contrôle continu De la 'Noopolitik' (1999) à 'Byting Back': une création de concepts et de dispositifs de contrôle des populations", available at: http://archivesic.ccsd.cnrs.fr/sic_00292207/fr, 2007.

[JUA 10] JUANALS B., NOYER J.-M., *Technologies de l'information et intelligences collectives*, Hermes-Lavoisier, 2010.

[KAP 06] KAPLAN F., OUDEYER P.-Y., "Discovering communication", *Connection Science*, vol. 18, pp. 189–206, 2006.

[KAP 07] KAPLAN F., "In search of the neural circuits of intrinsic motivation", *Frontiers in Neuroscience*, vol. 1, pp. 225–236, 2007.

[KIP 01] KIPLING R., *Kim*, Macmillan & Co, 1901.

[KIP 08] KIPP M.E.I., CAMPBELL D.G., "Patterns and Inconsistencies in Collaborative Tagging Systems: An Examination of Tagging Practices", *Annual General Meeting of the American Society for Information Science and Technology*, Austin, Texas, 3-8 November 2008.

[KIT 14] KITCHIN R., *The Data Revolution. Big Data, Open Data, Data Infrastructures and Their Consequences*, Sage, London, 2014.

[KNO 94] KNOESPEL K., "L'écriture, le chaos et la démystification des mathématiques", in ABRIOUX Y. *et al.* (eds), *Littérature et Théorie du Chaos*, Presse Universitaire de Vincennes, 1994.

[KRU 91] KRUGLER P.N., SHAW R.E., VIVENTE K.J *et al.*, "The role of attractors in the Self-Organization of Intentional systems", in HOFFMAN R.R., PALERMO D.S. (eds), *Cognition and the Symbolic Processes, Applied and Ecological Perspectives*, Psychology Press, 1991.

[KRU 12] KRUGMAN P., "Technology or Monopoly Power?", The New York Times, December 9, 2012.

[KRU 16] KRUGMAN P., "Robber Baron Recessions", The New York Times, April 18, 2016.

[KUP 08] KUPIEC J.J., *L'origine des individus*, Fayard, 2008.

[KUP 12] KUPIEC J.J., "L'AND seul n'est rien", *Libération*, available at: http://www.liberation.fr/sciences/2012/09/13/l-adn-seul-n-est-rien_846143, 2012.

[KUR 06] KURZWEIL R., *The Singularity is Near: When Humans Transcend Biology*, Penguin, New York, 2006.

[LAN 02] DE LANDA M., *Intensive Science and Virtual Philosophy*, Continuum International Publishing Group, 2002.

[LAR 80] LARUELLE F., "Homo Ex Machina", *Revue de Métaphysique*, vol. 3, 1980.

[LAR 00] LARUELLE F., "Alien sans aliénation,, programme pour une philo-fiction", *Philosophie et Science-Fiction*, Vrin, Paris, 2000.

[LAS 10] LASCOUMES P., *Favoritisme et corruption à la française, petits arrangements avec la probité*, Presses de Sciences-Po, 2010.

[LAT 84] LATOUR B., *Pasteur: guerre et paix des microbes, suivi de Irréductions*, La Découverte, 1984.

[LAT 85] LATOUR B., "Les 'vues' de l'Esprit", *Réseaux*, vol. 5, no. 27, pp. 79–96, 1985.

[LAT 88] LATOUR B., *The Pasteurization of France*, Harvard UP, 1988.

[LAT 95] LATOUR B., TEIL G., "The Hume machine: can association networks do more than formal rules?", *Stanford Humanities Review*, vol. 4, pp. 47–66, 1995.

[LAT 12] LATOUR B., *Enquête sur les modes d'existence. Une anthropologie des Modernes*, La Découverte, 2012.

[LAZ 06] LAZZARATO M., "Le 'pluralisme sémiotique' et le nouveau gouvernement des signes", available at: http://eipcp.net/transversal/0107/lazzarato/fr, 2006.

[LEC 11] LECOURT D., *Humain, post-humain*, Presses Universitaires de France, 2011.

[LEC 15] LECUN Y., BENGIO Y., HINTON G., "Deep learning", *Nature*, vol. 521, pp. 436–444, 2015.

[LER 64] LEROI-GOURHAN, *Gesture and Speech*, MIT Press, 1964.

[LEV 93] LEVY P., *Les technologies de l'intelligence, L'avenir de la pensée à l'ère informatique,* La Découverte, Paris, 1993.

[LEY 98] LEYDESDORFF L., "Theories of Citation?", *Scientometrics*, vol. 43, 1998.

[LEV 13] LEVY P., "Le médium algorithmique", available at: http://pierrelevyblog. files.wordpress.com/2013/02/00le_medium_algorithmique.pdf, 2013.

[LIC 58] LICKLIDER J.C.R., "Man–Computer Symbiosis", *IRE Transactions on Human Factors in Electronics*, 1958.

[LIP 25] LIPPMANN W., *The Phantom Public*, Transaction Publishers, 1925.

[LYN 10] LYNN B.C., LONGMAN P., "Who Broke America's Jobs Machine? Why creeping consolidation is crushing American livelihoods", available at: http://www.washingtonmonthly.com/features/2010/1003.lynn-longman.html, 2010.

[LYO 73] LYOTARD J.-F., "Ante diem rationis", in EIZYKMAN B. (ed.), *Science Fiction et capitalisme, Critique de la position de désir de la science*, Repères – Science humaine – Idéologie, 1973.

[LYO 79] LYOTARD J.F., *La condition post-moderne*, Edition de Minuit, 1979.

[LYO 88] LYOTARD J.-F., *The Differend*, University of Minnesota Press, 1988.

[MAD 75] MADISON G.B., *La Phénoménologie de Merleau Ponty*, Klinksiek, Paris, 1975.

[MAI 09] MAIGNIEN Y., Les *nouvelles frontières numériques des sciences*, Adonis, 2009.

[MAL 04] MALABOU C., *Que faire de notre cerveau?*, Éditions Bayard, 2004

[MAL 11] MALABOU C., *Que faire de notre cerveau?*, Bayard, 2011.

[MAL 14] MALABOU C., *Avant demain. Épigenèse et rationalité*, Presses Universitaires de France, 2014.

[MAL 16] MALABOU C., *Before Tomorrow, Epigenesis and Rationality*, John Wiley & Sons, 2016.

[MAN 03] MANN S., NOLAN J., WELLMAN B., "Surveillance & Society", available at: http://ojs.library.queensu.ca/index.php/surveillance-and-society/, 2003.

[MAR 58] MARX K., *Outlines of the Critique of Political Economy*, 1857–1858.

[MAT 72] MATURANA H., VARELA F.J., *Autopoïésis*, University of Chili, 1972.

[MAT 74] MATURANA H., *Stratégies Cognitives, L'Unité de l'homme*, Centre de Royaumont, 1974.

[MEN 09] MENGUE P., *Utopie et devenirs deleuziens*, L'Harmattan, 2009.

[MER 09] MERZEAU L., "De la surveillance à la veille", *Cités*, vol. 3, pp. 67–80, 2009.

[MER 12] MERLEAU-PONTY M., *Phenomenology of Perception*, Routledge, London, 2012.

[MIL 60] MILLER G.A., *Plans and the Structure of Behavior*, Holt, New York, 1960.

[MOR 14] MOROZOV E., *Pour tout résoudre cliquez ici : L'aberration du solutionnisme technologique*, FYP Éditions, 2014.

[MOU 10] MOULIER-BOUTANG Y., "Droits de propriété intellectuelle, terra nullius et capitalisme cognitif", *Multitudes*, vol. 2, pp. 66–72, 2010.

[MUT 01] MUTSCHKE P., QUAN HAASE A., "Collaboration and cognitive structures in social science research fields. Towards socio-cognitive analysis in information systems", *Scientometrics*, vol. 52, no. 3, pp. 487–502, 2001.

[NEG 00] NEGRI A., HARDT M., *Empire*, Exils, Paris, 2000.

[NEL 65] NELSON T., "A file structure for the complex, the changing, and the indeterminate", *Association for Computing Machinery: Proceedings of the 20th National Conference*, pp. 84–100, Cleveland, OH, 1965.

[NEW 58] NEWELL A., SHAW J.C., SIMON H.A., "Elements of a theory of human problem solving", *Psychological Review*, vol. 65, pp. 151–166, 1958.

[NIS 11] NISSENBAUM H., "A contextual approach to privacy online", *Dædalus, the Journal of the American Academy of Arts & Sciences*, vol. 140, no. 4, 2011.

[NOY 95] NOYER J.-M., "Scientométrie, infométrie: pourquoi nous intéressent-elles", available at: http://gabriel.gallezot.free.fr/Solaris/d02/2noyer_1.html, 1995.

[NOY 05] NOYER J.-M., "Préface" in CHANIER T. (ed.), *Archives ouvertes et publication scientifique Préface de Jean-Max Noyer. Comment mettre en place l'accès libre aux résultats de la recherche*, L'Harmattan, 2005.

[NOY 10] NOYER J.-M., *Technologies de l'information et intelligences collectives*, Hermès-Lavoisier, 2010.

[NOY 11] NOYER J.-M., CARMES M., "Les interfaces machiniques comme problème sémio-politique", *Actes de la Troisième Conférence Document Numérique et Société*, pp. 193–216, 2011.

[NOY 12] NOYER J.-M., CARMES M., "Le mouvement 'Open Data' dans la grande transformation des intelligences collectives et face à la question des écritures, du web sémantique et des ontologies", ISKO, available at: http://www.grico.fr/wpcontent/uploads/2012/10/ISKOMaghreb2012_P9_NoyerCarmes-Copy.pdf, 2012.

[NOY 13] NOYER J.-M., "Les vertiges de l'hyper-marketing: datamining et production sémiotique", in CARMES M., NOYER J.-M. (eds), *Les débats du numérique*, Presses des Mines, Paris, 2013.

[NOY 14] NOYER J.-M., "Encyclopédisme en éclats: réflexions sur la sortie des "essences"", *Cosmopolis*, 2014-3-4, 2014.

[NOY 15] NOYER J.-M., "Désirs de Data", in SEVERO M., ROMELE R. (eds), *Traces Numériques et Territoires*, Presses des Mines Paris Tech, 2015.

[OLD 08] OLDENBURG S., GARBE M., CAP C., "Similarity cross-analysis of tag/co-tag spaces in social classification systems", *Proceedings of the 2008 ACM Workshop on Search in Social Media*, pp. 11–18, 2008.

[ORI 09] ORIGGI G., "La Sagesse en réseaux : la passion d'évaluer", available at: http://www.laviedesidees.fr/Sagesse-en-reseaux-la-passion-d.html, 2009.

[ORI 15] ORIGGI G., *La réputation*, Presses Universitaires de France, 2015.

[OTL 34] OTLET P., *Traité de documentation : le livre sur le livre, théorie et pratique*, Éditions Mundaneum, Brussels, 1934.

[PAP 11] PAPADOPOULOS D., "The imaginary of plasticity: neural embodiment, epigenetics and ecomorphs", *The Sociological Review*, vol. 59, no. 3, 2011.

[PEI 97] PEIRCE C.S., *Pragmatism as a Principle and Method of Right Thinking: The 1903 Harvard "Lectures on Pragmatism"*, TURISI P.A. (ed.), State University of New York Press, Albany, NY, 1997.

[PEN 14] PENTLAND A., *Social Physics: How Good Ideas Spread – The Lessons from a New Science*, Penguin Press, 2014.

[PET 06] PETRAEUS D.H., AMOS J.F., Counterinsurgency, Field Manual nos. 3–24, 2006.

[PIN 09] PINFIELD S., "Journals and repositories: an evolving relationship", *Learned Publishing*, vol. 22, pp. 165–75, 2009.

[QUE 10] QUESSADA D., "De la sousveillance. La surveillance globale, un nouveau mode de gouvernementalité", *Multitudes* vol. 1, pp. 54–59, 2010.

[RAT 11] RATTI C., TOWNSEND A., "The social Nexus", *Scientific American*, vol. 305, pp. 42–48, 2011.

[RAY 94] RAYWARD B., "Visions of Xanadu: Paul Otlet (1868–1944) and hypertext", *Journal of the American Society for Information Science*, vol. 45, no. 4, 1994.

[RAY 06] RAYWARD B., FURNER J., LA BARRE K. *et al.*, "Paul Otlet, documentation and classification", *Proceedings of the American Society for Information Science and Technology*, vol. 43, no. 1, pp. 1–6, 2006.

[REG 14] REGALADO A., "Google Wants to Store Your Genome. For $25 a year, Google will keep a copy of any genome in the cloud", *MIT Technology Review*, 2014.

[REN 88] RENOUVIER C., *Uchronie*, Fayard, Paris, 1988.

[RIF 12] RIFKIN J., *La troisième révolution industrielle : Comment le pouvoir latéral va transformer l'énergie*, Les liens qui libèrent, 2012.

[ROS 74] ROSENSTIEHL P., PETITOT J., "Automate asocial et systèmes acentrés", *Communications*, vol. 22, pp. 45–62, 1974.

[ROS 10] ROSA H., *Accélération? Une critique sociale du temps*, La Découverte, 2010.

[ROS 13] ROSA H., *Social Acceleration: A New Theory of Modernity*, Columbia University Press, 2013.

[SAS 03] SASSO R., VILLANI A., *Vocabulaire de Gilles Deleuze*, Les Cahiers de Noesis, 2003.

[SAV 09] SAVULESCU J., BOSTROM N., *Human Enhancement*, Oxford University Press, 2009.

[SHE 81] SHELDRAKE R., *Une nouvelle science de la vie*, Rocher, 1981.

[SHE 98] SHELDRAKE R., The *Presence of the Past: Morphic Resonance and the Habits of Nature*, Inner Traditions Bear and Company, 1998.

[SHE 00] SHELDRAKE R., *The Presence of the Past: Morphic Resonance and the Habits of Nature*, Inner Traditions, 2000.

[SHE 03] SHELDRAKE R., *Une nouvelle science de la vie*, Éditions du Rocher, 2003.

[SHU 14] SHULMAN C., BOSTROM N., "Embryo selection for cognitive enhancement: curiosity or game-changer?", *Global Policy*, vol. 5, pp. 85–92, 2014.

[SIB 09] SIBERTIN-BLANC G., LEGRAND S., *Esquisse d'une contribution à la critique de l'économie des savoirs*, Edition Le clou dans le Fer, 2009.

[SIM 58] SIMON H.A., SHAW J.C., NEWELL A., "Elements of a theory of human problem solving", *Psychological Review*, vol. 65, pp. 151–166, 1958.

[SIM 70] SIMON H.A., NEWELL A., "Human problem solving: The state of the theory in 1970", *American Psychologist*, vol. 26, pp. 145–159, 1970.

[SIM 07] SIMONDON  G., *L'Individuation psychique et collective*, Aubier, Paris, 2007.

[SLO 05] SLOTERDIJK P., *Ecumes, Sphères III*, Maren Sell Editeurs, 2005.

[SLO 06] SLOTERDIJK P., *Le palais de cristal, à l'intérieur du capitalsime planétaire*, Maren Sell Editeurs, Paris, 2006.

[SLO 09] SLOTERDIJK P., "Rules for the Human Zoo: a response to the Letter for Humanism", *Environment and Planning D: Society and Space*, vol. 27, pp. 12–28, 2009.

[SLO 10] SLOTERDIJK P., "The operable man. On the ethical state of gene technology", *The Domestication of Being*, 2010.

[SLO 11a] SLOTERDIJK P., "Co-immunité globale, Penser le commun qui protège", *Multitudes,* vol. 45, 2011.

[SLO 11b] SLOTERDIJK P., *Le palais de cristal*, Poche, 2011.

[SLO 13] SLOTERDIJK P., *Crystal Palace, In the World Interior of Capital*, Polity Press, 2013.

[SMA 73] SMALL H.G., "Co-citation in the scientific literature: a new measure of the relationship between two documents", *Journal of the American Society for Information Science*, 24, 1973.

[SMA 95] SMALL H.G., "Navigating the citation network", in KINNEY T (ed.), *Proceedings of the 59th Annual Meeting of the American Society for Information Science*, Medford, NJ, 1995.

[SMI 99] SMITH J.W.T., "The deconstructed journal — a new model for academic publishing", *Learned Publishing*, vol. 12, pp. 79–91, 1999.

[SMO 08] SMOLIN L., "On Chris Anderson's The End of Theory", available at: http://www.edge.org/discourse/the_end_of_theory.html, 2008.

[SOU 09] SOURIAU E., *Les différents modes d'existence*, Presses Universitaires de France, 2009.

[STA 89] STAR S.L., GRIESEMER J.R., "Institutional ecology: 'translations' and boundary objects: amateurs and professionals in Berkeley's Museum of Vertebrate Zoology 1907-39", *Social Studies of Science*, vol. 19, 1989.

[STE 11] STENGERS I., *Thinking with whitehead*, Harvard University Press, 2011.

[STI 94] STIEGLER B., *La technique et le temps: Tome 1, La faute d'Épiméthée*, Éditions Galilée, Paris, 1994.

[STI 98] STIEGLER B., *Technics and Time, Volumes 1 and 2*, Stanford University Press, 1998.

[STI 01] STIEGLER B., *La technique et le temps: Tome 3*, Galilée, Paris, 2001.

[STI 04] STIEGLER B., *De la misère symbolique: Tome 1. L'époque hyperindustrielle*, Éditions Galilée, Paris, 2004.

[STI 12] STIEGLER B., "Le marketing détruit tous les outils du savoir", available at: http://www.bastamag.net/Bernard-Stiegler-Le-marketing, 2012.

[SUR 04] SUROWIECKI J., *The Wisdom of Crowds: Why the Many Are Smarter Than the Few and How Collective Wisdom Shapes Business, Economies, Societies and Nations*, Doubleday, New York, 2004.

[SZA 94] SZAFRANSKI R., "Neocortical Warfare? The Acme of Skill", available at: *https://www.rand.org/content/dam/rand/pubs/.../MR880.ch17.pdf*, 1994.

[TAR 95] TARDE G., *Les lois de l'imitation*, Éditions Kimé, 1895.

[TEI 95] TEIL G., LATOUR B., "The Hume machine: can association networks do more than formal rules?", *SEHR*, vol. 4, 1995.

[TES 09] TESTARD-VAILLANT P., BETTAYEB K., "La lecture change aussi nos cerveaux", *Science et Vie*, September 2009.

[VAN 01] VAN DER VEER MARTENS B., "Do citation systems represent theories of truth?", *Information Research*, vol. 6 no. 2, 2001.

[VAR 89] VARELA F., *Autonomie et connaissance*, Seuil, Paris, 1989.

[VAR 93] VARELA F., *L'inscription corporelle de l'esprit, sciences cognitives et expérience humaine*, Seuil, 1993.

[VAR 99a] VARELA F., *Autonomie et Connaissance*, Seuil, Paris, 1999.

[VAR 99b] VARELA F., THOMPSON E., ROSH E., *L'Inscription corporelle de l'Esprit, sciences cognitives et expérience humaine*, Seuil, Paris, 1999.

[VIA 13] VIAL S., *L'être et l'Ecran, Comment le numérique change la perception*, Presses Universitaires de France, Paris, 2013.

[VID 11] VIDAL D., "Robotique et principe de virtuosité", *Ateliers d'anthropologie*, vol. 35, available at: http://ateliers.revues.org/8787, 2011.

[VIN 91] VINCK D., *La gestion de la recherche. Nouveaux problèmes, nouveaux outils*, De Boeck, Bruxelles, 1991.

[VIR 86] VIRILIO P., *Speed and Politics: An Essay on Dromology*, Semiotext, New York, 1986.

[WEI 12] WEISSMAN J., Exology of the city, available at: www.fractalontology.wordpress.com, 13 September 2012.

[WHI 79] WHITEHEAD A.N., *Process and Reality (Gifford Lectures)*, Macmillan, 1979.

[WOL 08] WOLF M., *Proust and the Squid: The Story and Science of the Reading Brain*, Harper Perennial, 2008.

[WOU 99] WOUTERS P., "Beyond the holy grail: from citation theory to indicator theories", *Scientometrics*, vol. 44, 1999.

[ZAC 05] ZACKLAD M., "Introduction aux ontologies sémiotiques dans le Web Socio Sémantique", *Archives SIC*, 2005.

[ZAC 07] ZACKLAD M., "Classification, thésaurus, ontologies, folksonomies : comparaisons du point de vue de la recherche ouverte d'information", *Actes de la Conférence CAIS/ACSI*, Montreal, Canada, 2007.

[ZIN 76] ZINOVIEV A., *Les Hauteurs béantes*, L'Age d'Homme, Lausanne, 1976.

[ZIN 78] ZINOVIEV A., *L'Avenir radieux*, L'Age d'Homme, Lausanne, 1978.

[ZUN 12] ZUNSHINE L., *Getting Inside your head: What Cognitive Science Can Tell Us about Popular Culture*, Johns Hopkins University Press, 2012.

# Index

Other titles from

in

Information Systems, Web and Pervasive Computing

## 2016

BEN CHOUIKHA Mona
*Organizational Design for Knowledge Management*

BERTOLO David
*Interactions on Digital Tablets in the Context of 3D Geometry Learning*
*(Human-Machine Interaction Set – Volume 2)*

EL FALLAH SEGHROUCHNI Amal, ISHIKAWA Fuyuki, HÉRAULT Laurent,
TOKUDA Hideyuki
*Enablers for Smart Cities*

GAUDIELLO Ilaria, ZIBETTI Elisabetta
*Learning Robotics, with Robotics, by Robotics*
*(Human-Machine Interaction Set – Volume 3)*

HENROTIN Joseph
*The Art of War in the Network Age*
*(Intellectual Technologies Set – Volume 1)*

KITAJIMA Munéo
*Memory and Action Selection in Human–Machine Interaction*
*(Human–Machine Interaction Set – Volume 1)*

LAGRAÑA Fernando
*E-mail and Behavioral Changes: Uses and Misuses of Electronic Communications*

MONINO Jean-Louis, SEDKAOUI Soraya
*Big Data, Open Data and Data Development (Smart Innovation Set – Volume 3)*

VENTRE Daniel
*Information Warfare – 2$^{nd}$ edition*

VITALIS André
*The Uncertain Digital Revolution*

# 2015

ARDUIN Pierre-Emmanuel, GRUNDSTEIN Michel, ROSENTHAL-SABROUX Camille
*Information and Knowledge System
(Advances in Information Systems Set – Volume 2)*

BÉRANGER Jérôme
*Medical Information Systems Ethics*

BRONNER Gérald
*Belief and Misbelief Asymmetry on the Internet*

IAFRATE Fernando
*From Big Data to Smart Data
(Advances in Information Systems Set – Volume 1)*

KRICHEN Saoussen, BEN JOUIDA Sihem
*Supply Chain Management and its Applications in Computer Science*

NEGRE Elsa
*Information and Recommender Systems
(Advances in Information Systems Set – Volume 4)*

POMEROL Jean-Charles, EPELBOIN Yves, THOURY Claire
*MOOCs*

## 2012

BUCHER Bénédicte, LE BER Florence
*Innovative Software Development in GIS*

GAUSSIER Eric, YVON François
*Textual Information Access*

STOCKINGER Peter
*Audiovisual Archives: Digital Text and Discourse Analysis*

VENTRE Daniel
*Cyber Conflict*

## 2011

BANOS Arnaud, THÉVENIN Thomas
*Geographical Information and Urban Transport Systems*

DAUPHINÉ André
*Fractal Geography*

LEMBERGER Pirmin, MOREL Mederic
*Managing Complexity of Information Systems*

STOCKINGER Peter
*Introduction to Audiovisual Archives*

STOCKINGER Peter
*Digital Audiovisual Archives*

VENTRE Daniel
*Cyberwar and Information Warfare*

## 2010

BONNET Pierre
*Enterprise Data Governance*

BRUNET Roger
*Sustainable Geography*

CARREGA Pierre
*Geographical Information and Climatology*

CAUVIN Colette, ESCOBAR Francisco, SERRADJ Aziz
*Thematic Cartography – 3-volume series*
*Thematic Cartography and Transformations – volume 1*
*Cartography and the Impact of the Quantitative Revolution – volume 2*
*New Approaches in Thematic Cartography – volume 3*

LANGLOIS Patrice
*Simulation of Complex Systems in GIS*

MATHIS Philippe
*Graphs and Networks – 2nd edition*

THERIAULT Marius, DES ROSIERS François
*Modeling Urban Dynamics*

## 2009

BONNET Pierre, DETAVERNIER Jean-Michel, VAUQUIER Dominique
*Sustainable IT Architecture: the Progressive Way of Overhauling Information Systems with SOA*

PAPY Fabrice
*Information Science*

RIVARD François, ABOU HARB Georges, MERET Philippe
*The Transverse Information System*

ROCHE Stéphane, CARON Claude
*Organizational Facets of GIS*

## 2008

BRUGNOT Gérard
*Spatial Management of Risks*

FINKE Gerd
*Operations Research and Networks*

GUERMOND Yves
*Modeling Process in Geography*

KANEVSKI Michael
*Advanced Mapping of Environmental Data*

MANOUVRIER Bernard, LAURENT Ménard
*Application Integration: EAI, B2B, BPM and SOA*

PAPY Fabrice
*Digital Libraries*

## 2007

DOBESCH Hartwig, DUMOLARD Pierre, DYRAS Izabela
*Spatial Interpolation for Climate Data*

SANDERS Lena
*Models in Spatial Analysis*

## 2006

CLIQUET Gérard
*Geomarketing*

CORNIOU Jean-Pierre
*Looking Back and Going Forward in IT*

DEVILLERS Rodolphe, JEANSOULIN Robert
*Fundamentals of Spatial Data Quality*

Lightning Source UK Ltd.
Milton Keynes UK
UKHW02n2238180218
318073UK00003B/49/P